DEATH
& THE WORLD RELIGIONS
How Religion Informs End-of-Life Decisions

Walter N. Sisto

Kendall Hunt
publishing company

www.kendallhunt.com
Send all inquiries to:
4050 Westmark Drive
Dubuque, IA 52004-1840

This book is dedicated to Jenny, the love of my life.
Without you, none of this would be possible.

CONTENTS

INTRODUCTION

This text has been written to provide healthcare professionals with a meaningful and succinct introduction to how religion informs end-of-life care. I am greatly indebted to my students at D'Youville College whose insights and challenging questions in the context of our course *Challenges of Death* prompted the writing of this text. Many of these students are healthcare majors who challenged me to explain how to care for patients of different religions from their own and the importance of religion for dying persons. In my search for a text that addressed this issue, I was surprised to discover that although a panoply of articles on effective healthcare for dying members of religious traditions exists, very few texts synthesize this scholarship for nonspecialists. This text synthesizes this material to provide my readers with an accessible introduction to important scholarship on this topic.

Besides filling this gap in scholarship, in this text I will argue that the world religions do a very good job of helping their members cope with death. In fact, for many believers, religious teaching informs their healthcare choices. For this reason, healthcare professionals who are knowledgeable and sensitive to the unique needs of their patients' religious traditions will provide more effective healthcare, because they will address what Charles Corr defines as the physical, social, psychological, and spiritual dimensions of personhood. Thus, effective healthcare for members of these religions must be aware and vouchsafe to the best of their ability the customs and practices associated with each religion.

To this end, the majority of this text provides an introduction to the history and basic tenets of each major world religion, in addition to examining how each religion addresses the four dimensions of a person and how caregivers can effectively care for patients who are active members of their religious tradition. My chapters on the world religions end with qualitative interviews with death experts representative of each tradition. By "death expert" I mean religious leaders who have substantial experience preparing members of their community for death, officiating at funerary rituals, and helping family members bereave the dead.[1] Note that I interviewed primarily religious leaders from the Western New York/Southern Ontario region who are well known in this region for their expertise. I chose local religious leaders so as to provide former and current students in healthcare who are taking my course on the challenges of death with firsthand accounts of what they can expect from members of these religious communities in their care. However, it is important to note that end-of-life rituals, practices, and teachings are not regionally specific, and thus the information gathered from the interviews and my research is relevant to care for members of these traditions outside the Western New York/Southern Ontario region.

Nevertheless, the persons interviewed in this book are not only experts in their religious tradition but also have many years of experience ministering to the dying; much of what they say is representative of their respective religions. I ask pragmatic and tough questions, so as to facilitate a more intimate understanding of a particular religion or practice in question.

These chapters will help prepare healthcare professionals to more effectively communicate and understand patients who are members of these traditions. Needless to say, within every religious community there are varying degrees of religiosity, as well as cultural and religious expressions that are not addressed in this text. This is not to mention how the decline in health and physical pain can complicate religious expression. In essence, these chapters examine what is an ideal death for an active member of each religion (e.g., that the patient is terminally ill and desires to die a good death as defined by her religion). Therefore, the information supplied in the text should be used as a guide as opposed to a mandate for care for members of the world religions.

For the purpose of clarity, this text is divided into two main parts. Part One introduces the study of dying, death, and the afterlife. It is subdivided into three chapters that immerse readers into the psychology, ethical dilemmas, and controversy about what happens to consciousness when we die. Chapter One analyzes various studies on the death process with specific attention to how people die and the process of dying. Readers will be introduced to Elizabeth Kübler-Ross' five stages of coping with death but also criticism of her ideas and recent perspectives on the process of death. This chapter also introduces Charles Corr's theory of coping with death that I employ in later chapters to analyze how religious persons define a good death and how to effectively care for these persons. After that the reader is provided with a basic overview of the process and language about dying, as in Chapter Two I introduce the debate as to when it is ethical to die and how to care for the dying.

---

1. All interviews were edited with the consent of the interviewee.

This chapter includes arguments about when death occurs, the ethics surrounding euthanasia, and hospice philosophy. This chapter ends with an interview with Monica Sleap, a native of Buffalo and graduate of D'Youville College, who is an experienced hospice nurse. She offers her unique insights and experiences on the dying process and caring for those who are dying. Chapter Three ends our immersion into the dying process with a critical examination of current research on the near-death experience phenomenon (NDE), as well as an examination on how to care for patients with NDEs.

My chapter on near-death experiences, which provides good reason to believe that there is life after death, also provides a segway to the second part of this book. In Part Two we will examine what the major religions teach about the afterlife, what they define as a good death, and how to care for the dying. Part Two begins our discussion of these important topics with a study of the ancient religions of Egypt and Mesopotamia. I have chosen theses religions for my study because they provide a primer to the study of the aforementioned topics, as many of the ideas in these religions are similar to or directly appropriated by the world religions. Note that by "world religions" I mean the religions with the largest populations that are not confined to a particular geographical region. Chapters five through ten will examine respectively Hinduism, Buddhism, Judaism, Christianity, and Islam. Because Tibetan Buddhism is popular in the United States and teachings on dying, death, afterlife, and bereavement have a wide appeal to a non-Buddhist audience, I have included an additional chapter on this tradition.

Be aware that the world religions that I discuss are also known as axial religions. Axial religions originated between 470 BCE and 636 CE. It is important to note that traditionally, beginning with Karl Jasper, the axial period was associated with the change in thinking that occurred between 800 and 200 BCE. However, scholarship today generally finds Jasper's association of this period with 800-200 BCE to be too confining, for it fails to consider the teachings and movements begun by Jesus and Muhammad, who are the founders of the world's two largest religious communities. In this book when I refer to the axial period I mean that period associated with human beings reaching a new level of consciousness that begins with Socrates and ends with the death of the Prophet Muhammad.

Axial period is characterized as such because it is an epoch in which there was a profound shift in human consciousness: people began to ask critical questions about the meaning of human existence and sought answers to what it means to be human. Regarding this revolution in thought Anthony Black writes:

> What distinguishes the axial stage is an approach to the self and to the cosmos that is more reasoned, brooding, reflective, self-conscious, and at the same time more articulate. There was, indeed, a fuller awareness of the interior person (which also found expression in literature and the plastic arts). But there was also (as we shall see) a po-

litical and social dimension that Jaspers all but ignored. There was discontent with the execution of daily concerns, a search for better ways of organizing society, and a greater demand for self-sacrifice. People were seeking both to understand and, at the same time, to change the way life is; they were looking for changes in attitude as well as conduct.[2]

This was a departure from Egyptian and Mesopotamian ways of thinking that were largely reactive and passive. They, for instance, explain the phenomena of existence with their cosmological myths but do not have a strong tradition of meaningful reflection on the phenomena itself or offer substantive responses to the meaning of human life in light of this reflection.

In addition to the term "axial religions," I also employ the terms "eastern religions" and "western religions" throughout this text. These traditional appellations can be problematic, since it is no longer clear to many what constitutes east or west or what is the agreed point that demarcates east from west. Not only are eastern religions growing in the West, but in the East, western religions are growing. China is a great example of this latter phenomenon; albeit traditionally an eastern country populated by a majority of eastern religions, today it is home to one of the largest and fastest growing populations of Christians. If Christianity continues to grow at the rate it is growing in China, in a few decades China will have the world's largest Christian population.

For the purpose of this text, by "eastern religions" I mean religions that trace their origin to Hinduism and share the basic precepts of Hinduism, such as the belief in reincarnation and the law of karma. Hinduism and Buddhism are eastern religions. In contradistinction to "eastern religions" by "western religions" I mean "Abrahamic religions" or those religions that trace their origins to the prophet Abraham. In chronological order, these religions are Judaism, Christianity, and Islam.

---

2. Anthony Black, "The 'Axial Period': What was it and what does it signify?" (*The Review of Politics* 70.1 (Winter 2008): 23-39), 27.

CHAPTER ONE

DYING AND DEATH

Introduction

When I was a young boy, my father said, "There are only two things in life that you must do, pay your taxes and die." In the course of my adult life I have met many who have neglected to pay their taxes, but none who have been able to escape death. Since the fabled Gilgamesh and his epic journey to find immortality, humankind has struggled with the universal fact that we all will die, and we will at some point directly (our own death) or indirectly (the death of a relative or friend) experience death. This chapter provides a broad overview for what death is and how we should respond to it.

Defining Our Terms

"What is Death?" The answer to this question may seem self-evident, but in the context of ordinary discourse, when we talk about death we mean different things. Certain religious traditions teach the need for followers "to die to themselves" in order to be saved. Moreover, on more than one occasion I have heard people accuse living people of "being dead to the world." At the same time, we refer to death as the cessation of biological life.

Part of the problem is that colloquial death-talk lacks context or reference. Nevertheless, in the English language when we speak about death, we mean at least three kinds of death: biological death, psychological death, and spiritual death.

Biological death refers simply to cessation of life. Nevertheless, given advances in medical technology, the fact that patients can remain "alive" in an irreversible comatose state, and questions as to when it is ethical to harvest organs from donors, in 1968, Harvard Medical School published what it deemed as the essential criteria for death. These criteria are known as the brain death criteria, which includes lack of receptivity and response to external stimuli; absence of spontaneous muscular movement and spontaneous breathing; absence of observable reflexes, including brain and spinal reflexes; absence of brain activity, signified by a flat electroencephalogram (EEG).[1] Nonspecialists commonly refer to biological death as brain death. In the course of this discussion I will do likewise.

Psychological death refers to a "reversible termination of one's personal aliveness."[2] The result is an emotional deadening. Although commonly observed during bereavement and grief, it is a common response to the death event. Spiritual death is observed in the context of religious traditions. It is a phenomenon that is associated with all of the axial religions that I will discuss in the subsequent chapters.

Spiritual death refers to the cessation of habits, desires, and attachments to activities that are not conducive to enlightenment or salvation. For western religion practitioners it also refers to the clinging on to the absolute God (e.g., choosing God's will over and against will of the believer). For eastern religion practitioners it means to reject and suppress all attachments associated with desire for worldly goods. In this chapter, I am primary concerned with biological death and the literature regarding how one should respond to this phenomenon.

Death Statistics

According to the *Centers for Disease Control and Prevention (CDC)* the average life expectancy for citizens in the United States is 78.7 years. The CIA ranks U.S. citizens' life expectancy as fifty-first out of two-hundred and thirty-three countries and territories.[3] Interestingly, while Monaco, Macau, and Japan have the highest life expectancies of 89.63, 84.46, and 84.19, respectively, Chad and South Africa have the lowest life expectancy of 49.07 and 49.48. This disparity in life expectancy is echoed

1. Kenneth Kramer, *The sacred art of dying: How world religions understand death* (Mahwah, NJ: Paulist Press, 1988), 13-14.
2. Ibid, 18.
3. "The world factbook: Country comparison: Life expectancy at birth," Central Intelligence Agency, https://www.cia.gov/library/publications/the-world-factbook/rankorder/2102rank.html (January 17, 2014).

in the leading causes of death between high-income and low-income countries. In 2011, the top ten causes of death in the United States were:

1. Heart disease
2. Cancer
3. Chronic lower respiratory diseases
4. Stroke (cerebrovascular diseases)
5. Accidents (unintentional injuries)
6. Alzheimer's disease
7. Diabetes
8. Nephritis, nephrotic syndrome, and nephrosis
9. Influenza and pneumonia
10. Intentional self-harm (suicide)[4]

Note that in the United States the tenth highest cause of death was suicide. In 2011 alone, 38,304 persons took their own lives. We should pause and reflect about what this figure says about the wealthiest and most powerful country in the world. Moreover, these statistics are in stark contrast to the top ten causes of death in low-income countries, such as Chad. These include:

1. Lower respiratory infections
2. Diarrhoeal diseases
3. HIV/AIDS
4. Ischaemic heart disease
5. Malaria
6. Stroke (cerebrovascular disease)
7. Tuberculosis
8. Prematurity and low birth weight
9. Birth asphyxia and birth trauma
10. Neonatal infections[5]

With exception to heart disease and stroke, people from low-income countries and the United States die differently. Malaria and tuberculosis are virtually eliminated in the United States, and death resulting from birth that are the eighth, ninth, and tenth leading causes of death does not make the top ten list for the United States. Yet deaths related to giving birth are situated in the bottom of the top ten leading cause of death in low-income countries. Perhaps these facts are evidence of an injus-

---

4. "Deaths and mortality," Centers for Disease Control and Prevention 2011, http://www.cdc.gov/nchs/fastats/deaths. htm (January 21, 2014).
5. "The top ten causes of death," World Health Organization 2011, http://www.who.int/mediacentre/factsheets/fs310/en/ (January 17, 2014).

tice in the distribution of wealth worldwide and how that distribution limits access to technology, education, medication, and vaccines that can prevent or reduce death rates related to the aforementioned causes of death. This is not the context to systematically argue this point; however, the fact remains that countries like the United States that have wealth, therefore access to technology that prevents many of the top ten causes of death in low-income countries, do not die in the same way as human beings in poor countries.

Attitudes Toward Death

This difference in the causes of death is also evident in the difference in attitudes toward death. Whereas Americans tend to be fearful or afraid of death, citizens of low-income countries tend to have different attitudes since they experience death, especially the death of youth, on a regular basis. Thus when I speak about death and dying, I am primarily speaking from the perspective of a member of the high-income country, the United States, that has all of the amenities modern healthcare has to offer.

One constant in research on death, dying, and bereavement is that Americans generally fear death and avoid it at all costs. Elisabeth Kübler-Ross argues that the denial of death in our society "has given neither hope nor purpose but has only increased our anxiety and contributed to our destructiveness and aggressiveness."[6] She asks an important question that I think we should pause for a second and consider: "What happens in a society that puts more emphasis on IQ and class-standing than on simple matters of tact, sensitivity, perceptiveness, and good taste in the management of suffering [at the end of life]?"[7]

Death is an uncomfortable topic that Americans rarely want to discuss and in fact avoid the term "death" and employ euphemisms such as "passed away," "sleeping," or "expired."[8] Ruth Davis Konigsberg in *The Truth about Grief; The Myth of Its Five Stages and the New Science of Loss* offers an intriguing study about how "death" became an unmentionable in American society. She outlines several factors that have contributed to this pathos that include advancements in medical science, which made natural death (especially the death of youth) uncommon, secularism, pursuit of happiness, and couch potatoes.[9] While advancements in medical science, especially medical practices that have contributed

---

6. Elisabeth Kübler-Ross, *On death and dying: What the dying have to teach doctors, nurses, clergy and their own families* (New York: Scribner, 1969), 29.
7. Ibid., 25-26.
8. Charles Corr and Donna Corr, *Death & dying, life & living,* 7th ed. (Belmont, CA: Cengage Learning, 2013), 94.
9. Ruth Davis Konigsberg, *The truth about grief; The myth of its five stages and the new science of loss* (New York: Simon & Schuster, 2011), 31.

to low-infant mortality rates, in particular, have provided American with the luxury of not having to see death on a constant basis, secularization of culture entailed that Americans are no longer immersed in a culture that stresses dying, death, and belief in afterlife. The result is that bodily decomposition has become a topic that is too horrible to discuss.[10] Individualism and specifically the pursuit of individual happiness have also led to an avoidance of the topic of our mortality and death since death is the ultimate frustration to our happiness.[11] Thus as a culture we expect people to avoid speaking about the topic of death and restrain emotions when a loved one dies.[12]

This discomfort with death is evident in how people die in the United States. Whereas for the greater part of human history death occurred in the home, perhaps in the same home in which the dying person was born, today people die in white-washed hospital rooms. We objectify death and dying. Death and dying remain at a distance, and we do our best to go about living our lives as "normally" as possible amidst the dying experience. The benefit of this approach is that death becomes less of an inconvenience and something that we do not have to face until we are forced to encounter it (e.g., when we have to face the reality of our own mortality or the mortality of those around us). The drawback of this approach is that our society fails to provide the natural network of support for the dying and the bereaved. This is not to say that support systems do not exist, but rather that one has to actively seek out these systems. There are always exceptions, and as we will learn many of the major religions that are practiced in the United States have a subculture that supplies a necessary support system. Orthodox Judaism is a good example because in this tradition there is a prescribed time period for mourning and everyone in that community plays a role. Albeit less conscious of these cultural mores, this is how societies functioned in the past. However, in the United States today, these social mores are no longer dominant. Thus, not only do Americans often find themselves ill-prepared for death, but society affords very little time and resources especially to the bereaved. Evidence of this is found in benefits that companies afford to their workers, specifically the prescribed length of time that workers can take off from work to attend to the dead (with exception to Google, which allows its workers to take up to three months of unpaid time off). Most businesses, however, offer little or no paid leave/unpaid leave for bereavement. When positions offer leave for deaths, it comes with conditions. For example, in a former post my position offered two days of paid leave if there was a death in the family; however, the dead had to be a resident in your home! Thus, I was unable to use these days to attend the funeral of a family member who died suddenly. Because our society tends to avoid death rather than address it, members of our society lack the social support systems to aid in their healing and grief and feel pressured to return to normalcy as quickly as possible. This is not to say that our society lacks a death system, a sociopolitical network by which we understand the death, dying, and bereavement, but rather the death system in the United States

10. Ibid., 31.
11. Ibid., 31.
12. Ibid., 32.

can at times tend to express a fear or anxiety toward death. Nevertheless, the death system that we find in North American society is quite complex and includes important occasions associated with death, "hallowed ground," symbols of death, and death professionals.[13]

We need only recall the terrorist attacks on the Twin Towers in New York City on September 11, 2001. That September or "9-11" was an episodic event that is ingrained into the American psyche. I lived outside of New York City and vividly recall not only the events of 9-11, but the first time that I went to visit the site of the Twin Towers. For me and my friends that site became "hallowed ground." New York City is called the "city that never sleeps," and it is known for its loudness, but in those days and weeks following 9-11, there was an eerie silence over that section of Lower Manhattan. Today 9-11 has become a memorial day. The picture of the Twin Towers and "9-11" are in a sense sacred symbols in our culture that elicit emotion. I recall that immediately after 9-11, there was pressure from the public placed on the film and video game industry not to depict the event in their media. Moreover, there was virulent debate on whether to rebuild the Twin Towers. The event of 9-11 transformed the remains of the buildings as a sacred space. This experience of the sacred permeated that area to the point where it is not uncommon to find people commenting about the silence around that area of the city. Moreover, for many months two beams from the wreckage that formed in the shape of a cross stood at ground zero, further cementing the experience that the space was holy ground. For many, these two beams became a sacred symbol that referred not only to 9-11 but also to the suffering and death of Jesus, offering comfort to the bereaved.

September 11 also illustrates that our society has death professionals. The obvious examples are the funeral directors who provide a space for the bereaved to mourn their dead. When bodies were discovered, they embalm the body, dress it, and place it in a casket to be displayed for loved ones to pay their final respects before it is cremated or buried. The sanitization regarding the remains of the dead further demonstrates the uneasiness Americans have with death. Thus, we dress our dead in their best outfits and put makeup on them in order to make them look alive and vibrant, perhaps more alive and vibrant then they looked in life![14]

The process by which 9-11 became sacrosanct was largely unstated and implicit. This is usually how death systems function; they reflect our social mores that are rarely explicitly stated. People refer to them as "what you should do." By and large what exactly we should do we have learned from watching and hearing about how other people do those things. We are products of environment and culture. The signs of respect that the rescue workers gave to the remains of people who died on 9-11 is another example of these cultural practices.

---

13. Cf. Corr, 72, 70-71.
14. Cf. Kameran MacKendrick, *Fragmentation and memory: Meditations on Christian doctrine* (New York: Fordham University Press, 2008, 116.

Nevertheless, although we have lost the societal support systems, according to Philippe Ariès there are at least five main attitudes toward death in Western society[15] that include Tame Death, Death of Self, Remote and Imminent Death, Death of Other, and Forbidden Death. Tame Death is the belief that death is inevitable and there should be no attempt to evade it. Death of Self is what I have referred to above as spiritual death. Remote and Imminent Death sees death as highly ambivalent and attempts to distance oneself from it. Death of the other refers to attention on the dead person and attempt to reconnect with that person. Thus, the most famous example involves Harry and Bess Houdini, husband and wife. Bess attempted to contact Harry (then deceased) via séance every Halloween from 1927 to 1936. Forbidden Death goes beyond ambivalence and attempts to isolate the dying because this perspective tends to view death as either dirty or indecent. Ariès notes that these are snapshots of western attitudes. Thus, when faced with the topic of death it is not uncommon for a student to find all or some of these attitudes reflective of his/her experiences. These snapshots of our attitudes toward death paint a somewhat bleak picture of death as a negative experience.

Dying Process

The academic study of death and emphasis that we find in healthcare programs on understanding death and dying owes a great debt to the life and work of Elizabeth Kübler-Ross. Kübler-Ross was not only responsible for the first popular, systemic treatment of the psychological and emotional effects of the dying process on the dying and their relatives/friends, but was one of the most vocal proponents of death awareness. Although in recent years some of her scholarship is no longer relevant to experts in thantology, her lasting contribution is her view that all of those involved in care for the dying must better understand the death process so as to be more compassionate and effective in the care for the dying. By "dying process" I am concerned with the human psyche and the emotional/psychological trauma that dying creates as opposed to the physiological signs that death is approaching or occurring.[16]

---

15. By western society he means Europe and North America.
16. According to Kathleen A. Moneymaker there are signs that death is approaching and occurring. Some of the indicators that death is approaching for a terminally ill patient may include breathing irregularities, intensified pain, feelings of "letting go," and discoloration of hands and feet (bluish-white color). Some indicators that death is occurring are moaning associated with breathing, sense of vacancy, eyes open wide, and the loss of bowel or bladder control. (Kathleen A. Moneymaker, "Understanding the dying process: Transitions during final days to hours," *Journal of Palliative Medicine* 8.5 (2005): 1079.)

The Five Stages

In 1969 Kübler-Ross wrote *On Death and Dying* where she proposed her now famous five stages of grief, commonly known as the Kübler-Ross model. Her model addresses the grief that one *may* experience when dying or grieving the loss of a loved one. I have italicized the qualifier "may" because Kübler-Ross also stressed that every experience of death or loss is unique, and that the stages are not intended to exhaust the death experience, but rather are based on observations she made during her work with terminally ill patients. The five stages are Denial, Anger, Bargaining, Depression, and Acceptance.

Denial. This refers to the lack of acceptance of the patient's condition by the patient. It is a protective mechanism that is temporary, and it is usually accompanied by numbness and shock. Kübler-Ross defines it positively as "nature's way of letting in only as much as we can handle."[17] As the patient proceeds to make sense of the situation, denial dissipates and the emotions that were oppressed begin to surface.[18]

In the context of care for a patient, Kübler-Ross suggests that healthcare professionals and family be honest with the patient and his or her deteriorating condition. To do otherwise may empower false ground for their denial and prolong this stage of suffering. Tolstoy, in *The Death of Ivan Illych*, illustrates lucidly the ill effect that the lack of knowledge about the reality of one's condition can cause more harm than good. Ivan agonized constantly over "the lie" perpetuated by his physicians and wife, and rather than coming to terms with his condition suffered and resented his loved ones until the very end.

Anger. This is a usually the first emotion to surface after denial. It surfaces "once you are feeling safe enough to know you will survive whatever is to come."[19] It can function as a foundation to begin accepting your condition because you are angry at something. Insofar as there is an object of your anger, you now have an anchor from which you can begin to make sense of your emotions.[20] Kübler-Ross places anger at the front lines of emotion that is usually followed by sadness, loneliness, and panic.[21] It is not logical, and it can manifest itself with anger toward healthcare professionals, family, friends, illness, God, etc.

Unfortunately, during this stage providing care for the patient may be cumbersome and difficult.[22] Recognizing the difficulty in caring for someone who may be unjustifiably angered at the caregiver,

---

17. Elisabeth Kübler-Ross and David Kessler, *On grief and grieving: Finding the meaning of grief through the five stages of loss* (New York: Scribner, 2005), 10.
18. Ibid., 11.
19. Kübler-Ross, 11.
20. Ibid., 15.
21. Ibid., 12.
22. Ibid., 16.

caregivers must do their best to remain nonjudgmental. Do not take it personally—it is a part of the dying process! Nevertheless, for the terminally ill the more you immerse yourself into this experience (e.g., letting yourself be angry and trying to understand who or what you are angry at), the more it will begin to dissipate.

Bargaining. This stage may take various forms. It allows patients to believe that they can make sense of their illness. This may involve a false hope that patients can extend their life. A person in this stage may for instance be consumed with searching the internet for a cure or new treatments that can extend his or her life. Many ask God to prolong their life in return for "attending service more often," "performing good works," and "being a better person." Kübler-Ross warns that guilt is often the companion of bargaining.[23] It is not uncommon to say "if only I had exercised more, eaten right, etc." She also suggests that bargaining can function as a "way station" that gives our "psyche time to adjust."[24] We bargain and experience guilt because we are gradually adjusting to the reality of our mortality. Needless to say, caregivers in this stage must be supportive but realistic and honest.

Depression. This is characterized as preparatory grief. It should not be confused with clinical depression. One of the most challenging aspects of this stage is that preparatory grief, especially in the terminally ill, can have the same symptoms as depression.[25] A recent study purports that between 22 and 75 percent of all dying patients suffer from clinical depression.[26] To complicate matters there is no "gold standard" for differentiating preparatory grief from clinical depression.[27] Fleeting thought of suicide, crying, and withdrawal are natural responses to impending death. The serious issue occurs when these thoughts persist and there is an active desire to end one's life. Moreover, common signs of depression include statements like "I am a total failure," "I am an unnecessary burden to others," and "Nothing gives me pleasure."[28]

Nevertheless, because it is difficult to distinguish the two, patients exhibiting these signs should be evaluated by a professional. Caregivers must therefore be as supportive and understanding as possible and aware about their own limitations in caring for patients with these symptoms and be willing to seek help. Kübler-Ross stresses that it is not productive for a caregiver to tell the patient to see

---

23. Ibid., 17.
24. Ibid.,19.
25. Periyakoil Vyjeyanthis and James Hallenbeck, "Identifying and managing preparatory grief and depression at the end of life," *American Family Physician* 65.5 (March 2012): 883-890), 883.
26. EPEC/Institute for Ethics at the American Medical Association. Education for physicians on end-of-life care. Chicago, IL: American Medical Association, 1999 cited in Vyjeyanthis, 884.
27. Periyakoil Vyjeyanthis and James Hallenbeck "The development and initial validation of the Terminally Ill Grief or Depression Scale (TIGDS)," *International Journal of Methods in Psychiatric Research* 14.4 (2005): 202-215), 212.
28. Ibid., 207.

"sunny side of things."[29] Only by allowing the patient to express her sorrow over losing everything she values can the process of acceptance start. This stage is the hardest stage for the patient and caregiver, since patients may be willfully unresponsive or not want to be visited. Perhaps the only upshot to preparatory grief is that it is indicative that the patient be in the process of accepting her condition. We know this because it is the imminence of death that is the cause of the depression.

Acceptance. In this stage the person comes to terms with their medical condition and life expectancy. This does not necessarily mean that the patient is happy and content with their situation, but rather that they have accepted their mortality and are now preparing themselves for their end of life. Kübler-Ross says that this stage is "void of feelings."[30] In this stage a person may or may not find meaning in their suffering, yet they are at peace with the reality of their imminent death. For caregivers, this stage is a great blessing as the patient is easier to care for, since she is at peace with their medical condition and willing to have conversations about end-of-life care.

The strength of Kübler-Ross's theory is that it is clear and concise. It provides the dying and the bereaved with a road map of what to expect. Her scientific approach to dying was unprecedented and remains the best known and widely used theory on grief today. Nevertheless, Kübler-Ross' theory has been criticized by her peers for her research and passive approach to death. Kübler-Ross' theory was based on her clinical experiences with terminally ill patients. Beyond her life experience, she provides no empirical evidence to support her claims: a substantial study of the psychosocial aspects of the dying experience is needed. Moreover, to complicate matters, Kübler-Ross does not absolutize these five stages and admits that these are not the only emotions that one will experience; and there is not necessarily a linear progression from one stage to the next. Although these qualifications make her theory more inclusive and less rigid, they also call into question her selection of some but not other emotions. Since she lacks evidence to support her theory, her selection of Denial, Anger, Bargaining, Depression, and Acceptance is arbitrary.

However, the most pressing criticism of her work is the framework of her theory. Namely, is it really helpful to segment the dying process into stages? The clarity that stage-theories offer has drawbacks. First, given the fact that Kübler-Ross admits that people may bounce from one stage to another or occupy more than one stage at the same time, segmenting death in stages may seem unnecessary. Moreover, her theory fails to empower the dying to take an active role in their dying process because their experience of dying is assigned to predetermined stages. The result is that her theory fails to take into account the complexity of the human person, and may give false hope to the dying person or a caregiver that acceptance of death will be reached. Life and death are more complex and ambiguous than Kübler-Ross' theory can encompass. Take, for instance, a terminally ill patient who has not been able to accept her death due to an untimely death. Does her failure to accept her death mean that she

29. Kübler-Ross, *Death and dying*, 98.
30. Ibid., 124.

had a bad death? Is it helpful to intimate to the dying that acceptance will occur once they suffered the requisite anger and depression associated with death? Rather than taking control of their death, the dying are left in a kind of limbo waiting for the next stage to arrive. The effect is that caregivers as well as the dying can be detrimental, since they may think that there is something wrong with them.

In defense of her theory, a 2007 empirical study of the stages of grief provides an evidence base for stages of grief.[31] Moreover, Kübler-Ross stresses that her theory is misunderstood. She never intended her stages to exhaust the death experience or to be seen as a clear-cut progression. Rather they are "tools to help us frame and identify what we may be feeling."[32] Moreover, she argues that "we do not enter and leave each individual stage in a linear fashion. We may feel one, then another, and back again to the first."[33] Her goal is not to tell the dying what will happen to them but rather give them basic concepts for better understanding their experience.

We cannot underestimate the healthcare community that is highly reliant upon Kübler-Ross' stages of grief and that stages of grief continue to be taught to nursing students who remain on the front lines of care for the dying.[34] Influential organizations like the National Cancer Institute not only provides resources to Kübler-Ross' research but teaches that there is a "numbers of stages that people go through as they cope with loss."[35] Kübler-Ross remains an ubiquitous figure in terms of how healthcare professionals approach coping with death. Despite Kübler-Ross' influence there is consensus among scholars who challenge the assumptions Kübler-Ross associated with grief and dying.[36]

BEYOND "STAGES" OF DEATH

With this consensus in mind, Charles Corr drops the language and concepts of stages and proposes a task-based approach to death. As opposed to providing a road map through death, based on his research on death and dying, he writes that dying affects these four dimensions of a person's life: the physical, psychological, social, and spiritual dimensions. The dimensions are not arbitrary but reflect what he has found to be the four components that cause the dying the most stress when they break down. Corresponding to each area, he provides a task that the dying should be aware of and attend to in order to be empowered and better at peace with their death. His usage of "task"

31. Cf. Paul K. Maciejewski, Baohui Zhang, Susan D. Block, and Holly G. Prigerson, "An empirical examination of the stage theory of grief," *The Journal of the American Medical Association* 297.7 (February 2007): 716-723.
32. Kübler-Ross, *On grief and grieving*, 7.
33. Ibid., 18.
34. Cf. Alison E. Holman, Jennifer Perisho, Ada Edwards, and Natalie Mlakar, "The myths of coping with loss in undergraduate psychiatric nursing books," *Research in Nursing and Health* 33 (2010): 486-499.
35. "Grief, bereavement, and coping with loss," *National Cancer Institute*, http://www.cancer.gov/cancertopics/pdq/supportivecare/bereavement/Patient/page3#Keypoint10 (June 19, 2015).
36. Holman, 487.

as opposed to "stage" is important because while "stage" implies a linear progression,[37] "task" refers to an aspect of a person's life that requires attention. It is not a stage-oriented theory that focuses on progression or regression of a patient's psychological condition, but rather provides aspects of a person's existence that the dying and caregivers should be continually aware of in order to help the dying through the dying process. They have the benefit of aiding caregivers whose terminally ill patient or loved one is unconscious, because they help the caregiver to see things from the point of view and offer a plan for modifying activity so that their activity better addresses the patient's current situation.[38]

Corr stresses that these tasks are important to focus on and the more attention that is given to them, the more empowered and better the dying will feel; however, there is no order or time limit for accomplishing them. Nevertheless, the tasks are potential areas of work, and thus they "may or may not be undertaken and that some may be more or less necessary or desirable."[39] Corr is proposing general guidelines that allow the person to decide which tasks are important for them. What is most important is not the task itself but rather the active role the patient is taking in the illness. From the perspective of caregivers, Corr's tasks provide guidelines to more effectively use their time and energy to help the dying to feel empowered and to an extent in control of their death, which has the effect of protecting their integrity and dignity. Rather than passively waiting for the patient to move from one stage to the next, now the caregiver has specific points to address with the patient.

Corresponding to the area of a person's social-psychological and spiritual existence, Corr proposes four tasks: physical, psychological, social, and spiritual tasks.

Physical Task. The physical task refers to the bodily needs of a person and minimizing physical stress that is consistent with a person's value/belief system.[40] Here we find the subjectivity involved in attending to this task, as it is up to the patient to determine what medications or treatments are consistent with his or her values. For instance, a Jehovah Witness and a Christian Scientist may not want specific medical treatments, such as cardiopulmonary resuscitation, to be used even if the withholding of this treatment will result in death.[41] This is an important task because such patients will be unable to focus on other areas of their life that they deem important if they are in severe physical distress. The challenge is to manage pain well; that is, to use the right amount of medication to control pain. Therefore, the goal is analgesia (controlling pain) not anesthesia (unconsciousness).[42] Drug therapy is not the only option to control the chronic pain, but constructive psycho-

---

37. Cf. Corr, 155.
38. Ibid., 158.
39. Ibid., 162.
40. Ibid., 157.
41. Marianne Matzo and Deborah Witt Sherman, *Palliative care nursing: Quality care to the end of life* (New York: Springer Publishing Company 2010), 23.
42. Corr, 172.

logical and physical therapy are also options to be explored, as they can help patients increase their threshold for pain, so as to avoid overmedication that can result in lack of clarity in consciousness that is necessary to address the other tasks.[43] The caregiver, especially professional caregivers, must do their best to understand the patients' needs and values when administering palliative care.

Psychological Task. This task refers primarily to the autonomy of a person, which Corr means as "the ability to be in charge of one's own life."[44] One of the most challenging aspects of dying is the breakdown of one's ability to make one's decisions and actions. I not only mean the ability to vocalize one's opinion, but also the ability to do mundane activities that you and I take for granted (e.g., clean oneself, shave). What it means to "be in charge of one's own life" is different for each person. This could mean allocating decision making to a particular person or being able to continue to do something that a person enjoys, such as tasting a favorite food.[45] Needless to say, caregivers should do their best to give patients the opportunity to make decisions. This could entail simply asking patients if they want something done. The goal here is to maintain their dignity by treating them as a person and maintaining human interaction to the best degree possible, as opposed to treating the dying as an object for which to be cared. For caregivers, this means to be a good listener, compassionate, and to touch![46] Sometimes a simple physical gesture is all that is needed to convey one's concern for a person's dignity and quality of life. Nevertheless, the values of that person must always be taken into account, and thus it may be grossly inappropriate to touch a person, who is from a specific religious tradition that views groups of people as unclean.

Social Task. This task refers to sustaining and enhancing relationships that a dying patient values.[47] This entails relationships to society and individuals and the values apportioned to each. Regarding the former, this may entail allowing a patient to follow his or her favorite professional sports team. However, dying may also reorient/change interests. The latter refers to interpersonal relationships. Simply, this can mean maintaining relationships that are valued by the person. At times this may cause conflict especially when the patient chooses to forego burdensome treatment in hopes for a cure that the family wants the patient to undergo. This is a conflict over the task of curing an illness (i.e., the physical task for the family) and forgoing burdensome treatments (i.e., the physical task for the person).

This task also refers to interacting with social systems, albeit charitable organizations, the government, and religious institutions. Thus, there are specific treatments that state governments do not permit that the patient may want, such as death-inducing drugs.

---

43. Ibid., 172.
44. Ibid., 158.
45. Ibid., 159.
46. Ibid., 176-177.
47. Corr, 159.

Caregivers need to be sensitive to the identities of their patients and allow them to voice their concerns about their relationships to other people and society. The dying need an opportunity to ask those questions like, "What will happen to my children when I am gone?" that the caregiver may not be able to answer. The goal for caregivers is to help the dying think about goals that they may have and ways to accomplish these goals. Corr notes that it can be disempowering to accomplish this task for them. Thus, although there may be a good intention in contacting a dying person's disaffected relative,[48] this may be counterproductive as it takes away the ability of the patient to act on the thought that he or she may not be prepared to act on.

Spiritual Task. Spiritual task concerns the meaningfulness of life, the connectedness to others, and transcendence. People who are devoted members of a religious community will look to their religious tradition for guidance regarding these important topics. Although for many dying patients religion will play an important role, this is not necessarily the case. Atheists, those who are self-described as "religious nones,"[49] and agnostics may ask the same questions about existence after death, the meaning of life, their lasting contribution to the world, but they will undoubtedly arrive at different conclusions. For these reasons the spiritual task is not just for religious people, but for all people, and it underlies the other social dimensions.[50] In other words, how you answer the question, "What is the meaning of life?" will affect how you approach pain management (physical dimension), vouchsafe your autonomy (psychological dimension), and maintain relationships (social dimension). For devoutly religious people, their faith tradition will more explicitly inform these other aspects of their life, orienting one's relationships and activities so that they reflect belief in the afterlife—the social and psychological aspects).

It is of interest to note that the topic of how "religious people" cope with death versus "non-religious" people is a hot topic of debate. In my research I have not found a clear consensus among experience-based studies that demonstrate religious people are better at coping with death than nonreligious people. I think part of the problem is that "religious" and "nonreligious" can be numinous terms that mean very different things to different people. Even among "religious" people there are various levels of devotion to a particular deity or tradition, and not all religious people cope with death and dying in the same manner. Nevertheless, there is good research that "religious coping" overtime yields positive effects (e.g., less stress, depression, and anxiety about death).[51] Note that the evidence we have for "religious coping" yielding positive effects is dependent upon views about God that "reflect a secure relationship with God, a belief that there is a greater meaning to be found,

---

48. Corr, 180.
49. Cf. Heidi Glenn, "Losing our religion: The growth of 'Nones'" (National Public Radio, January 13, 2013), March 28, 2013, http://www.npr.org/blogs/thetwo-way/2013/01/14/169164840/losing-our-religion-the-growth-of-the-nones.
50. Corr, 180.
51. Cf. K. I., Pargament and H. Abu Raiya, "A decade of research on the psychology of religion and coping: Things we assumed and lessons we learned," *Psyke & Logos* 28 (2007): 742-766.

and a sense of spiritual connectedness with others."[52] The same study notes that religious coping that views the world as threatening yields harmful effects. A 2012 in-depth study of ninety-eight persons coping with loss by Mellissa M. Kelley and Keith T. Chan confirmed this finding and suggested that the belief in a God that is benevolent, available, and responsive "generates resilience in the face of significant loss."[53]

Regardless of whether patients identify with a religious tradition, caregivers need to be careful not to impose their values upon the dying, as the spiritual quest is each patient's spiritual quest and not the caregiver's quest. E.M. Brady suggests that when dying persons ask caregivers about spiritual questions they are "often striving to tell their own stories."[54] If caregivers are asked to share their ideas on this topic, they should be aware that the patient may be looking for an opportunity to talk about these issues rather than listen to a response. The caregiver's goal after attentively listening may be to "bring the person to the source of help or bring the helpful resource to the person."[55] This may entail giving the patient a Bible, contacting a religious leader, or providing opportunities for the person to express creativity or transcendence. The spiritual task is rarely completed before death. Nevertheless supporting the dying in their search for the answers to their meaning and transcendence can be of great comfort to them.

Although his model for coping with death lacks the clarity of Kübler-Ross' theory, Corr's task emphasizes the importance of the autonomy and personality of the dying patient that helps to safeguard against objectifying the dying patient in his or her experiences. Corr's model builds on Kübler-Ross' emphasis on the unique subjectivity of the dying that must be respected.

Coping with Death and Bereavement

Thus far, I have examined death and two different models of the socio-psychological dying process. However death involves not only the personal loss of life, but the loss of a loved one by those who remain living. In this section I will focus on the process of bereavement and additional models to help the bereaved in their grief. Following Corr, I use "bereaved" and "grief" in two different senses. Corr defines bereavement as "the state of being deprived of something" and grief as "one's reaction to loss."[56] In the context of death bereavement refers to a loss of a valued person and grief is a normal

---

52. Ibid., 748.
53. Melissa M. Kelly and Keith T. Chan, "Assessing the role of attachment to God, meaning, and religious coping as mediators in the grief experience," *Death Studies* 36 (2012): 199-227), 222.
54. E. M. Brady, "Telling the story: Ethics and dying," *Hospital Progress* 60 (1979): 57-62, quoted in Corr, 180.
55. Corr, 181.
56. Corr, 238.

reaction to those experiencing this loss. Everyone who values someone who dies experiences some form of sorrow for this loss; and this experience is grief.

There is no consensus on how one should grieve among scholars. The only consensus is that grieving is individualized, and thus there is no "golden rule" for what constitutes good or bad grieving or too long or too short grieving. This is not to say that grief cannot lead to depression or that grief can be unrealistic. Although grief can affect behavior, physiology, and feelings, it is not a disease or unhealthy process. Rather it is "a sign of health itself."[57] We ought to be gravely concerned when we fail to grieve for our loved ones. This may seem a shock, since our society generally does not encourage displays of grief and, as mentioned, fails to provide support for the bereaved. Nevertheless, grief is a natural response to death and should not be suppressed as it is one manner in which the bereaved can accept their loss and celebrate or express love for the person who has died.

As noted, there are several theories on the process of grieving. Before I address them it is important to note that both Kübler-Ross' five-stage theory and Corr's task-based theory may also be applied to coping with the loss of a loved one. However, the most popular theory of mourning or grieving the loss of a loved one is the phase-based theory that Parkes proposes that entails four phases: shock and numbness, yearning and searching, disorganization and despair, and acceptance.[58] Shock and numbness refers to the initial reaction to the death. Think for instance about how people initially responded to 9-11. Many people stood in the streets of Manhattan staring in silence at the death and destruction. Yearning and searching refers to unrealistic desires for the loved one to return to familiar habits and the pattern of life. The bereaved may yearn for their loved one to return to the routine of work or be reminded of their loved one by a familiar smell or sight. This begins the adjustment of the bereaved to life without their loved one. Disorganization and despair refers to the next phase in this adjustment, namely figuring out how to go about living without their loved one. This means having to make difficult decisions and experiencing the stress and at times despair that may ensue. The bereaved have to figure out how to pay their bills without a second paycheck, how to find comfort when all those around them are also grieving, and so forth.[59] When the bereaved find their way forward they enter into the final stage of mourning, which is reorganization. Here they have created new habits without their loved one. They have learned how to survive and perhaps thrive without their loved one.

Although the phase-based theory has appeal because it is clear and seems to confirm many people's lived experience, it suffers from many of the problems for which Kübler-Ross' theory was criticized. Moreover, although this theory is based on research as opposed to personal experience, the focus is primarily on elderly widows, who are not representative of all mourners. For these reasons Worden,

---

57. Cf. Corr, 242.
58. Cf. Corr, 249.
59. Ibid., 250.

in a recent study, offers a task-based theory that emphasizes the individuality and activity of the mourner. The tasks that Worden argues that the bereaved should attend to are: to accept the reality that your loved one has died; to process the pain of grief without being overwhelmed by the pain of loss or suppressing those feelings that will only lead to prolonged grief; to adjust to the world without the deceased and acknowledge what was lost and gain new necessary skills (e.g., washing dishes); and to find an enduring connection with the dead while beginning a new life.[60] The final task refers to finding an appropriate place in the bereaved life for their dead. This is individualized and may include visiting the gravesite at certain times and events. Again these tasks are important features of grieving that may help mourners accept the death of their loved ones. Nevertheless these tasks are individualized insofar as they rely on mourners to avoid or to attend a specific task that the mourners deem appropriate.

Caregivers, Helpers, and Friends of the Bereaved

To this point I have provided general theories for understanding and responding to the death and bereavement process. Because death and bereavement are individualized experiences I have intentionally avoided specific advice and remained general. However I think it is important to discuss briefly but more specifically what caregivers and friends of the bereaved can do, namely "caregivers and the dying" and "friends of the bereaved."

SUGGESTIONS FOR CAREGIVERS

Corr provides five practical suggestions for caring for the dying: Remember, Recognize, Respect, Reinforce, and Reminiscence. I teach a course on the challenges of death, and invariably almost every semester I am asked by a student how should a healthcare professional respond to the questions of their patient's about the afterlife. Many of these students may not be a member of any religious community or not feel comfortable expressing their views on this topic. Corr suggests that we **remember** that you are different from your patient. You do not know your patient's background fully and thus you should be cautious if you choose to answer this question. If you do choose to answer, do not speak as an authority with "absolute truth" but rather as an individual who has found a meaningful answer to this question.[61] Thus you should preface your response with "In my experience." You should **recognize** that death is a profound experience for that individual that you cannot enter into, and **respect** the fact that you cannot comprehend what that person is going through. This

---

60. Cf. J.W. Worden, *Grief counseling and grief therapy: A handbook for the mental health practitioner*, 4th ed., New York: Springer, 2008.
61. Corr, 183.

means to be "authentically present" to your patient and pay attention to the subtle clues to be left alone or a need for companionship.[62] This will require a bit of a balancing act, especially from a professional caregiver to be compassionate but avoid personal attachments. For your own psychological well-being and that of your patient, you need to be the best nurse, physician assistant you can be for that person, not an adopted son or daughter. Thus, you need to treat the person as a human being and show that you genuinely care, which will be evident in the little things that you do well. On this note, make your care relevant to your patient by always including him or her in a dialogue. Show your respect by telling your patient what you are doing (e.g., washing, administering medication) and why you are doing it. In so doing you will **reinforce** the person's dignity and decision-making capacity. One way to accomplish this is to ask the patient questions about not only his or her feelings but also preferences, desires, and values. Instead of asking, "How do you feel?" you may ask, "Has *medication x* relieved any of your discomfort?" Being specific in your question asking will help the patient feel valued and indicate you took the time to understand the patient's treatment/condition and ways to better relieve his or her discomfort. Finally, help patients **reminisce** about their life.[63] It is important to be an active-listener. In terms of addressing their spiritual dimension, you may ask them if they want their stories recorded for posterity. [64] This is also a great suggestion if you have time to spend with the dying person, but may feel uncomfortable and at a loss for words. You can simply ask: "What was it like growing up in the 1950s?" or "What were the most exciting things that you have done?"

SUGGESTIONS FOR COMFORTING THE BEREAVED

Often a death in a community/family can leave not only the immediate family disoriented, not knowing what to do, but also extended family, friends, and relatives. Before we examine specific steps for you to take, it is important to note that you cannot "fix" the situation or make everything better. It is not what you say that is most important or may help ease the bereaved person's grief but what you do. Harvard Medical School has identified the following eleven ways to comfort someone who is grieving[65]: name names, offer hope, make phone calls, write a note, help out, be sensitive to difference, make a date, listen well instead of advising, express your feelings, handle anger gently, and keep your promises.

Name names. It is important that when speaking of the deceased that you call the deceased by his or her name. This may cause tears, but it is far worse to avoid saying the deceased person's name,

---

62. Ibid., 183.
63. Ibid., 183.
64. Ibid., 183.
65. Harvard Health Publications: Harvard Medical School, "11 ways to help someone who's grieving," http://www.health.harvard.edu/healthbeat/11-ways-to-comfort-someone-who%E2%80%99s-grieving (January 29, 2014).

which may inadvertently confirm the bereaved person's fear that that his or her deceased loved one is lost forever.

Offer hope. There is a time and place to offer hope. But you should reassure the bereaved that things will get better. At the time this may not be what the bereaved wants to hear, but it is often the people who offer hope that the bereaved remember and are thankful for as they reorganize their life without their loved one.[66]

Make a call. Immediately after the tragedy call and express your support. Since most people stop calling because they want to give the bereaved space to mourn, the bereaved may need you now more than ever. However, "[t]ry to steer clear of such phrases as 'It's God's will' or 'It's for the best' unless the bereaved person says this first." As we have learned, death is a deeply individualized experience and thus we ought not to make sense of if for the bereaved person even if we deeply believe that it is God's will.

Write a note. It is very difficult to convey your sympathy, especially immediately after the death. Writing a note or perhaps sending an email or Facebook message lets the bereaved know that they are not alone and that you care for them. In the message, if you knew the person that died, mention something funny or kind about them; if not, then simply offer your prayers and/or thoughts.[67]

Help out. There are myriad responsibilities that the bereaved must attend to in regard to the death, including calling relatives, an employer, a doctor or county coroner; getting a death certificate; submitting a will to appropriate parties; contacting agencies about the deceased person's benefits; contacting religious organizations, if applicable; planning a funeral; and more.[68] Helping with any of these tasks or even basic tasks like cooking dinner will greatly reduce stress and allow the bereaved to take time to grieve.

Be sensitive to difference. As mentioned there is no gold standard for mourning. Practice self-restraint if you do not agree how your loved one is grieving or how the funeral or memorial was performed.

Make a date. Facing difficult times, people generally enjoy companionship. Suggesting a low-stress activity such as movie, walk, coffee once a week, dinner especially during extensive times when the bereaved is alone, may be a great help to the bereaved. Usually the weekends are the most difficult

---

66. Ibid.
67. Ibid.
68. Cf. "What to do when a loved one dies: Our advice can keep a sad even from becoming more painful," *Consumer Reports* 2012, http://www.consumerreports.org/cro/magazine/2012/10/what-to-do-when-a-loved-one-dies/index.htm (January 14, 2014).

times because that may have been the time that the bereaved allocated exclusively to spending time with the deceased love one.[69]

Listen well instead of advising, and express your feelings. "[P]eople work through grief and trauma by telling their story over and over."[70] Do not give advice unless asked to do so; however, if you are grieving the person's death it is appropriate to let them know so. But do not assume that you know how they feel.[71]

Handle anger gently. It is not uncommon for anger to be directed at you because you are the "closest target."[72] Do your best to be understanding, and after the person has calmed down let the person know any concerns that you have.

Keep your promises. Death can often feel like abandonment. The last thing the bereaved needs is to be abandoned by you.

Conclusion

This chapter has provided a broad overview to the study of death, dying, and bereavement in American society. It has offered a variety of popular theories for readers to better understand the complexity of the dying process. The goal has been to introduce readers to the topic and process of death so as to familiarize them with the dying process, to better prepare them to understand the complexity of the ethical issues related to dying. The chapter lays the foundation for my examination of how religious people cope with death. Religion helps people die well because it addresses the four dimensions of dying persons.

---

69. "11 ways to help someone who's grieving," *Harvard Health Publications: Harvard Medical School*, http://www.health.harvard.edu/healthbeat/11-ways-to-comfort-someone-who%E2%80%99s-grieving (January 29, 2014).
70. Ibid.
71. Corr, 294.
72. *Harvard Health Publications*.

CHAPTER TWO

END-OF-LIFE DECISIONS AND CARE

Introduction

While advances in healthcare have raised life expectancy, they have also engendered debates and moral dilemmas about end-of-life care for many families in the United States. This chapter provides a succinct overview of the moral dilemmas and discussions regarding end-of-life decision making. For the purpose of clarity this chapter is divided into three parts: the bioethics of dying, hospice care, and an interview with Monica Sleap, a hospice expert. The bioethics of dying will primarily focus on the ethical decisions related to euthanasia and withholding or withdrawing life support. With attention to hospice care and philosophy, the second section discusses end-of-life care. This chapter concludes with an interview with Monica Sleap that will provide a firsthand account about the challenges and blessings that accompany care for the dying. Her lived experience provides a great overview of many of the issues discussed in this text.

Part One: Bioethics of Dying

WHEN DO WE DIE?

In the last chapter I introduced the neurological (brain death) criteria or the standard used by the majority of health professionals and legal entities to define biological death. It is important to note that a growing number of bioethicists and health professionals no longer find this standard an adequate metric for death. Not only are we aware of cases where patients were declared "brain dead" but lived, but also as recent research demonstrates patients could be labeled brain dead but not lose all brain function.[1] Take for instance a patient that was declared brain dead but retained spinal reflexes; this is indicative of lower brainstem function. Moreover, the neurological criteria is premised on the belief that when brain death occurs sentient function is lost, which is the loss of personhood, that in turn justifies taking the patient off life support since the person is dead. The problem with this premise is that sentient function also relies on the nervous system that is not addressed by the neurological criteria. Finally, scholars like Hans Jonas argue that the criteria were introduced to expedite the need of organ harvesting for transplants as opposed to advancement in scientific research.[2]

There is no consensus as to a new standard to replace the neurological criteria. Nevertheless in recent years, a variety of alternative standards have been proposed.[3] One important standard is the cardiopulmonary standard that refers to the irreversible cessation of cardiopulmonary function. What makes this standard attractive is that it was used for the greater part of human history to determine death. Signs of death included the lack of pulse, heartbeat, and/or breathing. Proponents of this view may argue that "breathing and maintaining circulation" indicate life, and therefore only when these mechanisms are lost has life ended.[4] Alternative cardiopulmonary standards equate life with the function of the heart in conjunction with the lungs, and brain. Death occurs only when all of these organs cease to function. The upshot is that these standards may better protect patients from being denied services that may prolong their life; however, they also make ending the life of a patient in a vegetative state with little or no brain function cumbersome.

A number of scholars reject the notion of equating human life to the proper functioning of one or several organs or biological mechanisms as reductionist. They argue that a person may only be

---

1. Cf. R. D. Troug and J. C. Fackler, "Rethinking brain death," *Critical Care Medicine* 20.12 (1992): 1705-1713.
2. Cited in William E. May, *Catholic bioethics and the gift of human life,* 3rd ed. (Huntington, IN: Our Sunday Visitor, 2013), 297.
3. For a list and succinct overview of the different standards proposed, see "The definition of death," *Stanford Encyclopedia of Philosophy* 2011, http://plato.stanford.edu/entries/death-definition/ (January 27, 2015).
4. Cf. Ibid.

declared dead when that person "has lost the capacity for any sort of consciousness [beyond reasonable doubt]."[5] This is difficult to determine and requires careful and repeated testing.

The widespread criticism of the neurological criteria as well as the inability to form a consensus as to how to determine when it is legally and morally permissible to declare that a patient is dead, and advances in healthcare science, have led many lawmakers to question whether or not the neurological criteria is suitable for declaring someone dead. Although the neurological criteria remains standard, states such as New Jersey and New York have made important addendums to state law regarding the legal definition of death based on this standard. Both states allow doctors to take into consideration their patient's religious and moral views when determining if a patient is deceased.[6]

Euthanasia

Is it ethical to end our own life if we are terminally ill? Should the state legalize euthanasia? Is letting someone die a form of euthanasia? All of these questions are important questions that Americans struggle to answer. This struggle is nowhere more evident than in American media's excessive preoccupation with the right-to-die debate. In the past few years the American media has inundated the public with high-profile cases including Terri Schiavo (2005), a woman in a vegetative state who was starved to death by the state of Florida at the request of her husband; Jahi McMath (2013-), a thirteen-year old girl who was declared brain dead but whose family legally forced her hospital to keep her "alive" with life-sustaining machines[7]; Marlise Machado Muñoz (2013), a brain-dead pregnant mother that the state of Texas, against the wishes of her husband, kept her body functioning during her pregnancy; Brittney Maynard (2014), a vocal advocate for the right to physician-assisted suicide and terminally ill women who moved to Oregon in order to end her life on her own terms; and Martin Pistorius (2015), the "Ghost Boy" who not only "broke free" of his vegetative state after a decade but also argued that he was completely conscious during the time of his vegetative state.

A 2014 Pew Study revealed that ethics involved in ending the life of a terminally ill person is a divisive issue in the United States. This study discovered that although 63 percent of Americans think that there are "circumstances in which doctors and nurses should allow a patient to die,"[8] Americans

---

5. May, 309.
6. "Why hospitals and families still struggle to define death," *NPR* 2014, http://www.npr.org/blogs/health/2014/01/10/261391130/why-hospitals-and-families-still-struggle-to-define-death (January 28, 2015).
7. As of 2014, Jahi was moved a facility in New Jersey where she is undergoing treatment.
8 "5 facts about Americans' views on life-and-death issues," Pew Research Center 2014, http://www.pewresearch.org/fact-tank/2014/01/07/5-facts-about-americans-views-on-life-and-death-issues/ (January 20, 2015).

were almost evenly divided as to whether or not an attending physician should have the ability to prescribe a drug that would end the life of a terminally ill patient; 49 percent of Americans think physician-assisted suicide should be illegal, and 47 percent think it should be legal.[9]

These findings are very interesting when we consider that around 90 percent of Americans profess membership in an organized religion. A 2013 Pew Study of sixteen major religious communities in the United States found that with exception to the Unitarian Universalist Association and the United Church of Christ, they reject physician-assisted suicide as inconsistent with their ethic on life.[10]

WHERE IS PAS LEGAL, AND WHAT ARE THE STIPULATIONS?

As of January 2015, five states legislate that terminally ill patients have the right to end their lives. These states include Oregon (1997), Washington (2008), Montana (2009), Vermont (2013), and New Mexico (2014). Euthanasia, or more specifically physician-assisted suicide (PAS), is regulated by each state. Nevertheless most states follow Oregon law because it was the first state to lobby successfully to legalize PAS and the state law has been upheld by the Supreme Court as constitutional. Therefore Oregon's law on PAS is worth our consideration.

In Oregon, the request for PAS can be as quick as fifteen days from the initial request to die; however, on average the process takes three months. There is a basic standard of eligibility for euthanasia that includes being a resident of Oregon, at least eighteen years of age, diagnosed with a terminal illness that has a life expectancy of six months or less, and capable of making one's own decisions.[11]

 An eligible patient must first request from a physician that is licensed in the state of Oregon to be euthanized. The patient must make at least two oral requests. The second request cannot be made until fifteen days after the first request. This allows the patient enough time to reconsider the decision. Afterwards, in the presence of two individuals, the patient will sign the request for PAS. A second physician must confirm the prognosis of the first physician. At this point various forms are completed by the patient requesting euthanasia and then sent to the Oregon Health Authority. These forms include questionnaires that help determine that the choice for euthanasia is not coerced and that the dying patient is of sound mind. Regarding the former, on the "Request for Medication to End My Life in a Human and Dignified Manner" form, the patient must have two witnesses verify

---

9. Ibid.
10. "Religious groups' views on end-of-life issues," Pew Research Center 2013, http://www.pewforum.org/files/2013/11/end-of-life-religious-groups-views.pdf (January 28, 2015).
11. "Death with dignity: Oregon revised statue," *Oregon Health Authority,* http://public.health.oregon.gov/ProviderPartnerResources/EvaluationResearch/DeathwithDignityAct/Pages/ors.aspx (January 29, 2014).

that the "person is of sound mind and not under duress."[12] One witness must not be a family member that "shall not be entitled to any portion of the person's estate upon death and shall not own."[13] Although Oregon's state law does not require that people requesting PAS have a psychological evaluation, according to state law, if the physician or consulting physician thinks that the person may be suffering from depression or a psychological disorder, the medication cannot be administered until a counselor has determined that these disorders are not affecting the patient's judgment.[14] Before the medication can be prescribed, the prescribing physician must inform the patient of alternatives to PAS, such as hospice, and request that the patient contact next-of-kin about the decision. At any point the patient can decide not to pursue PAS. If all the protocols are followed, the patient is given a prescription of secobarbital in capsule form or pentobarbital in liquid form to be consumed at a time when the patient deems it appropriate to die.[15]

What Is Euthanasia?

Part of the challenge with discussing euthanasia is that it can mean different things to different people. Above I have used euthanasia and PAS as synonyms. Although there is consensus that PAS is euthanasia, there is not that same consensus when we examine whether letting someone die is PAS. Even among those that accept that letting someone die is not necessarily euthanasia, there are instances where many would argue that it is PAS. Thus I think it is helpful to be as specific as possible when referring to euthanasia.[16] Following William Mattison, I will argue that an action is euthanasia if it fulfills these criteria: [17]

1. **The terminally ill patient must have the *intention* to die in order to end suffering.** This is different from the intention to take a person off life support in order to end a burdensome treatment. It is not easy to determine intentionality, especially when a variety of intentions are present. Mattison offers some advice as to how to determine the primary motivating intention:

---

12. "Request for medication to end my life in a humane and dignified manner," *Oregon Health Authority,* http://public. health.oregon.gov/ProviderPartnerResources/EvaluationResearch/DeathwithDignityAct/Documents/pt-req.pdf (January 29, 2014).
13. Ibid.
14. "127.825 counseling referral," Oregon Laws 1999, http://www.oregonlaws.org/ors/127.825 (January 29, 2014).
15. Cf. "Physician-Assisted Suicide: Ongoing Challenges to Pharmacists," *Medscape* 2011, http://www.medscape.com/viewarticle/742070_3 (January 28, 2015).
16. I have opted against employing the traditional distinction between passive and active euthanasia because of the latent ambiguities in these terms, and the fact that "euthanasia" in popular idiom has appropriated a negative connotation. My definition attempts to capture what people mean when they speak about euthanasia.
17. My definition for euthanasia is adapted from William C. Mattison III, *Introducing moral theology: True happiness and virtues* (Grand Rapids, MI: Brazos Press, 2008), 372-374.

Create a thought experiment that eliminates other intentions. Suppose that you were the proxy entrusted with making the decisions to continue or discontinue life support for a loved one. Think for instance about how you would react if after taking the person off life support, she lived. If you would jump for joy, then your intention was not for the person to die, but rather to end burdensome treatment, knowing that ending this treatment will most likely result in death. Whereas if you would be angry that she did not die, then your primary motivating intention is for her to die. In most religious traditions this intention is immoral.

2. **Euthanasia is an action or omission of an action that causes death.** We tend to think of euthanasia as physician-assisted suicide. However, for many people euthanasia may also be the omission of basic care. The dilemma surrounding Terri Schiavo illustrates this, as her parents accused Terri's husband and the state of Florida of murdering their daughter since they took away her basic care (e.g., feeding tube and intravenous therapy). In medical ethics basic healthcare is generally referred to as ordinary means or the "kind of treatment which offers reasonable hope of benefitting the subject without imposing unacceptable burdens on the subject."[18] Thus, starving a terminally ill person to death would violate ordinary means, as food benefits the subject without imposing an unacceptable burden. Terri's parents argue that this is what befell their daughter. This is omission of an action that causes death. This differs from "extraordinary means" or burdensome/useless treatments. These treatments have one or all of these characteristics: they are futile, not worthwhile since the patient has reason to think that she no longer has an obligation to prolong her life; the burden is not warranted by the promised benefits, it is more than the patient can cope; and it poses excessive financial risk.[19] A clear example of an extraordinary means is keeping a person "alive" who has lost the capacity for consciousness. Nevertheless there is not a clear-cut standard for defining what constitutes an ordinary or extraordinary means since it depends upon the circumstances of the individual patient to some extent.

3. **The patient is suffering and terminally ill.** Thus patients who are suffering but clinically depressed or suffering with a likelihood of healing do not qualify for euthanasia. Killing one of these patients is not euthanasia but murder. For this reason states that legalize euthanasia have an eligibility requirement that includes "six months or less to live."[20]

Pro Euthanasia (PAS) Arguments

There are a variety of arguments used to justify the legalization and morality of PAS. One of the most popular arguments is the autonomy argument, which is sometimes referred to as the quality of

---

18. May, 270.
19. Cf. Ibid.
20. "Death with dignity: Attending physician form," *Oregon Health Authority*, http://public.health.oregon.gov/Provider-PartnerResources/EvaluationResearch/DeathwithDignityAct/Documents/at1form.pdf (January 31, 2014).

life argument or death with dignity argument. The Canadian High Court that legalized euthanasia in 2015 provides a succinct explanation of this argument: "an individual's response to a grievous and irremediable medical condition is a matter critical to their dignity and autonomy."[21] In other words, respect for personal autonomy entails respect for the ability to choose PAS. The argument rests on the presupposition that life can lose its dignity. The dignity of life is relative to the ability to act autonomously; because dying persons lose basic motor functions and the ability to communicate, they lose the ability to act autonomously, and they therefore no longer have dignity. Proponents for this argument also appeal to intense pain involved in many terminal illnesses as persons lose their ability to make autonomous decisions. The pain to which I refer is not exclusively physical pain, but also emotional and psychological distress. PAS offers a way out of this suffering. It is the best option in a bad circumstance: PAS allows the individual to maintain autonomy to the best extent possible because, at the very least, persons can die on their own terms, sparing themselves the suffering and loss of autonomy they fear to lose.

This argument is a logical extension of the basic human rights to autonomy and privacy.[22] Think about how many decisions that you have the legal right to make (e.g., what you want to eat, where you want to work or live, and what you want to believe/worship). Americans pride themselves on their rights. Yet as Peter Singer, a contemporary controversial bioethicist, argues, it is inconsistent to say that we respect people's rights to autonomous existence so long as their actions do not interfere with another person's expression of autonomy, but then prevent them from making autonomous decisions that do not hurt other persons.[23] Therefore we must either legalize PAS, or admit our irrationality about personal autonomy; Singer thinks consistency is the best option.

In my experience in lecturing and researching this topic, another popular argument in favor of euthanasia is actually a counterargument that rejects the common iteration that PAS is against "God's will since God is the author of life." Proponents of this argument exploit the fact that monotheists believe that God has a will for each of us that includes not only how we are to live but that we will die. They may grant that PAS frustrates God's will because it is a medical service that ends life. However, just about every lifesaving treatment frustrates God's will since it interferes with the death process that presumably God initiated. There is no doubt that terminally ill patients would die much sooner without modern medical intervention. Thus the rejection of PAS based on it frustrating God's will is inconsistent with how most monotheists exploit modern medicine. Therefore, to be consistent, persons who posit that PAS is against God's will must also reject all of the lifesaving treatments that

21. "Physician-assisted suicide ban overturned by Canadian Supreme Court," *CBS NEWS* 2015, http://www.cbsnews.com/news/physician-assisted-suicide-ban-overturned-by-supreme-court-of-canada/ (February 6, 2015).
22. James B. Martin-Schramm, "Death, duty, and dignity" in *Christian ethics: A case method approach*, 4th ed. (pp. 305-326). Edited by Laura A. Striver, Christine E. Gudorf, and James B. Martin-Schramm (Maryknoll, NY: Orbis Books, 2012), 322.
23. Cf. Peter Singer, *Practical ethics*, 2nd ed. (Cambridge: Cambridge University Press, 1993), 175-217.

also frustrate God's will. Because few monotheists are willing to do this, then they must either reject modern medicine or be irrational. The response to this argument is that "doing God's will" actually involves a synergism between the Divine and human wills rather than a passive determinism that is suggested above. Moreover, within the Judeo-Christian traditions God wills life, not death. Medication that saves life is consistent with God's will.

Another popular argument in favor of euthanasia applies the golden rule—"treat others the way you want to be treated"—to the euthanasia debate. The argument is that if you do not legalize euthanasia, then you will force people to suffer the physical and psychological trauma of dying when they do not want to experience these things. The argument attempts to appeal to our humanity: no person of sound mind wants others to suffer for the sake of suffering. We should legalize euthanasia since to do otherwise is a violation of the basic principle of human relationships: treat others like you want to be treated. The retort to this argument is usually to stress that I do not want to die; therefore by logic of the golden rule, I should not support laws that cause death.

Contra Euthanasia (PAS) Arguments

Arguments against euthanasia fall into two general categories: common good arguments and sanctity of life arguments. Whereas the former arguments are inductive arguments that examine the negative effect that the legalization of euthanasia will have on culture and its citizens, the latter attempts to demonstrate that life and suffering are valuable experiences. Although I have divided these theories for clarity, they are interrelated. And thus many will argue that the legalization of PAS will lead to a culture (common good) that devalues human rights (value of life).

COMMON GOOD ARGUMENTS.

The Roman Catholic bishops of the United States succinctly summarize the common good argument:

> If our right to life itself is diminished in value, our other rights will have no meaning. To destroy the boundary between healing and killing would mark a radical departure from longstanding legal and medical traditions of our country, posing a threat of unforeseeable magnitude to vulnerable members of our society. Those who represent the interests of elderly citizens, persons with disabilities, and persons with AIDS or other terminal illnesses, are justifiably alarmed when some hasten to confer on them the "freedom" to be killed.[24]

---

24. "Euthanasia statement," United States Catholic Conference of Bishops 1991, http://www.usccb.org/issues-and-action/human-life-and-dignity/end-of-life/euthanasia/statement-on-euthanasia-1991.cfm (February 10, 2014).

In accord with the bishops' statement, opponents of the legalization of euthanasia often argue that legalization of euthanasia will not only force healthcare professionals to violate the Hippocratic oath but put them in positions where they may have to violate their own conscience. PAS is counterintuitive because it goes against the basic role of medical doctors: to heal the sick. Moreover if euthanasia becomes culturally acceptable there will be no or very little incentive to advance palliative care and end-of-life treatment. This is an acute concern in the United States, because profit margins motivate what medicines are produced and what kind of research is financed.[25] If PAS becomes legal and culturally acceptable, pharmaceutical companies and research institutions will have incentive to stop producing and pursuing research for drugs that offer more effective symptom control. The result will be inadequate care for the terminally ill. In 2001, members of the American College of Physicians-American Society of Internal Medicine rejected PAS for this reason, arguing that PAS "undermine[s] efforts to marshal the needed resources, and will ensure humane and dignified care for all persons facing terminal illness or severe disability."[26] They argue that the reason why persons resort to PAS is "inadequate care." Doctors and medical researchers should be focused on this problem, to make pain more manageable. They fear that doctors will be/are in a position where they become delivers of death as opposed to committed to the healing or management of the pain of their patients. The result is a healthcare system and society that no longer is concerned about the common good or creating a society that values human life and the quality of care for the terminally ill. Because legalized euthanasia is a recent phenomenon, it is unclear whether or not these fears have manifested.

Slippery-Slope Arguments.

Related to the common good argument against legalizing PAS is the slippery-slope argument. Proponents of this argument posit that legalizing euthanasia will erode the moral fiber of our society. Not only will physicians become "dealers of death" as opposed to committed to "health" and "care," but persons on the margins of society, the poor, the elderly, and disabled will be pressured into opting for euthanasia. Supporters of this position refer to recent examples of non-terminally ill persons who have been euthanized because of a perceived decrease in quality of life. For example, a woman in the Netherlands who lost her sight was euthanized because blindness caused her "unbearable suffering."[27] A 2005 study indicates that in the Netherlands 400 people a year request PAS because

---

25. Cf. Marcia Angell, *The truth about drug companies: How they deceive us and what to do about it.* New York: Random House, 2004.

26. Lois Snyder and Daniel P. Sulmasy, "American College of Physicians-American Society of Internal Medicine's Position Paper: Physician Assisted Suicide," *Annals of Internal Medicine* 3.135 (August): 209-216.

27. "Woman, 70, is given euthanasia after going blind," *Dutch News* 2013, http://www.dutchnews.nl/news/archives/2013/10/women_70_gets_euthanasia_after.php/ (February 2, 2015).

they are "weary of life."[28] Interestingly, the authors of this study concluded that there is an alarming trend of "therapeutic nihilism."[29] This refers to physicians' lack of interest or ability to seek to treat or offer pain management options when they are approached about PAS by terminally ill patients. These physicians immediately support such patients' decision to kill themselves. Alarmingly in "only two thirds of the cases in this study the physicians did not treat the patient and in half of the cases treatment was not even considered."[30] Supporters of this position may argue that the slippery slope is evident not simply by the increased amount of persons seeking PAS but also in the lack of health professionals' commitment to caring as opposed to killing their patients.[31] Similar trends are evident in Oregon; according to the 2013 Death with Dignity Report, between 1998 and 2013 there has been over a 400 percent increase in the amount of persons requesting PAS.[32] However, like the Netherlands, these deaths still make up a small percentage of deaths per year in Oregon.

With respect to the legalization of PAS pressuring the poor and persons with disabilities to be euthanized, there is no clear evidence that this is the case in Oregon. Nevertheless Belgium, which has recently received a lot of scrutiny for its liberal euthanasia laws that includes euthanasia of terminally ill children[33] and high-profile cases such as Marc and Eddy Verbessem, who were granted their wish to be euthanized because they became aware that a genetic condition they had that would lead to blindness and cause "extreme discomfort and unhappiness,"[34] perhaps offers evidence for PAS prejudicing against the most vulnerable in society. Els Van Hoof, a Belgium senator, argues that this has occurred, reporting that, "[i]n the beginning they presented a law that included mentally ill children…During the debate, supporters of euthanasia talked about children with anorexia, children who are tired of life - so how far does it go?"[35] Nevertheless, a 2009 study of euthanasia in Belgium (from 2002-2007) warns that developments do not necessitate slippery slope.[36] Nontermi-

28. Mette L. Rurup, T. Martien Muller, Bregje D. Onwuteaka-Philipsen, Agnes Van Der Heide, Gerrit Van der Wal, and Paul J. Van der Maas, "Requests for euthanasia or physician-assisted suicide from older persons who do not have a severe disease: An interview study," *Psychological Medicine* 35 (2005): 665–671.

29. Rurup, 679.

30. Ibid., 671.

31. Cf. "Euthanasia in the Netherlands: Rick Santorum's bogus statistics," *The Washington Post* 2012, http://www.washingtonpost.com/blogs/fact-checker/post/euthanasia-in-the-netherlands-rick-santorums-bogus-statistics/2012/02/21/gIQAJaRbSR_blog.html (February 2, 2015).

32. Cf. "Oregon death with dignity-2013," *Oregon Health Authority* 2014, http://public.health.oregon.gov/ProviderPartnerResources/EvaluationResearch/DeathwithDignityAct/Documents/year16.pdf (February 2, 2015).

33. Cf. Charlotte McDonald-Gibson, "Belgium extends euthanasia law to kids," *TIME* 2014, http://time.com/7565/belgium-euthanasia-law-children-assisted-suicide/ (February 2, 2015).

34. Cf. Nancy L. Segal, "Twin reunions: The science behind the fascination/Twin Research Reports: Altitude and hypoxia; twin pregnancy outcomes; space mission/media highlights: Chinese twins reunited; twin loss discovered; hidden twins; twin euthanasia; twin savior," *Twin Research and Human Genetics* 16.5 (2013): 1008-1013.

35. European Institute of Bioethics cited in Linda Pressly, "Belgium divide on the euthanasia of children," *BBC News Magazine* 2014, http://www.bbc.co.uk/news/magazine-25651758 (February 10, 2014).

36. Tinne Smets, Johan Bilsen, Joachim Cohen, Mette L. Rurup, and Luc Deliens, "Legal euthanasia in Belgium characteristics of all reported euthanasia cases," *Medical Care* 47.12 (December 2009): 1-6.

nal patients are a small minority of persons (6 percent) dying from PAS, and the majority of persons opting for PAS in euthanasia in 2002 and 2007 were terminally ill younger patients and patients with cancer. Although the argument that legalized euthanasia will prejudice the most vulnerable persons in society is not specifically addressed in this study, the authors conclude that there is no evidence to date that euthanasia prejudices, at least, against the elderly.[37] Nevertheless, part of the problem with discussing euthanasia statistics is what J. Pereira argues is a culture of tolerance in Oregon and countries that legalize euthanasia where physicians repeatedly fail to follow the protocols and provide accurate documentation and are not prosecuted.[38] In fact, the authors of the 2009 study note that all of their data is based on officially reported cases and therefore cannot exclude Pereira's thesis.

Pereira provides data evidencing that legalized PAS does in fact prejudice against the disabled, particularly the mentally disabled (i.e., clinically depressed individuals). As I mentioned in the last chapter, clinical depression is common among terminally ill patients; perhaps as many as 75 percent of the dying experience clinical depression. Moreover, since preparatory grief may resemble clinical depression, diagnosing it in the dying is difficult. To complicate matters in Oregon, a psychological evaluation by a professional is not mandatory. Only in cases where the administering physician, who is not a psychologist and has little or no training in mental health,[39] suspects the dying to have a mental illness are these evaluations performed. In these instances, depressed persons can still be euthanized if the attending physician determines that their choice for PAS is not influenced by their depression.

Interestingly, a 2008 study of fifty-eight Oregonians requesting PAS found that one in four persons requesting PAS is clinically depressed.[40] The study also found that persons who should have been ineligible due to their depression were euthanized. It is clear that the Death with Dignity Act inadequately protects mentally ill patients, but this does not necessitate a slippery slope. Nevertheless, the fact that a single mentally ill person, albeit terminally ill, is killed by PAS is enough cause to reflect on the value of euthanasia, as it is prejudicing against clinically depressed persons. The result is an evaluation over whether or not the freedom to kill ourselves is more valuable than the protection of the mentally ill.

---

37. Ibid., 5.
38. Pereira, J., "Legalizing euthanasia or assisted suicide: The illusion of safeguards and controls," *Curr Oncol.* 18.2 (April 2011): e38–e45, The National Center for Biotechnology Information, http://www.ncbi.nlm.nih.gov/pmc/articles/PMC3070710/ (February 2, 2015).
39. In Oregon any M.D. or D.O. who is registered to practice medicine in the state of Oregon may participate in physician-assisted suicide. ("Facts about the Death with Dignity Act," Oregon Health Authority, http://public.health.oregon.gov/ProviderPartnerResources/EvaluationResearch/DeathwithDignityAct/Documents/faqs.pdf [January 20, 2014].) Moreover, in many medical schools clinical psychiatry is not stressed. For instance, Harvard Medical School's curriculum requires medical students to take only one introductory course in clinical psychiatry, PS700M.9 MMHC - Psychopathology and Intro to Clinical Psychiatry. Does one introductory graduate course in clinical psychiatry prepare a medical doctor to properly assess the mental health of a dying patient?
40. Linda Ganzini, Elizabeth R. Goy, and Steven K. Dobscha, "Prevalence of depression and anxiety in patients requesting physicians' aid in dying: Cross sectional survey," *British Medical Journal* (2008), The National Center for Biotechnology Information, http://www.ncbi.nlm.nih.gov/pmc/articles/PMC2562435/ (February 2, 2015).

Sanctity and Importance of Human Life.

That human life has an intrinsic value and importance is a central tenet in all of the major world religions. This argument reproaches the autonomy argument as wrongheaded since it values human life on the basis of a quality, but fails to appreciate the intrinsic beauty and value of human life. The sanctity of life argument is most often found in a theological or religious context. In the Judeo-Christian religious traditions, God is the author of life and life is sacred. Life is a gift from God of which we are stewards. Thus the Catholic bishops write, "as a responsible steward of life one must never directly intend to cause one's own death, or the death of an innocent victim, by action or omission."[41] Many Muslims agree with the bishops, arguing that PAS is forbidden by this verse: "[d]estroy not yourselves. Surely Allah is ever merciful to you" (Surah 4:29). Killing oneself, even to end suffering in the case of terminal illness, is tantamount to rejecting God's gift. What follows is that the preservation of life is a universal right that needs to be protected.

Although Hindus and Buddhists reject euthanasia as immoral, they do not do so based on the sanctity of human life, but rather the principle of nonviolence (*ahimsa*) that dictates that harm against oneself or others produces bad karma and rebirth.[42] To an extent, both traditions derive the prohibition of euthanasia without an objective moral order or supreme deity. Moreover, for Buddhists, "rights language" albeit from God or nature, such as the "right to life," is foreign since this language presumes that human life has some absolute value.[43] Euthanasia is a serious problem not because it devalues a person's rights or violates a principle per se, but rather because it stems from desire. It is a failure to grasp the basic teaching of the Buddha that desire is the cause of all suffering.[44] Desire for PAS will result in bad karma and rebirth. For members of these traditions, although human life is not intrinsically sacred, it is the most important opportunity we have to be liberated from suffering. PAS wastes this opportunity.

Suffering Arguments.

Many opponents of euthanasia argue that suffering at the end of life has value. These persons are not masochists but rather point to the fact that suffering can strip away all of our distractions from what is really important in life. In my experiences ministering to the terminally ill, I recall a man that I met who was involved in a traumatic accident that left him paralyzed from the neck down: he lost everything over the next few years—his job, his home, even his wife. On many occasions he wanted to die.

---

41. Ibid.
42. Cf. Robert E. Florida, *Human rights and the major world's religions: Volume 5: The Buddhist tradition* (Westport, CT: Preager Perspectives, 2005), 11
43. Ibid., 17.
44. Cf. D. Lizardi and R. E. Gearing, "Religion and suicide: Buddhism, Native American and African religions, atheism, and agnosticism," *J Relig Health* 49 (2010): 377–384.

Overtime, after accepting that God had a plan for him, his suffering led him to a better understanding of the meaning of his life and reconciliation with those whom he loved. Even though he was in physical pain, he died at peace with his life. If euthanasia were legal in the state of New Jersey, he would have qualified for it and ended his life at the beginning of his terminal illness. But this choice would have robbed him of the meaning and joy he received from his painful dying experience.

My friend's experience is reiterated in the Buddhist and Hindu traditions that stress the necessity of suffering to expiate bad karma so as to attain a good rebirth or the joy of liberation. The Western traditions tend to see suffering as an opportunity to grow closer to God and family. For instance, in the Catholic Christian tradition, suffering at the end of life is an opportunity to participate with Christ in his suffering. Standing within this tradition, Pope John Paul II begins his famous work on the value of human suffering, *Salvifici Doloris,* with a quotation from the letter of St. Paul to the Colossians, stating that "[i]n my flesh I complete what is lacking in Christ's afflictions for the sake of his body, that is, the Church"[45] (Col 1:24). Pope John Paul II reveals that suffering, particularly suffering due to illness and/or dying, is not meaningless because Jesus Christ in his suffering gives it meaning. Suffering can be an opportunity, as it was for my friend above, to understand what is most important and to grow in union with a God who loves to the point of suffering. Moreover God does not allow us to suffer beyond our strength (Cf. 1 Cor 10:13).[46] PAS robs people of the salvific role of suffering. Nevertheless both arguments are difficult for persons who reject religion or do not share the tradition of redemptive suffering.

Letting a Person Die

Life is often more complicated than we would like it to be. Above I have outlined the popular arguments and counterarguments for PAS. Nevertheless, more Americans die from overdosing on morphine and the removal of life support than from PAS every year. Supporters of the legalization of euthanasia argue that PAS simply makes explicit this practice and pushes back the moment in time when a physician may intervene to help a patient die.[47] This position is based on the presumption that death of a terminally ill patient via morphine or cessation of life support is a form of PAS. Overdose of morphine or ceasing life-sustaining treatment is not necessarily PAS.

---

45. Pope John Paul II, "Apostolic Letter *Salvifici Doloris* of the Supreme Pontiff John Paul II to the Bishops, to the Priests, to the Religious Families and to the Faithful of the Catholic Church on the Christian Meaning of Human Suffering," The Holy See 1984, http://www.vatican.va/holy_father/john_paul_ii/apost_letters/documents/hf_jp-ii_apl_11021984_salvifici-doloris_en.html (February 2, 2015).
46. Cf. Martin-Schramm, 321.
47. Cf. Gine Kolata, "When morphine fails to kill," *New York Times* 1997, http://www.nytimes.com/1997/07/23/us/when-morphine-fails-to-kill.html (February 13, 2015).

Morphine.

Morphine is a highly effective painkiller. It is so effective that some opponents of PAS argue that morphine makes euthanasia antiquated since it reduces suffering and makes pain manageable. Nevertheless the use of morphine also poses an interesting moral dilemma, as morphine is an additive painkiller, to which the human body builds tolerance over time. Just like drug addicts who need a higher dosage of drugs to reach the same level of pleasure that they once attained with previous dosages, people taking morphine will need to continually increase the dosage of morphine to receive the same level of previous pain relief. Nonetheless a 2005 study of 441 hospitals between 2001 and 2003 revealed that patients who were treated with morphine had a much higher percentage of premature death.[48] For us the question is: In cases where patients died from overdosing on morphine, is this an example of PAS?

Unfortunately, the application of our definition of euthanasia above does not easily resolve this dilemma, as the intention of the healthcare professional administering the drug at least at face value seems to be immoral. Healthcare professionals may not know which dose will kill the patient, but they are aware that eventually if morphine is continually increased, this will result in the patient's death. However, it seems odd to argue that nurses administering morphine to patients to relieve their unbearable pain are killing the patients. One way to navigate through this dilemma is to apply the doctrine of double effect (DDE), an argument used to determine if an action that has more than one consequence is morally justified. In our case, the action in question is giving morphine to a terminally ill patient resulting in two effects: (1) pain relief, and (2) death. Note that there are four criteria included in this theory, and if the actor fails all or at least one of the criteria, the action is immoral. These are the criteria:

1. The act itself must be morally good or at least indifferent.
2. The agent may not positively will the bad effect but may permit it.
3. The good effect must be produced directly by the action, not by the bad effect.
4. The good effect must be sufficiently desirable to compensate for the allowing of the bad effect

Let us take the example of the nurse who administers a lethal dose of morphine to a terminally ill patient who is in unbearable pain. The act of administering morphine is itself morally indifferent, as morphine is a painkiller. The nurse passes the first criterion. With regard to the second criterion, the nurse is aware that morphine will most likely kill the patient, but she is administering it to relieve the patient's pain. Relieving pain is a good effect. She passes the second criterion. Moreover, the relief from suffering (good effect) is produced directly by the administration of morphine and not

---

48. Julie Mckeel, "CRUSADE: Increased risk of death with IV morphine use?" Duke Clinical Research Institute 2005, https://www.dcri.org/research/news/2005-news-archives/crusade-increased-risk-of-death-with-iv-morphine-use (February 2, 2015).

directly by the death of the patient (bad effect). Morphine relieves suffering even though this relief also poisons the patient to death. The nurse passes the third criterion. Finally, the relief of suffering in the case of a terminal illness (good effect) which is extraordinarily painful is sufficiently desirable to allow for the patient's potential death (bad effect). In this case the nurse passes all four criteria.

Nevertheless you may be wondering why we need such a convoluted theory to determine what most of us agree is ethical and in fact happens frequently. The goal of this theory is to navigate through the ambiguities of end-of-life morality. In fact, it can be used in a variety of instances to help differentiate euthanasia from letting someone die, which I address below. But it also helps to capture what most people intuitively think is moral and immoral but lack the ability to express their ideas clearly. It allows us to differentiate the use of morphine to relieve pain from PAS. Like the use of morphine, PAS creates two effects—the death of the patient (bad effect) and the relief of suffering (good effect). However, PAS fails the doctrine of double effect and is therefore immoral because it fails the first three criteria: suicide is immoral; the bad effect is positively willed, not simply permitted; and the relief of suffering is caused by the death of the patient (bad effect). The doctrine of double effect allows us to better differentiate a nurse that intends to kill her patient from a nurse that kills his patient treating the patient's pain. Even though the former nurse passes criteria 1, 2, and 4, she fails criteria 3 because she wills the death of the patient and is using morphine as a means to kill the patient. This action is immoral and illegal. Note that even in states that legalize euthanasia, administering morphine for the sole purpose to kill a patient is illegal: PAS is protected by the law if and only if all the regulations are followed.

Letting Die versus PAS

The doctrine of double effect allows us to better differentiate when an action is euthanasia. Its value is particularly evident when we examine the dilemma that thousands of American families make every day: When is it morally permissible to let someone die?

Jahi McMath provides an important test case. After undergoing a tonsillectomy to treat sleep apnea, something went terribly wrong, and Jahi was declared dead based on the neurological criteria. The hospital and parents were involved in a legal battle over whether or not to remove Jahi's life support. The state of California ruled in their favor to keep Jahi on life support.

Nevertheless for us the question remains: Was the hospital's attempt to remove Jahi's life support after she was declared "brain dead" an attempted murder? The hospital passes the first criterion of DDE because several physicians declared her as brain dead and life support in the case of a brain dead patient is a useless or extraordinary treatment. Note that if her parents are correct that Jahi is responsive, improving, and has brain function then the hospital would fail this criterion since life support in this case would be an ordinary means. (See the above for my definition of ordinary versus extraordinary means.) For many, including the U.S. Catholic bishops, there is no moral obligation to force patients to undergo useless or burdensome treatments. The second criterion states, "The agent may not positively will the bad effect but may permit it." To my knowledge there is no good reason to believe that the physicians' intentions were to kill Jahi, as they attempted to save Jahi's life repeatedly. Moreover a state-appointed neurologist confirmed the conclusion of the hospital physicians. Thus the bad effect is not death, since on the basis of the neurological criteria Jahi is dead. The hospital passes the second criterion. With respect to the third and fourth criteria that are dependent on the good effect, to end burdensome treatment, being directly produced by the action and being sufficiently desirable to compensate for the cessation of Jahi's vitals (bad effect), the hospital passes both because Jahi is already dead. The good effect ending burdensome treatments is sufficiently desirable to permit the cessation of her life support, and the cessation of her life support is not directly willed but rather permitted as an indirect action effected by taking her life support away. In this instance, taking life support away is not PAS.

Part Two: Hospice Care

Hospice provides care for the terminally ill during the final stages of the dying process. It allows the terminally ill to retain their integrity and autonomy to the best degree possible. Although hospice is an alternative to legalized euthanasia, it is not necessarily opposed to PAS. In Oregon, since the legalization of PAS, hospice care has continued to expand and offer care to the terminally ill. Nevertheless hospice is a philosophy that emphasizes life and maximizing the present quality of life, and thus euthanasia is not within its purview. Therefore patients enrolled in hospice that choose PAS cannot remain at a hospice facility or under hospice care.

What Is Hospice?

Hospice is a form of palliative care that provides pain relief to the terminally ill and that stresses making the dying process as dignified as possible. More specifically, hospice is a philosophy for caring for the dying persons and their families that emphasizes holistic care that focuses on the well-being of the person who is at the end of their life as opposed to finding a cure for their illness or simply giving medication to dull their pain. It represents an alternative model to dying to the institutional environment (hospital or nursing home). Because it stresses maximizing life during the end of life, care can take a variety of forms and be offered at a variety of locations (e.g., at a hospice facility or in the home of the dying).

The National Hospice and Palliative Care Organization (NHPCO), which is the largest nonprofit membership organization representing hospice and palliative care programs and professionals in the United States, writes:

> At the center of hospice is the belief that each of us has the right to die pain-free and with dignity, and that our families will receive the necessary support to allow us to do so... Hospice focuses on caring, not curing and in most cases care is provided in the patient's home. Hospice care also is provided in freestanding hospice centers, hospitals, and nursing homes and other long-term care facilities.[49]

This stress on "caring, not curing" is attractive to many terminally ill patients and their families because it provides a setting and care for the patient "to die pain-free and with dignity" but also ongoing support for family members. Hospice reconceptualizes end-of-life care as care for the patient and family unit.[50] The result is an effective plan of care that incorporates the wishes of the patient and family. This stress on individualized care implicitly addresses Corr's four dimensions of the person (physical, social, psychological, and spiritual dimension).[51] Although these dimensions and related tasks are not explicitly posited in the mission or goals of the NHPCO, the fact that hospice care allows persons to retain their dignity by involving the patient, to the best of the patient's ability, in the decision-making process for their care is evidence that these dimensions are addressed. For instance, hospice not only allows patients to remain in their homes, which is very important for many people as it helps them retain their dignity (psychological task) and their societal connections (social tasks), but also hospice care provides palliative (physical task) and holistic care through the involvement of an interdisciplinary team, at the patient's request, that may include religious leaders, counselors, social workers, family, friends, and health professionals (spiritual, social, and psychological tasks).[52]

Perhaps for these reasons more people choose hospice care today than in the past. Hospice cares for 40 percent of dying people in the United States.[53] This percentage is expected to rise. The effective-

---

49. "Hospice care," National Hospice and Palliative Care Organization, http://www.nhpco.org/about/hospice-care (January 19, 2014).

50. "Patient and family-centered care (PFC)," National Hospice and Palliative Care Organization 2000-2010, http://www.nhpco.org/sites/default/files/public/quality/Standards/PFC.pdf (February 10, 2015).

51. For more information on hospice's principles and program of patient and family-centered care (PFC) see "Patient and Family-Centered Care (PFC)," National Hospice and Palliative Care Organization 2000-2010, http://www.nhpco.org/sites/default/files/public/quality/Standards/PFC.pdf (February 10, 2015).

52. Corr, 203.

53. Ibid., 226.

ness at hospice providing holistic care that addresses patients' needs is evidenced by recent studies that report higher rates of satisfaction with hospice as opposed to nonhospice facilities. In a 2004 study, 70.7 percent of families of hospice patients rated the care of their loved one as "excellent." Compare this to family members of nonhospice patients, whose loved one died in a nursing home or hospital. Less than 50 percent rated their care as "excellent."[54]

Beyond the attraction of hospice to patients who want to die at home or on their own terms, this high percentage is also due to the fact that Medicare covers hospice care and is less expensive than institutional care. Hospice reduces healthcare costs at an average of $2,309 per hospice patient as compared to nonhospice patients.[55]

Conclusion

In this chapter I have examined end-of-life care. Specifically I have defined what euthanasia is and attempted to differentiate it from "letting someone die." I used an important case study and philosophical terms like the doctrine of double effect to demonstrate the difficulty in differentiating the two. I also examined the controversy surrounding the legalization of euthanasia and arguments for and against its legalization. My chapter ended with a brief overview of end-of-life care, specifically hospice and palliative care. Below I have included an interview with Monica Sleap, an expert hospice nurse, whose experiences shall provide valuable insight into the role of the hospice nurse at the end of life, as well as the unique challenges and blessings associated with caring for the dying.

Interview

Monica Sleap is a 1979 graduate of D'Youville College receiving a BS in Nursing. Her career has spanned a multitude of nursing positions both in the Buffalo, New York area and in North Carolina. Her passion for hospice care and meeting the needs of dying patients and families stemmed from an important message received during the commencement address in 1979. Elisabeth Kübler-Ross' commencement address included: "The people who teach you how to live will be the terminally ill, the hopeless, the blind, the old men and women in nursing homes and dying children."

---

54. Cf. Ibid., 221.
55. Cf. Ibid., 221.

DEATH & THE WORLD RELIGIONS

After the sudden death of her daughter, Katie, in 2001, Monica joined a group of bereaved mothers at Salem College in Winston Salem, North Carolina, for a one-day writing workshop in 2002. This session led to many more writing events together including a book titled *Farther Along: The Writing Journey of Thirteen Bereaved Mothers* by Carol Henderson. Through writing symposiums, book readings, and their blog site fartheralongbook.com, the group has continued to support the community and one another in their grief journeys.

Currently, Monica works as a staff development nurse for National Hospice Company, working with all members of the hospice team in developing care plans for patients and families facing end-of-life care decisions.

Q: What is your role at Hospice?

A: I am a staff development nurse. My current role in hospice is to teach nurses, support staff and the aides about hospice. We start with Hospice 101 that teaches what hospice is about and what their role is.

Q: You have a unique perspective on hospice. You are not only a hospice professional but also a mother who has lost her daughter. How did hospice help you cope with her death?

A: Katie passed away in a car accident. In a winter storm she lost control of her car on the way to school and was killed instantly. I was not able to get hospice since she did not have an illness. But I had worked with hospice so after I knew that my training with bereavement would be the biggest help. Also I knew the people who worked with bereavement, so I was able to seek out counseling services as I needed them.

Q: Have you or can you achieve a sense of normalcy after losing a child?

A: I believe so. What has helped my husband and I is our sense of humor. This is not to make light of this tragedy, but rather our sense of humor helped lift us out of that terrible grief. We look at each other in shock but we find some way to get ourselves through our loss.

Q: What advice would you give to persons who have lost a loved one?

A: The year after Katie's death I joined a bereavement group. I remember that when I first got there I wanted to go back home. However, I stayed and met other bereaved mothers. It was only supposed to be for a day, but we have continued to meet at least twice a year over the past twelve years. We even published a book about our experiences.

Q: Did religion play a role in this healing/grieving process?

A: I would say so. I was raised Roman Catholic and our family is Roman Catholic. I think our up-bringing, our faith, and our relationships with our children carry us through tough times. I pray every day; I hope I carry on this tradition that I was taught when I was young.

Q: As a hospice professional who works with the dying regularly, does your faith carry over to your profession?

A: It sure does. But as a professional we have to take into consideration the faith of our patients and understand where they are coming from. I do not push my faith on my patients. We have to be diverse and accepting of all religions and cultures. I have to be a strong person in order to care for my patients. My faith gives me the peace and strength I need to care for someone else who is going through a tough time. If I did not have a great faith, I would not be able to help them.

Q: Is it appropriate to participate in a religious tradition if the patient or family invites you to do so?

A: Sure, it is appropriate. In many instances the chaplain in the hospice team leads prayer, and we are a part of this service.

Q: What advice do you give to nurses who have no faith or do not feel comfortable with the topics of religion and spirituality?

A: If you are comfortable, say "that is not my area of expertise, but on our team we have a wonderful chaplain who can talk to you about this. Would it be acceptable to have him visit today?" This is the beauty of the team. The nurse is not everything, and should not be everything to the patient. What is important is the team. It is really important that we rely on those persons that are experts in their fields, especially when that expertise is necessary. Nurses may have ten patients, so it is important to rely on other members of the team, as the nurse cannot be in all places at once.

Q: Does your Catholic faith pose any challenges for you when attending to the needs of persons from different religions?

A: No, it really doesn't. I let people be who they are and learn through them as well.

Q: Our society is uncomfortable with the topic of death. What prompted you to choose a career that puts you on the front lines, so to speak, of dying and death?

A: I remember at our commencement ceremony at D'Youville College, Dr. Kübler-Ross gave the commencement speech. She spoke about "walking among the daises" and about paying attention to those who really need us: the elderly in nursing homes and dying children. Her speech inspired me and made me realize that this was where my nursing career had brought me, as well as caring for these persons is almost something engrained in me.

What I found interesting about hospice was that it was almost completely opposite of what I learned in nursing school to heal and help people get better. In hospice you stop all the heroics and curatives, and just help people live the best they can for the days or months they have left.

Q: You mentioned Kübler-Ross. I know that you are familiar with her model of death, as well as the criticisms of her model. However, in your professional experience do you think her model is accurate? Is it helpful?

A: I think about this often. I think about how we get stuck in certain stages. Nevertheless in my own grieving I never really experienced the anger stage. I am an optimist and I think that there is always a greater plan.

In my professional experience I have seen these stages play out with the dying. But everyone goes through the death phase differently.

Q: Why is hospice important?

A: If there is no hope for the cure, which means that two physicians have to certify that there is six months or less to live, the patient is going to die. Hospice effectively addresses the needs of the patient at this point. Unlike a traditional hospital setting, hospice relies on a team of experts that care for the patient and family unit. Together the team, not solely the nurse, offers care and comfort for the patient and family. This is why hospice is so good! Healthcare professionals in traditional settings are trained to cure and lack the recourses, training, and an individualized plan of care, involving chaplains and social workers, committed to comforting the patient.

Some patients' health actually improves once hospice starts. They may be in a crisis in a hospital because the symptoms are not controlled. This means hospice must discharge them since they no longer meet the criteria. It is not always a perfect science.

Q: What is the greatest reward working with hospice?

A: When my dad was dying, he was under hospice care. Hospice allowed my family and me to help my mom care for my dad. It was a great reward for us all to be present to our father during the end of his life. I remember my Dad dying in peace at home with his family. I had a sense that if he was not in hospice, he would not have had this. I know that he got to the place he was supposed to go.

Q: What was one of your most challenging experiences as a hospice professional?

A: After Katie died, I was taking care of children that were dying. There were a set of twins who had Tay-Sachs disease. It was the most wonderful family. The problem was that in their tradition there were various rituals that must be performed. One of the twins, a little girl, died and we had to bathe her according to their custom. She was then dressed and laid on a bed with flowers around her. She stayed there for days while the family celebrated her life. At the same time her brother was dying. I remember walking over beer caps to get to the little boy. He died two weeks later and we had to go through the ritual again. Can you imagine celebrating the life of one child while the second is dying? To complicate matters the family did not speak English. We needed an interpreter at all times. This made the experience even more challenging.

Q: In the face of such difficulty, how do you remain professional?

A: You can get too close to your patients. I have seen it on many occasions. In doing staff development, I come in; I look at charts; I look at frequency of visits, and then I do home visits with nurses, chaplains and social workers. Sometimes you will get a glimpse that something is wrong when the patient and family only want a certain nurse to come, and they do not want the rest of the hospice team. You have to have the entire team involved: this is what hospice is all about. You will hear for instance that this particular nurse is bringing groceries to the house. This is not appropriate. This is when we step in to talk to that nurse or in some cases—not too often—pull the nurse out of that family. The nurse may need counseling or may have unmet needs.

Q: Hospice professionals have to be professional and caring, but not personally involved. This seems like a fine line. How do you prevent yourself from becoming too close?

A: Medicare requires a plan of care for every patient. In that plan of care it separates out the goals and needs of the patient and family. You have to have interventions and then your goals. This lays out exactly what you should be doing. For instance, hospice nurses are not allowed to get medications for the patient from the pharmacy or even transport medications. If what you are doing is not within that plan of care, you are going outside those boundaries. Those actions are inappropriate.

Q: It seems to me that helping dying persons on a daily basis must be emotionally and spiritually draining. How do you keep from burning out?

A: You may have to have a change of assignment. Medicare requires that you have a meeting with your team at least every fifteen days. If someone is having a hard time caring for a patient, then the team will look into finding another nurse to care for the patient. You don't see a lot of nurses in hospice for a long time for this reason. Our hospice is very good at providing support for those feeling that they are burned out.

Q: There have been a few studies on "religious coping." In your own experience have you found that religious people die better than nonreligious people, or vice versa?

A: I can't say that I have seen a big difference between both. This is because of the team. If the patient has questions about the afterlife or life's existence, then the chaplain or social worker would be called in. In many cases nonreligious people do talk to these persons. It is hard to say if they die with faith. It is by no means black and white. They may not want to meet the chaplain. We are only required to have the nurse and social worker. The social worker can be the person that helps guide them about these questions about transcendence. We attend to their autonomy to the best of their ability.

Q: Hospice seems to offer effective personalized care. Have you ever had a request from a patient that made you feel uncomfortable?

A: The hospice where I work has a memorial fund. This fund is used for requests of the dying to do something like see their favorite singer perform. It is almost like "Make a Wish." We accommodate reasonable requests. We can add air conditioning to a room to make a patient feel comfortable, but we cannot redo their home. Some of the most uncomfortable situations were when the family of the patient called for a refill of their mother's medications. The medications should have lasted for a few weeks. This is the concern: the family member is using mom's medications. It is not only difficult to refill the medications, but now you have to be concerned that the patient is not getting the medication.

Q: What qualities are you looking for in a potential hire?

A: You want to have at least one year of nursing experience. You need good communication skills with a team, a good knowledge of medications and symptom control, and flexibility. About 80 percent of hospice is home care. You really have to be good at moving your calendar around. You have to fluctuate your visit frequency based on patient-family need. For instance, you may have a patient that you scheduled to visit three days a week, but that patient may not want you to visit any more. At the same time you may have a patient that you were only seeing once a week, but now that patient begins to die, requiring you to be with them more frequently. You have to move them into your schedule. Some patients die sooner than expected and some do not. Finally, you need to think about your team, and how they can support your patient and meet your goals.

Q: On average how many patients does a hospice nurse visit?

A: Ten to twelve patients is the average in a home setting. Now there are also hospice homes, which is an inpatient unit. There are actually four levels of care in hospice: (1) routine care—this is care for the patient wherever they call home; (2) inpatient care—this is at a hospice home, but it is only for symptom control. Once the symptoms are controlled, you are moved back to the home setting;

(3) continuous care—let's say that you have a symptom that is out of control; a nurse working with the team will provide care to control the symptoms on a twenty-four-hour basis; and (4) respite care—you give five days of rest for the family. The patient goes into a facility to give the family a rest before returning to the home.

Q: What happens when a patient enters hospice but decides that hospice care is not appropriate?

A: Medicare has a revocation statement. Unless the patient has an altered mental capacity, only the patient can revoke the care. This is an important point that I teach to hospice workers in our program: in normal circumstances only the patient can revoke hospice care. If a patient's care improves and they no longer meet the criteria for hospice, we cannot revoke that care. The patient has to do so.

Q: Part of the criteria to enter hospice is that two doctors have to verify that the patient has six months to live. Is it possible for a patient stay in hospice for years if the patient's doctors continue to verify that the patient has six months or less to live?

A: This does happen. The patients' health decreases and then stabilizes. Sometimes there is an underlying health issue that is not addressed because the patient is near death. This issue may be the cause of the fluctuation in health.

Q: Today the legalization of euthanasia is a hot topic. Are euthanasia and hospice a contradiction in terms? Can both perspectives on end-of-life care coexist?

A: In hospice in order for the facility to remain viable you need a budget. If you brought euthanasia to a hospice home, my fear is that the focus would no longer be the well-being of the patient, but rather the dollars and cents. It could create a climate where symptom control is no longer seen as a worthwhile end; the hospice team is pressured to end the patient's life in order to fill the next bed. I also wonder what that may look like to patients in a hospice home that reject euthanasia. Euthanasia is not what we are about. We are about celebrating the life of a patient and living life to the fullest. Euthanasia would be a contradiction in terms of how we support the patient and family in the hospice home.

Q: You have had a lot of great experiences as a hospice nurse. What is the worst experience you have had in your role as a hospice nurse?

A: Sometimes a patient comes into hospice after the hospital has been treating, treating, treating, and now there is nothing left to treat. There is not enough time to control the symptoms. I had one instance where a patient was discharged home and the patient and family did not want to be bothered by us until the next day. I always teach my nurses that as soon as a patient is discharged you have to get the patient's consent to come under hospice care. Care cannot begin until this occurs. In this case, the patient refused to sign anything; he wanted to be left alone. We respected his wishes, but we knew that he needed care immediately. In the middle of the night he went into a pain crisis. We had to set up the patient with hospice and get morphine from a night pharmacy. It is a complicated process to get a controlled substance. By the time we got there this poor gentleman was in pain while dying, and this should not have happened. Tragically, the patient's family saw him die in pain. Dying in pain is an image you will never forget.

Q: What advice do you want to give to persons interested in pursuing careers where they will encounter dying people?

A: You need a very good sense of self: you're at peace with yourself, and you can help your patients get to a place where they are comfortable with their end-of-life experience. You do this also with the family, as not only will the family eventually be the ones to whom you communicate, but they are the primary caregivers. You are only there intermittingly. You have to teach the family how to care for the patient. You need to be able to empathize but not sympathize. This means to say: I do not simply feel for you, but I am here for you until the end! Let's make the end as best as it can be!

CHAPTER THREE

NEAR-DEATH EXPERIENCE

There is little doubt that the topic of near-death experience (NDE) is polarizing. Dr. Raymond Moody, who coined the term "near-death experience" and inaugurated the scientific study of NDE in his book *Life After Life*, argues that discussion about NDE is at an impasse that has been dominated by three voices, which he categorizes as the parapsychologists, the skeptics, and the fundamentalists.[1] The dictum: "To those whom believe, no proof is necessary and to those whom disbelieve, no proof is possible" seems to carry over to the popular debates about NDEs. Therefore, for paranormalists who believe in the afterlife, NDEs provide good reason for the obvious, that the human consciousness continues after death. Skeptics, however, argue that NDEs are at best the experience of the dying brain or at worst fabrications by charlatans. Although fundamentalists accept that NDEs are evidence of the afterlife, they argue that NDEs are the work of the Devil and reject research on the topic.

It is my hope that we can approach the study of NDE with an open mind because the scientific study of NDEs is important for at least three reasons. First, millions of persons in North America claim to have had an NDE. Due to the sheer mass of NDE accounts, NDEs cannot be ignored as wishful thinking or simply fabrications. NDEs are phenomena that warrant further scientific study. Second, NDEs have the potential to allow for a better understanding about what happens to consciousness during and after the death process. Moreover, they raise further questions about the suitability of the

1. Raymond A. Moody, *The last laugh: A new philosophy of near-death experiences, apparitions, and the paranormal* (Charlottesville, VA: Hampton Road Publishing Company, 1999), 12-13.

neurological criteria to define death, and when it is appropriate to harvest organs from brain-dead patients. Third, NDErs report to have positive psychological side effects from their NDE including "less materialism, less afraid of death, and more altruism."[2] Whether or not the NDE is the result of Divine intervention, these psychological side effects are mediated by changes in the expression of genes and proteins.[3] Researchers are concerned about the physiological mechanisms involved with these positive effects of NDEs; this discovery has the potential to allow for the panoply of treatments for psychiatric disorders. The hope for researchers is to be able to recreate the effects of NDEs without the trauma of dying. For these reasons, NDEs has been the subject of scientific investigation for over forty years. In this chapter we shall introduce and examine the research on NDEs as well as how to care for patients who claim to have had an NDE.

What Are NDEs?

Due to popular texts, blockbuster movies like *Heaven Is For Real* (2013), and the interest in NDEs by influential persons like Oprah Winfrey, popular culture has been inundated by images and stories about NDEs. Some skeptics, in fact, argue that the "Oprah effect" is so pervasive that people who purport to see the phenomena of outer worldly events cannot be taken seriously. For many the topic of NDEs conjures images of tunnels that lead to a bright light! Albeit recent studies have revealed that although these images are indeed reported by many NDErs, they are not necessary to qualify for an NDE.

Defining an NDE is not an easy task, as not only are no two NDEs identical but there is no widely accepted definition among scholars studying this phenomenon. In this chapter when I speak about NDEs I will mean an "[event] that take place as a person is dying or, indeed, is already clinically dead."[4] Despite the fact that NDEs are highly individualized there is a discernible pattern among reported NDEs. One of the most popular scales that researches use to discern if an experience is an NDE is "the Greyson scale" created by Dr. Bruce Greyson that attributes a numerical value to specific experiences. He listed sixteen characteristics of an NDE and attributed a score of 0 (no experience), 1 (experience), or 2 (intense experience) to each characteristic. For an experience to classify as an NDE it has to score 7 or higher. Dr. Jeffery Long, however, proposes a more succinct and less rigorous list of the most frequent characteristics of an NDE that include these twelve characteristics:

2. Sam Parnia, *What happens when we die: A groundbreaking study into the nature of life and death* (Carlsbad, CA: Hay House, 2006), 177.
3. Parnia, 177.
4. Jeffery Long and Paul Perry, *Evidence of the afterlife: The science of near-death experiences* (New York: Harper Collins, 2010), 5.

1. Heightened senses
2. Intense and gradually positive emotions or feelings
3. Passing into or through a tunnel
4. Encountering a mystical or brilliant light
5. Encountering other beings (religious figures, deceased relatives, angels, etc.)
6. A sense of alteration of time or space
7. Life review
8–9. Encountering heavenly realms and/or special knowledge
10. Encountering a boundary or barrier between this world and the next world
11. A return to the body
12. Out-of-body experience (OBE): Separation of consciousness from the physical body[5]

Interestingly, among NDErs that were under anesthesia or lacked oxygen, as opposed to no memory or a clouded memory of events that would be expected from persons in these situations, these NDErs report lucid experiences whereby their senses were heightened. One feature of the heightened sense phenomena is the ability to see in 360 degrees with perfect clarity. NDErs also report that they felt as if they were no longer constrained by time and space. They argue that their NDE was ineffable, transcending our vocabulary, and that what they experienced was "so much more real than anything I have experienced in my entire life."[6] This feeling of embracing reality may also be coupled with a positive emotion that is generally expressed as all-encompassing love. Adjectives such as peaceful and joyful are commonly employed by NDErs to describe this loving embrace. Dr. Longs' ubiquitous study, Near Death Experience Research Foundation (NDERF), which included accounts from over 1,600 NDErs, discovered that nearly three quarters of the NDErs experienced these emotions.[7]

Surprisingly, the same study discovered that the tunnel experience, which is probably the most well-known NDE characteristic, was reported by only 33.8 percent of respondents. Nevertheless the tunnel experience usually culminates with a bright light that theistic persons describe as God. This light is bright, luminous, and beautiful, drawing the human spirit to itself.

Although many NDErs report to have encountered a religious figure (e.g., Jesus, the Blessed Mother, Angels, etc.), in NDERF most people claim to have encountered deceased relatives.[8] When the relatives are known they are usually depicted as young men or women; if it is a child that has died, the child is known but encountered as an adult. In cases where the identity of the relative is not known, it is not uncommon for the NDEr, at a later date, to see their deceased relative in an old photo.

---

5. Cf. Long, 6-7.
6. Ibid., 8.
7. Sixty percent argued that they felt that space and time were altered (Long, 13).
8. Ibid., 12.

In NDERF, 22.5 percent of NDErs reported a life review. Recently, the Catholic Church in many parts of the country has launched the "Catholics Come Home" campaign to welcome back non-practicing Catholics into the Church. One of the commercials for this campaign depicts several deceased persons alone in an auditorium watching a movie of their lives. From the commercial it is evident that the greatest pain in watching the movie is seeing how they treated other people in their life. This commercial depicts what many NDErs describe as a life review. The NDErs in NDERF did not interpret this as an act of judgment by God, but rather a self-judgment whereby you are able to see how you treated others from an objective vantage point. Depending on the type of person, this experience can either be pleasant, almost like a well-deserved pat on the back or the worst form of painful self-judgment.

Half of all NDErs in the NDERF study argued that they were given a glimpse of heaven and new knowledge about reality. Usually the content of this new knowledge is related to the interconnectedness of all things. It is of interest to note that although the images of heaven vary, they all describe a paradise-like realm. NDErs, in fact, who have the choice, do not want to return to earth because they want to exist in this realm. In 31 percent of the cases, the NDEr comes to a boundary and has the opportunity to either cross over into the afterlife, which means that they will not return to life on earth, or return to life on earth. In many cases the NDEr is either dissuaded from staying in the afterlife since they have more to accomplish on earth or have family or loved ones that depend on them to whom they desire to return.

Out-of-body experience (OBE) is the final and one of the most well-known characteristics of NDEs. OBE is usually described by NDErs as the experience of levitating above the physical body whilst observing their dead body and the events occurring below them. What is most remarkable about an OBE is that NDErs' reports accurately describe the events and conversations by medical personnel and family members around their body. OBE accounts from persons blind from birth are particularly interesting since these persons have no analogy for sight. For this reason, researchers believe that blind persons from birth dream without images. Yet, these NDErs accurately report not only the NDErs' appearance, which is the first time they have seen themselves, but also the persons and things around.[9]

From a scientific perspective, OBEs are important because they provide one of the only elements of an NDE that is more amenable to testing. Unlike the other eleven characteristics of NDE that are circumscribed by the subjective experience of the NDEr, OBEs involve observations that can be verified as inaccurate or accurate by people in the vicinity of the NDEr.

---

9. Cf. K. Ring and S. Cooper, "Near-death and out-of-body experiences in the blind: A study of apparent eyeless vision," *Journal of Near-Death Studies* 16 (1998): 101-147.

For these reasons, scientists have devised tests that not only involve placing targets in rooms that can only be seen from the ceiling, presumably where the spirit or consciousness would be hovering, but also include in-depth interviews with the NDErs that determine if the recall from the OBE is consistent with the attending nurses' and physicians' observations and notes.[10]

The most recent and largest study on OBE was completed in 2014 that involved 2,060 patients from fifteen hospitals that tested the accuracy of purported OBEs of cardiac arrest survivors. In October 2014, the study was published and provided good reason to believe that consciousness continues after the cessation of cerebral functions. The authors of the study reported that in one instance a cardiac arrest patient

> described the perception of observing events from the top corner of the room and continued to experience a sensation of looking down from above. He accurately described people, sounds, and activities from his resuscitation...His medical records corroborated his accounts and specifically supported his descriptions and the use of an automated external defibrillator (AED). Based on current AED algorithms, this likely corresponded with up to 3 min of conscious awareness during CA and CPR.[11]

In a recent interview Dr. Sam Parnia, director of the study, commented on this OBE and the importance to further study of NDEs:

> [I]t has often been assumed that experiences in relation to death are likely hallucinations or illusions, occurring either before the heart stops or after the heart has been successfully restarted, but not an experience corresponding with 'real' events when the heart isn't beating. In this case, consciousness and awareness appeared to occur during a three-minute period when there was no heartbeat. This is paradoxical, since the brain typically ceases functioning within 20-30 seconds of the heart stopping and doesn't resume again until the heart has been restarted. Furthermore, the detailed recollections of visual awareness in this case were consistent with verified events.[12]

---

10. For more information see these studies: M.M. Ghoneim, "Awareness during anesthesia," *Anesthesiology* 92 (2000): 597-602; Sebel C. Kerssens, "Awareness during general anesthesia," *Curr Rev Clin Anaesth* 24 (2002): 13-24; S. Parnia, K. Spearpoint, and P. B. Fenwick, "Near death experiences, cognitive function and psychological outcomes of surviving cardiac arrest," *Resuscitation* 74 (2007): 215-221; P. van Lommel, R. van Wees, V. Meyers, and I. Elfferich, "Near death experience in survivors of cardiac arrest: A prospective study in the Netherlands," *Lancet* 358 (2001): 2039-2045.

11. Sam Parnia, Ken Spearpoint, Gabriele de Vos, Peter Fenwick, Diana Goldberg, Jie Yang, Jiawen Zhu, Katie Baker, Hayley Killingback, Paula McLean, Melanie Wood, A. Maziar Zafari, Neal Dickert, Roland Beisteiner, Fritz Sterz, Michael Berger, Celia Warlow, Siobhan Bullock, Salli Lovett, Russell Metcalf, Smith McPara, Sandra Marti-Navarette, Pam Cushing, Paul Wills, Kayla Harris, Jenny Sutton, Anthony Walmsley, Charles D. Deakin, Paul Little, Mark Farber, Bruce Greyson, and Elinor R. Schoenfeld, "AWARE—AWAreness during REsuscitation—A prospective study," *Resuscitation* 85 (2014): 1799-1805), 1802.

12. "News Release: Results of world's largest near death experiences study published," University of Southampton, 2014, http://www.southampton.ac.uk/mediacentre/news/2014/oct/14_181.shtml#.VLQrcivF_96 (October 7, 2014).

Dr. Parnia is cautiously optimistic about his study and does not intimate that this incident is proof that the consciousness exists after death, note that only 2 percent of people reported an OBE. Nevertheless this study corroborated several smaller studies on the OBE phenomenon as well as a plethora of anecdotal accounts by NDErs and their families and caregivers.

NDEs Across Culture and Age

NDEs are global phenomena; albeit it is not known how many people purport to have an NDE worldwide. Dr. Long's ubiquitous study, *Near Death Experience Research Foundation* (NDERF) corroborated Dr. Greyson's research in the 1980s that NDEs are not cultural specific.[13] Muslims, Hindus, Christians, Jews, atheists, and nonreligious theists purport the same core experience. Nevertheless, what differs is the manner in which they interpret this experience. Thus, while Christians interpret the being of light as Jesus Christ, Hindus interpret it as their deity, and Muslims may interpret it as an angel. Moreover NDE is not simply a phenomenon exclusive to adults. Children also have NDEs, and although children interpret and process the experience differently, the content of the NDE of a child is the same as an adult.[14] For instance, the youngest recorded case of a child NDEr was a six-month-old baby that survived severe kidney failure. Parents of the child noticed that whenever the child went through a tunnel he had a panic attack. It was not until he was four, when his parent tried to explain that his grandfather was dying, that the child explained to his parents that he died and traveled through a tunnel.[15]

With respect to the United States, researchers suggest that 4 to 9 percent of the population have had an NDE. In other words, one out of five people who faced a potentially deadly situation had an NDE.[16] Notice the qualifier "potentially deadly," as NDEs are reported by not only terminally ill persons, but also persons about to die or experience a traumatic event (e.g., serious car accident).

Negative NDEs

Debate and discussion of NDEs are dominated by the positive and welcoming experiences of life after death. This is no doubt in part due to our culture that generally considers hell and stories about eternal

---

13. For more information on this study, please visit http://www.nderf.org/.
14. Parnia, 14.
15. Ibid., 14-15.
16. *Making sense of near-death experiences: A handbook for clinicians*, eds. Mahendra Perera, Kurrupiah Jagadheesan, and Anthony Peake (London: Jessica Kingsley Publishers, 2012), 11.

suffering and judgment to be uncouth. Strangely, negative NDEs are more common in non-Western NDErs; however, the reason above no doubt influences this fact. Therefore, it is likely that negative NDEs are underreported in North America.[17] There is no clear consensus as to how often negative NDEs occur; some scholars estimate that 1 to 5 percent of reported NDEs are negative and frightening.[18] Even positive NDEs can have frightening elements, such as the uncontrolled travel through the aforementioned tunnel; however, negative NDEs generally include one or both of two dominant images: first, the experience of void or intense emptiness/loneliness; second, hellish imagery. Hellish imagery may include encountering frightening creatures, beings that suffer, demons, and foreboding landscapes.[19] In a Tokyo study of NDEs, a sixty-six-year-old woman provides a good example of a negative NDE with hellish imagery:

> She described having a vision of a river, which separated her side from that of the Realm of Dead (or "Yomi"). She said: "As I got closer, at the very end of the other side of the river, I saw my mother who passed away 18 years ago. I could see only her face because a group of children monks, dressed in white and black, masked the rest of her body. The children were very noisy. I moved closer, to see my mother. She looked very worried and she said: 'Don't come here! Go back!' So I turned back and regained consciousness in the hospital. At that very moment, I heard a nurse calling my name."[20]

Interestingly, negative NDEs do not usually involve the torment; rather, they provide new insight into what awaits those who are not kind in life. For this reason, negative NDEs may have positive aftereffects, as they can allow NDErs to reevaluate their life to make changes so as not to experience the torments that they witnessed.

Explanations for NDEs

Several decades of research on NDEs reveal that there is no clear consensus among medical professionals as to the causes of NDEs. Yet there is no lacuna of opinions that seek to explain this phenomenon affecting millions of people. Within the scholarly community there are three leading explanations about NDEs: dying brain hypothesis, psychological hypothesis, and transcendental hypothesis. There are a variety of explanations within these categories. In the interest of time and space, I will only present the most prominent arguments for each explanation.

---

17. Ibid., 53.
18. Cf. R.J. Bonenfant, "A child's encounter with the devil: An unusual near-death experience with both blissful and frightening elements," *Journal of Near-Death Studies* 20.2 (2001): 87-100.
19. Cf. N. E. Bush, "Afterward: Making meaning after a frightening near-death experience," *Journal of Near-Death Studies* 21.2 (2002): 99-133.
20. *Making sense of near-death experiences*, 53-54.

Dying Brain Hypothesis

Proponents of this theory argue that NDEs are hallucinations caused by physiological changes that occur at the time of brain death. Dr. Blackmore argues that the lack of oxygen to the brain that occurs when the brain dies is responsible for NDEs, particularly the phenomena of visions, tunnel feeling, and seeing a light. His theory is supported by studies of the effects of G-forces on high-speed fighter pilots.[21] These studies found that at high speeds, sudden changes in direction can result in the "G-LOC" phenomenon, whereby due to the lack of blood flow to the brain, pilots report to be in a dreamlike state with a sense of detachment and euphoria.[22] The similarity between this experience and the positive experience associated with NDEs are obvious. Furthermore, Dr. Blackborn suggests that lack of oxygen to the brain, which occurs once the heart stops, activates cells in the back of the brain that may create the illusion that there is a light in the periphery which in turn gives rise to the tunnel experience;[23] this explains the tunnel experience and the light at the end of the tunnel.

The second influential theory that has received a lot of publicity in the past few years attempts to explain NDEs not in terms of the lack of oxygen but rather the increase of carbon dioxide levels in the blood when the oxygen levels decrease. In a 2010 study, researchers noted that after studying fifty-two persons who had heart attacks, eleven claimed to have an NDE. What is interesting is that "those patients who experienced the phenomenon [NDE], blood carbon-dioxide levels were significantly higher than in those who did not."[24] The researchers are nevertheless baffled as to how carbon dioxide interacts with the brain to produce NDEs and suggest that further studies are needed to examine these relationships.

Although both theories provide cogent explanations for NDEs and help explain the consistency of NDEs across cultures and religions, both theories share similar problems. First, as of yet, no scientific study has demonstrated how lack of oxygen or increased carbon dioxide creates NDEs, namely explain the pathophysiological mechanism of a NDE. Both theories are based on conjectures that are informed by studies unrelated to NDEs or evidence that NDErs have elevated amounts of carbon dioxide. Second, if NDEs were caused by either the lack of oxygen or increased carbon dioxide, why then do we find such a small percentage of dying patients experiencing NDEs. Both physiological factors are extremely common problems; if these were the causes of NDEs, then we would expect to find many more accounts of NDEs. Yet in studies of cardiac arrest patients who commonly have low oxygen levels or high carbon dioxide levels, only 8 to 10 percent experience NDEs. Third,

---

21. Parnia, 19-20.
22. Ibid., 20.
23. Ibid., 21.
24. James Owen, "Near-death experiences explained? Bright lights, angelic visions products of too much CO2 in the blood, study says," *National Geographic News* 2010, http://news.nationalgeographic.com/news/2010/04/100408-near-death-experiences-blood-carbon-dioxide/ (January 13, 2014).

with respect to sudden cardiac arrest patients, there is no cerebral activity after a few seconds and therefore should be no consciousness, yet NDErs are reporting conscious experiences. Fourth, there is evidence as to how the lack of oxygen affects consciousness: lack of oxygen results in an "acute confusional state" that involves a clouding of consciousness with little or no memory recall.[25] This is quite different from a NDE experience that is not only vivid, rational, ordered, but also a life-changing event that NDErs are able to recall decades after the event. Moreover, NDErs that have the tunnel experience and see a light never describe it in the fashion proposed by Dr. Blackmore.[26] Finally, if we grant either or both theories are correct, this does not account for the myriad of NDEs reported by NDErs that experienced their NDE before life-threatening danger.[27]

PSYCHOLOGICAL HYPOTHESIS

Adherents of this theory explain NDEs as a kind of depersonalization. Depersonalization refers to the process by which a patient creates a surreal environment that is disconnected from a trauma. Therefore NDEs function as an unconscious defense mechanism that helps the person cope with the reality of their experience dying.[28] The strongest evidence for this argument is the fact that many people have had near-fatal accidents and have reported experiences similar to NDEs. NDErs unconsciously construct a fantastic experience that appropriates various memories from their life experience. In addition, proponents of this argument explain away accurate OBEs as the result of consciousness of the patient unbeknownst to the attending physicians and/or simple recall of life-saving events on a medical television show such as *Grey's Anatomy*.

Although this theory is cogent, it remains untested. Also depersonalization is generally observed in women, ages fifteen to thirty, and is reported as a dreamlike state. However, NDEs are not gender or age specific.[29] Moreover, NDErs report vivid experiences, not dreamlike states.

TRANSCENDENTAL HYPOTHESIS

This viewpoint is premised on the fact that consciousness cannot be explained by psychological or physiological factors alone. Those espousing that they had an NDE are experiencing life outside their physical bodies. The consensus of the medical community does not support this theory. Scientists that will admit the problems with the theories proposed above, also admit that there is still much to be learned about the body before they can make an informed position about the afterlife.

25. Parnia, 21.
26. Ibid., 21.
27. Ibid., 21.
28. Ibid., 26.
29. *Making sense of near-death experiences*, 99.

Many scientists believe that the purview of scientific investigation is limited to the material world, which precludes the willingness to entertain or the ability to test if there is life after death. Nevertheless, studies like the Awareness (2014), mentioned above, provide very good reason to believe that the consciousness after death precludes a simple biological explanation. Dr. Long in his book *Evidence of the Afterlife* provides no less than nine proofs that NDEs are evidence that consciousness continues after death: "Proof 1: Lucid Death; Proof 2: Out of Body; Proof 3: Blind Sight; Proof 4: Impossibility conscious; Proof 5: Perfect Playback; Proof 6: Family Reunion; Proof 7: Children and NDEs; Proof 8: Worldwide Consistency; Proof 9: Changed Lives." Although his arguments are based on personal accounts by NDErs that were not corroborated with medical facts when available, his research provides a provocative argument that NDEs are evidence of an afterlife.

Perhaps it is not surprising that NDEs have defied biological explanations, as the nature of the mind or consciousness remains an enigma to scientists. Today neuroscientists are aware how the brain functions. They can in fact trace what your brain is doing as you read this sentence. But the fact that you understand this sentence or that you agree or disagree with what I have written in this chapter remains a mystery. Specifically, how do brain cells or electrical and chemical processes in your brain create thought? If cells cannot think, how then do thoughts arise at all? Thus researchers have mapped the mechanisms of the brain, but remain dumbfounded as how these mechanisms translate into thought and/or consciousness. If consciousness is an ethereal or spiritual entity, then how or why does this entity exist in and is influenced by the brain? One of the major difficulties in answering is that there is no consensus as to what consciousness is. This topic continues to be a matter of debate for scientists and philosophers. Nevertheless, if NDEs can provide evidence that some form of consciousness exists after death, then simple materialistic arguments that conflate the mind or consciousness with the brain will no longer be cogent.

Caring for an NDEr

Whether or not you are a health professional who advocates any or none of the explanations for NDEs proffered, it is very likely that health professionals will encounter NDErs in their career given the frequency of NDEs among ill persons. Therefore it is important to be aware of NDEs and how to effectively care for those patients who purport to have them. A 1995 study, in fact, found that although "70% of RNs, especially those in critical care areas and emergency rooms, stated that they were familiar with NDE. Ironically, results also showed that there was a low percentage of actual knowledge [about NDEs]."[30] In my personal conversations with nurses and health professionals, I

---

30. Cf. Suzanne M. Simpson, "Near death experience: A concept analysis as applied to nursing," *Journal of Advanced Nursing* 36.4 (2001): 520-526.

have found this statement to be accurate. Although most of these persons are familiar with NDEs, there is little knowledge about what exactly it is and even less knowledge about how to respond to patients who claim to have experienced an NDE.

Suzanne Simpson, a clinical nurse educator, recognizing the large amount of NDEs but also the lacuna of information for nurses to effectively care for these NDErs, offers several important suggestions for healthcare professionals that may encounter NDEs. She suggests medical staff and nurses be preemptive and avoid "suggestive or menacing language" such as, "He is not going to make it," as NDErs with OBE recall actions and conversations verbatim.[31] Any comments that could be embarrassing or lead the patient to believe that the health professionals are not completely committed to saving the patient's life should be avoided. If there are signs that a patient may have experienced an NDE, or that the patient speaks about such an experience, caregivers need to be nonjudgmental and cast aside their personal beliefs about NDEs. It is important to remember that not only is there no clear consensus among scholars studying the NDE phenomenon as to what the underlying mechanisms are that cause it, patients who have had an NDE are also most likely not interested in the health professional's opinion.

Simpson continues that healthcare professionals should create a nonthreatening environment but also look for signs after successful resuscitation that an NDE may have occurred by being active listeners and careful observers. Pay attention to some common cues that an NDE has occurred such as the patient post resuscitation "wanting to keep the lights on, talking about having a strange dream and appearing withdrawn and scared,"[32] and if you suspect that an NDE has occurred ask open-ended questions while speaking in a calm and supportive voice. Also be conscious of your nonverbal communications. Nevertheless, post-NDE care must cross a fine line between encouragement and overloading the patient with questions. One technique that researchers have found effective in post-NDE care is to tell the patient that many people report to have had a similar experience.[33]

Nevertheless, avoid jumping to the conclusion that the patient is confused or experiencing ICU psychosis. Unfortunately, many NDErs complain that that their health providers labeled them as psychotic after sharing their experience.[34] This is problematic as it can lead to negative emotions that inhibit recuperation. Therefore, health professionals need to exercise prudential judgment, as the characteristics of NDEs that I outlined above are very different from psychosis. If the latter is suspected, it is important to contact qualified personnel.

---

31. Ibid., 525.
32. Ibid., 525.
33. Ibid., 525.
34. Cf. C. Sutherland, "Changes in religious beliefs, attitudes, and practice following near-death experiences," *Journal of Near Death Studies* 9 (1990): 21-31.

Much like any patient who is dying and wants to talk about death, NDErs most likely want to share their experiences. They are not looking for approval, but they certainly do not desire rejection. Although our culture is more aware of NDEs than in the past, many NDErs feel that their experience will be ridiculed, so they do not share their experience for years. For this reason, caregivers should consider it an honor and evidence of their effective care if patients feel comfortable enough to share their experience with them.

It is important to note that it is acceptable not to have all of the answers. Being honest about this and having the willingness to connect your patient to those that have more experience on this topic than yourself is important. Healthcare providers are encouraged to suggest that patients not only contact the chaplain on-call but also NDE support groups. In many cases hospital chaplains have not only the most experience dealing with NDEs, but can help the patient process their experience, especially, if needed, within the context of their religious tradition.

Conclusion

This chapter provided a basic introduction to the phenomenon known as NDE. Whether or not NDEs are proof that we have an eternal spirit and that life continues after death is debatable; however, what is a fact is that millions of people have and millions of people will continue to experience NDEs. It is therefore imperative that healthcare workers be familiar with this phenomenon and be supportive when their patients share such experiences with them.

CHAPTER FOUR

EGYPTIAN AND MESOPOTAMIAN VIEWS ON DEATH AND THE AFTERLIFE

Introduction

The human struggle to understand death and what happens after death perhaps dates back to at least 30,000 BCE where we find Neanderthal graves of the dead stocked with tools, weapons, and food. Although there is no consensus as to when belief in the transcendent began, what is clear is that where we find human civilizations we find belief in the afterlife.

The appeal of religion both in ancient and modern times is no doubt due to the fact that it offers human beings meaning and hope about their existence and death. Recall Charles Corr's task-based approach to coping with death. Religion addresses the overarching dimension of human existence (spiritual dimension) that influences our physical, social, and psychological dimensions. Religion offers answers to the big questions: "Is there life after death?" and "Is there meaning in life?" How we answer these questions dictate to some extent how we address the other tasks of human existence. A discussion about human death would be incomplete without a discussion about religion. Only in doing so can we better understand the human experience of death and become more sensitive to the vast majority of North Americans who profess faith in a religious tradition and whose approach to their end-of-life issue is informed by their religious tradition.

This chapter begins with the religions of two civilizations that arose toward the end of the Neolithic age (circa 10,000–2500 BCE). The Neolithic age is the epoch of human history when human civilizations emerged around the great rivers of the world: the Indus River, Nile River, Euphrates River, and the Yellow River. Around these rivers agrarian societies developed that allowed human civilizations, cultures, and religions to flourish. In the interest of space this chapter will focus briefly on the Egyptian and Mesopotamian religions that had intricate funerary practices. I have chosen to focus on these two religions because they are both well known in popular American culture and more importantly provide a solid introduction to our study of the world religions. They also provide stark contrast to views on the meaning of death, life, and the afterlife that we find in the world religions. Nevertheless, these ancient religions also offer great examples as to how religion is conducive to negative or positive religious coping: while the Mesopotamian religion leads to realism, if not pessimism about life and death for the living, the Egyptian afterlife was the cause of optimism but also great anxiety for the living. This chapter familiarizes readers with the basic terminology and concepts about the afterlife that is used in subsequent chapters.

Ancient Egyptian Religion

BACKGROUND

Egyptian civilization began around 3000 BCE and ended around 395 CE.[1] My study will be limited to the New Kingdom period of the Egyptian civilization (1550–1070 BCE). Superficially, we might think that the ancient Egyptians were consumed with death and the afterlife, and this is not an unfounded observation. We are all familiar with the Egyptian dead; in particular, Egyptian mummies that inundate American pop-culture. Most American children have at one point donned toilet paper and murmured "Umm" with their arms outstretched! Many of my readers who were children in the late 1990s may remember "Mummies Alive," a cartoon that popularized the Egyptian cult of the dead. Moreover, when we think about landmarks in ancient Egypt we almost indelibly think about the Great Pyramids, which were tombs for the dead. They were the largest monuments in that society.

To the contrary, especially in the New Kingdom, Egyptians did not look forward to death or their "day of landing," since they enjoyed the pleasures of life.[2] This is not to deny that preparing for death

---

1. Nicola Harrington, *Living with the dead: Ancestral worship and mortuary ritual in ancient Egypt* (Oxford: Oxbow Books, 2012), XII-XVI.
2. William J. Murname, "Taking it with you: The problem of death and afterlife in ancient Egypt," in *Death and Afterlife: Perspectives of World Religions*, 35-49, ed. Hiroshi Obayashi (New York: Praeger, 1992), 35.

(i.e., planning lavish funeral services and tombs), were a part of Egyptian life. Nevertheless, Egyptians were focused on life, and their funerary customs were important inasmuch as they allowed them to continue their lifestyle in the afterlife. The Egyptian conception of death was what Philippe Aries categorized as a "death to self" mentality. Death itself was seen as an intruder, a negative experience; the goal of the funerary rites was to delimit this intrusion and maintain the connection with society and the family unit.[3] If the funerary rites were performed correctly, the afterlife would include the order and comfort that they experienced in life. Of course, if they were not performed correctly total annihilation of the deceased was possible. Thus, there is little doubt that Egyptians experienced some form of "death anxiety" characteristic of "death to self" mentalities.

The fact that the afterlife offered the possibilities of both eternal comfort and total annihilation was not in conflict, for the pleasures of the afterlife were only enjoyed after the dead successfully navigated through their day of judgment, avoiding total annihilation.

The Egyptian conception of paradise further demonstrates the close connection between the land of the living and the dead. This is evident in the term that Egyptians used for paradise, "the field of rushes." A rush is a flower-bearing plant indigenous to Egypt. The implication is that life in paradise replicated life on earth. Egyptians, in fact, believed that the dead plowed and harvested their land and worshipped the pantheon of gods and goddesses, who ruled them as the Pharaoh did in life.[4]

Before examining the Egyptian religion further I must mention an important caveat. Egyptian society was socially stratified; common Egyptians, who comprised the majority of Egyptian society, did not partake in the elaborate funerary cults mentioned below because they lacked the means to do so. At best they were observers of the cult or helped to carry out the funerary cult for the elite. Even though during the New Kingdom certain religious rites were disseminated to the populous (e.g., the ability of non-royals to acquire the *Book of the Dead*), it is unclear to what extent the commoner took part in the elaborate funerary rituals. The common Egyptian lacked the resources to preserve their bodies and personalize tombs. For the purpose of clarity, unless otherwise noted, when I write about the funerary rituals in Egypt, I am primarily speaking about those rites used by the rich and royalty of Egyptian society.[5]

---

3. Cf. Jan Zandee, *Death as an enemy: According to ancient Egyptian conceptions,* trans. W. F. Kalsens (Netherlands: Ayer Co Pub, 1960), 45.

4. "The underworld and afterlife in ancient Egypt," *Australian Museum* 2013, http://australianmuseum.net.au/The-underworld-and-the-afterlife-in-ancient-Egypt (March 12, 2014).

5. Archeological evidence reveals although the majority of ancient Egyptians lacked the means to have any of the funeral rituals mentioned above, common Egyptians had modest funerals without mummification. They buried their dead with items for use in the afterlife (Harrington, 31).

Gods and Goddesses and the Funerary Cult

The ancient Egyptian religion was a polytheistic religion that included a pantheon of gods and goddesses. In the context of the afterlife and funerary rituals, Osiris and Anubis were the most important gods. By the New Kingdom, Osiris was the god of the underworld that determined whether or not the human spirit was allowed to enter Paradise.

According to Egyptian mythology, Osiris was the first pharaoh of Egypt; unfortunately, he was the victim of fratricide: his brother Seth killed him and cut his body into fourteen pieces that he buried throughout Egypt. This was not the end of Osiris. Isis, his consort/sister located and reassembled his body for burial with exception to his phallus or penis.[6] This remains in the Nile, giving it fertility on which Egyptian society depended. Thus, Osiris was also the god of fertility. Anubis factors into this myth as the god who mummifies Osiris' corpse, allowing for Osiris' reanimation and new life as the king of the underworld. In some myths, Anubis abdicates his throne in the underworld to Osiris. Nevertheless, Osiris' death is not left unanswered, as Osiris' son, Horus, defeats Seth, thus avenging his father.

The Osiris legend informed the Egyptian funerary cult inasmuch as it provided justification for embalming the dead because it enshrined the importance of the corpse in the afterlife. Moreover, Osiris is the king of the underworld, the realm that all Egyptians enter. He was very important for Egyptians, since he decided whether or not the dead entered paradise. Nevertheless Anubis, not Osiris, was the most important deity for dying and bereaved Egyptians,[7] for just as he prepared Osiris for the afterlife, he facilitated the funeral and the transition of the dead to the afterlife.[8] For this reason he was worshipped in order to assist the dead: he was the patron god of tombs, the embalming process, and the recently dead.[9] Most importantly, although Osiris pronounced the final judgment, Anubis performed the test that informed Osiris' decision: it was Anubis who weighed the heart of the dead against the feather. Gaining favor with Anubis was of utmost importance, and if your heart weighed more than a feather, you would forfeit the afterlife.

---

6. "Osiris," *Encyclopedia Britannica* 2013, http://www.britannica.com/EBchecked/topic/433922/Osiris (March 12, 2014).

7. Elena Andra Cicarma, "The theriomorphism of Anubis. His etymology, mythological attendances and religious manifestations: The perceptions external of Egypt and subsequent religious assessments," *The Scientific Journal of Humanistic Studies* 5.9 (2013): 42-49), 45. Interestingly, Anubis is depicted as a black figure with a jackal's head. Jackals were associated with gravesites.

8. Ibid., 42.

9. Ibid., 45.

THE FUNERAL CULT

Although ancient Egyptians may not have shared the questions modern Western readers have about coping with dying and death, Egyptians prayed and recited spells to protect the dying from bad deaths (e.g., premature death and death by suffocation).[10] Needless to say, preparing the dead for a good afterlife was of utmost importance.

It is important to note that ancient Egyptian religion as well as the Mesopotamian religion was a religion that stressed *orthopraxy* over and against *orthodoxy*. While orthopraxy refers to the correct religious practices, orthodoxy refers to the correct religious beliefs. This does not mean that correct belief was not important for the Egyptians. Rather the emphasis in this religion at least for the wealthy and in the context of preparing for the afterlife was not the belief of the dead, but the traditions related to properly burying the dead.

Orthopraxy with reference to Egyptian funerary rights included important preparations like purchasing funerary items (e.g., *The Book of the Dead, Shabtis* or workers for the afterlife, and magic amulets to accompany the mummy), the coffin, and the building of a tomb in the land of the dead, the land west of the Nile.[11] Preparation for the afterlife required careful planning that ideally included these elements: mummification, a funeral procession, the "Opening of the Mouth" ceremony, offerings for the dead, a feast on behalf of the dead, and the closing of the tomb.[12]

MUMMIFICATION AND FUNERAL PROCESSION

By the time of the New Kingdom, Egyptians developed great skill in embalming the corpse. Their goal was to prevent as little decomposition as possible. Mummification of the corpse was a complicated process that entailed intricate removal of soft tissue and primary organs (lungs, liver, brain, stomach) that retained moisture that would cause decomposition. Afterwards the body was buried in natron, or naturally occurring soda ash, for seventy days. Once this period of preservation of the body was completed, the body was wrapped in resin-soaked linen and then wrapped again. As the embalmers wrapped the mummy, they placed various amulets for protection of the body in this world from grave robbers and in the next world from spiritual threats. One of the most interesting amulets is the heart scarab, which was an amulet in the shape of a beetle that had chapter thirty from the *Book of the Dead* inscribed on its underside. Egyptians placed the amulet over the heart to

---

10. Zandee, 70-75.
11. "The underworld and afterlife in ancient Egypt," *Australian Museum* 2013, http://australianmuseum.net.au/The-underworld-and-the-afterlife-in-ancient-Egypt (March 12, 2014).
12. "Funerals in ancient Egypt," *Australian Museum* 2009, http://australianmuseum.net.au/Funerals-in-ancient-Egypt (March 12, 2014).

ensure that the spell activated as Anubis weighted the deceased's heart. Afterwards the corpse was wrapped, coated in resin, adorned with a funeral mask depicting a person's greatest qualities, and then placed into its coffin.[13]

Once the embalmers completed the embalming process and placed the mummy in the coffin, the final funeral rituals began. A funeral procession met at the embalming hut and then carried the coffin to the banks of the Nile. This procession was a public display of mourning that involved a cohort of family members, friends, and professional mourners that chanted dirges and made vivid displays of mourning. Such displays included but were not limited to women showing their breasts and men raising arms in the air. After reaching the Nile, mourners boarded a boat with the coffin and crossed to the western side of the Nile where the procession continued to the tomb. At the tomb the priests performed various rituals including the "Opening of the Mouth" ceremony. Wearing a jackal's mask, representing Anubis, the priests touched the lips of the dead with a chisel that symbolized the freeing of the *ba* from the body. This ceremony enabled the *ba* to receive offerings from the living that would further sustain it.

Interestingly, the tomb was an extravagant display of wealth and prestige. However, it would be remiss to suggest that this was the only purpose of the tomb. Rather the tomb and all of items contained therein offered the dead a good afterlife. The artwork that adorned the walls was a magical backdrop for the dead that came to life to help the dead in the hereafter. Most importantly, the tomb provided a location for the living to continue the mortuary cult perpetually. In so doing not only were the dead ensured a good afterlife, but the living would receive protection from their dead loved one. For this purpose many tombs were also outfitted with more accessible dwellings or statues that would allow their family to visit them and continue the funerary cult. Family members were expected to continue to pray and make offerings on behalf of the deceased to the deities. Destruction or robbery of the tomb was catastrophic for an Egyptian, since it could have a negative effect on their ancestor's afterlife. For this reason, not only was grave robbery a serious criminal offense in the New Kingdom that received capital punishment but alternative tombs for the dead were created, so as to confuse grave robbers and preserve the original mummy.

After the coffin was placed in the tomb, more offerings were made for the dead, and then a feast was held to honor the dead. Finally, the tomb was sealed, which concluded the funeral.

---

13. Murname, 38.

The Book of the Dead

The Book of the Dead, or properly known as *The Chapters of Coming Forth by Days*, is one of the most interesting and important items for my study that was deposited in the tomb. It helped to guarantee that the deceased had an afterlife, but also today provides insight as to how the Egyptians viewed the afterlife.

Nevertheless *The Book of Dead* was not a book per se, but rather a list of spells; therefore, it should not be placed in the genre of sacred scripture, such as the Bible, Gita, Suttas of the Buddha, or Qur'an. Egyptians lacked a central holy text. *The Book of the Dead* was a loose collection of spells, prayers, and hymns for Egyptians that functioned as an instruction manual to successfully navigate the trials of the afterlife, avoiding the "Second Death" or spiritual extinction. Spells in the text would activate to protect the deceased or provide the deceased with correct responses to questions from various judges.

The trials to which *The Book of the Dead* refers by and large tested the virtue of the dead Egyptian. For Egyptians, virtuous living included abiding by their forty-two Negative Commandments. Knowing that most of the dead broke one or more of these commandments, this text offered a spell for the dead to recite that would demonstrate that they kept each commandment, that they were innocent of wrongdoing. Here is an example of a hymn that provided the dead with the correct response to four of the forty-two judges that they would face.

> Hail, Long-Strider who comes from Heliopolis, I have not done iniquity. Hail, Embraced-by Fire who comes from Kher-aha, I have not robbed with violence. Hail, Divine-Nose who comes from Khemmenu, I have not done violence to another man. Hail, Shade-Eater who comes from the caverns which produce the Nile, I have not committed theft.[14]

This hymn continues to address the remaining forty-two commandments and corresponding gods that judged whether or not their respective commandment was kept. *The Book of the Dead* supplemented the lack of virtue and knowledge about the afterlife of the dead person. Because the text was expensive, in the New Kingdom, Egyptians who could afford the text would have it customized to include specific prayers and information that the Egyptian priest deemed necessary for the wealthy person to enter into paradise.

Nevertheless, this trial period culminated in the weighing of the heart, which I mentioned above. Although this final test is not mentioned in the text, it is depicted in the vignette accompanying

---

14. "The Coming Into Day (The Book of the Dead): Chapter 125, The Judgment of the Dead," *World Cultures* 1997, http://richard-hooker.com/sites/worldcultures/EGYPT/BOD125.HTM (February 23, 2015).

chapter 125, also known as the final judgment. For Egyptians the heart is the essence of a person; for this reason the heart was the only organ left in the mummy. The weighing of the heart against a feather or truth itself gauged whether or not a person was truthful and righteous during life. A balanced scale symbolized that the dead person was truthful, since the dead's heart weighed as much as truth itself. Then Osiris would allow the deceased to enter paradise. Only persons who pursued truth were worthy to enter paradise. On the other hand, an unbalanced scale represented the sins of a person that weighed down the heart. An alligator-headed beast, Ammit, "the Eater of the Dead" devoured heavy hearts, which is a metaphor for the annihilation of the self.

The Egyptian Soul

Ancient Egyptians perceived the human being as a spiritual-corporeal complex entity. Dualistic notions of the self that bifurcate soul from body were not native to Egyptian theology. To complicate matters, Egyptian thought on the human person is inconsistent and ambiguous; thus terms like *ka* and *ba* are conflated but also treated as distinct entities. Here are some of the terms frequently employed to refer to the human person: *ba, ka, sah, akh*, name, and shadow. The *sah* is the body itself. Usually it referred to the mummified body. The terms *khet* and *khat* were also used to refer to the body; however, while the *khet* was the living body, the *khat* was the dead body. The *sah* was important because it allowed the dead to enjoy their offerings in their tomb. For this reason, Egyptians left jars of food for the dead in their tomb to sustain their *sah*. Nevertheless, there is no clear consensus among Egyptologists as to how the *sah* functioned and what happened to the dead if their corpses were destroyed.

If the *sah* provided the opportunity for the dead to be nourished, it was through the *ka* that the nourishment occurred. The *ka* is an impersonal life-force of a person.[15] It is a spiritual double that came into existence at birth,[16] and was released from the body at death. The *ka* was the means through which energy derived from offerings to the *sah* could nourish the *ba*. The *ba* was the intellect or personality of the person. When you think of a human soul or ghost, you are thinking about the *ba* in an Egyptian context. It was able to move from this world to the afterlife and back again. It is usually depicted as a human-headed falcon.[17] The *ba* most likely underwent the trials mentioned in the "Book of the Dead." Moreover, the "Opening of the Mouth Ceremony" allowed the *ba* to leave the body and rejoin the *ka*.

---

15. Harrington, 14.
16. Murname, 40.
17. Harrington, 3.

Nevertheless the goal of the funerary cult was the transformation of the *ka* and *ba* into an *akh*. The *akh* was an illuminated or ancestral spirit.[18] You do not have an *akh*, but rather you can become an *akh*. It is unclear when the *akh* comes into existence. When the *ba* and *ka* form the *akh*, the *ba* and *ka* do not cease to exist.[19] The *akh* was many things, but perhaps most importantly it was the transfigured or resurrected person.[20] The legend of Osiris provides a good indicator that Egyptian resurrection was a kind of reanimation. Scholars debate the meaning of resurrection and its importance to the ancient Egyptians as well as its influence on Judeo-Christian and Islamic notions of resurrection.[21] Nevertheless, belief that *akh* could become a beneficial spirit or a malevolent spirit or ghost was very important. This of course depended upon the proper performance of the funerary rituals and ancestral worship.

Associated with the *sah* is the "name" and "shadow." The "name" refers to a given name of a person. It contained the personal power of a person. The shadow refers to the shadow cast by the body. Egyptians believed that as the shadow follows a person in life, it continues to exist after death, living in the tomb.

Bereavement in Egypt

Egyptian society allowed Egyptian workers to take up to nine days off to mourn their dead. Moreover, ancient Egypt had a strong ancestral cult, whereby the ancient Egyptians continually made offerings and prayers to and on the behalf of their ancestors.[22] In her book, *Living with the Dead: Ancestor Worship and Mortuary Ritual in Ancient Egypt*, Nichola Harrington argues proper burial and arraigning the mortuary or ancestral cult guaranteed an afterlife for the dead.

Nevertheless, writing letters to the dead is perhaps one of the most interesting ancient Egyptian bereavement practices. Although it is unclear how widespread this practice was given the fact that only sixteen letters remain in existence, these letters evidence that at least in these cases Egyptians believed that their relationship with their loved ones transcended death and that familial responsibilities continued. While the living had to maintain their relationship with the dead through offerings for the dead, the *akh* was expected to return the favor. Thus, in these letters Egyptians ask the *ahk* of their loved one to intercede on their behalf in times of trials (e.g., to resolve grievances, infertility, and so forth). These letters are not always cordial; in one infamous letter a brooding hus

---

18 Cf. Ibid., 7.
19 Cf. Ibid., 7.
20 Jiří Janák, "Akh" in *UCLA Encyclopedia of Egyptology Open Version* (Los Angles: University of California, 2012), 2.
21 In Judaism, Christianity, and Islam the resurrection of the dead is central to their narratives, which occurs at the end of time as we know it. This was not the case in ancient Egypt.
22 Ibid., 33.

band chided his dead wife for her failure to grant him favors. In another letter one Egyptian makes his offering conditional on a favor being granted in advance!

> "Please become a spirit for me [before] my eyes so that I may see you in a dream fighting on my behalf." In return, he promises to "deposit offerings for you [as soon as] the sun has risen and outfit your offering slab for you." [23]

Perhaps this is the earliest evidence of the living extorting the dead! Ritual letter writing is evidence of an important coping mechanism for many to continue their relationship with the dead. In so doing, the living were able to reintegrate the dead into their lives but also continue their communication with loved ones. The funerary and ancestral cults were also an important characteristic of the ancient Mesopotamian religion.

Mesopotamian Religion

BACKGROUND

Much like the Egyptian religion, the Mesopotamian religion (2500 BCE to 500 CE) did not have a specific founder or a central holy text. It was the religion of the people inhabiting the area between the Euphrates and Tigris rivers, which today we know as Iraq and Iran. The religion itself consisted of a loose conglomeration of various local gods and goddesses, demons and monsters. Each city had a particular patron and protector god or goddess; and as the city increased or decreased in prominence, so did its patron deity. In these cities we find great temples or *Ziggurats* where the temple priests performed rituals for the protection of their city.[24] Relevant to the prominence of a city, at various times during the history of this civilization, certain gods rise and fall in prominence. Nevertheless, there were several major gods and goddesses associated with the natural and psychological elements. These included the deities Anu, the father god and god of the sky; Utu, the "sun god and the lord of truth and justice"; Nanna, "the moon god: Inanna was the goddess of love and war"; Ninhursag, "the goddess of the earth"; and Enki, "the god of fresh water as well as the lord of wisdom and magic."[25]

---

23. Ibid., 35.
24. "Gods, goddesses, demons and monsters," *The British Museum* 2014, http://www.mesopotamia.co.uk/gods/home_set.html (March 3, 2014).
25. "Life in Mesopotamia: Religion," *Oriental Institute of the University of Chicago* 2013, http://mesopotamia.lib.uchicago.edu/mesopotamialife/article.php?theme=Religion (March 1, 2014).

The gods and goddesses in ancient Mesopotamia (2500–500 BCE) were much more capricious and arbitrary than the deities in Egypt. This is evident in a popular creation myth whereby Enki created humankind out of clay so as to lessen the workload for the gods and goddesses, who grew tired of tending and tilling the soil. Not wanting to share their immortality with human beings, humankind was made mortal. Humankind, therefore, had no other purpose than to work the land for the god and goddesses. Unpredictability of the weather that included sporadic, violent flooding for the Mesopotamians most likely verified the capriciousness of their deities.[26]

AFTERLIFE

Mesopotamian belief in the afterlife is in stark contrast to the Egyptian belief on this topic. Mesopotamians did not have anxiety over a "Second Death"; however, their afterlife tradition provided little hope and comfort for the living. Perhaps the Mesopotamian religion resulted in "negative religious coping," as dying meant the loss of everything you hold dear and ignominious existence. Whereas the Egyptian afterlife offered hope of paradise, Mesopotamian afterlife was gloomy and sad. If not pessimists, the Mesopotamians were at least realists about their inevitable end. The *Epic of Gilgamesh*, an important and popular literary work of Mesopotamian civilization, reveals vividly the futility with which the Mesopotamians viewed the afterlife. This narrative relates the age-old quest to escape death and gain immortality, as Gilgamesh attempts to find immortality after watching his beloved friend, Enkidu, die. Before his death, Enkidu has a near-death experience where he visits the afterlife; he recounts that:

> There is the house whose people sit in darkness dust is their food and clay their meat. They are clothed like birds with wings for covering, they see no light, and they sit in darkness. I entered the house of dust and I saw the kings of the earth, their crowns put away forever; rulers and princes, all those who once wore kingly crowns and ruled the world in the days of old. They who had stood in the place of the gods like Anu and Enlil stood now like servants to fetch baked meats in the house of dust, to carry cooked meat and cold water from the water-skin.[27]

Note the dark and gloomy portrayal of the afterlife, for the afterlife was a "house of dust" whereupon the dead eat dusk and clay. This was a fate irrespective of their social significance. Justice in the afterlife is not central narrative in the Mesopotamian afterlife. If there was any justice it was in the fact that all people, rich or poor, have the same fate, and what you did in life matters little. Here

---

26. Here we find an important contrast with ancient Egypt in terms of how the order of the seasons and weather influenced their deities' decisions and belief in the afterlife. The seasons and weather were relatively predictable in Egypt. This predictability was attributed to the deities and contributed to the Egyptians' positive outlook as well as their belief in the order of the afterlife.

27. *The Epic of Gilgamesh*, trans., Nancy Sandars (New York: Penguin Books, 1960): 86-93.

is stark contrast to the Egyptian belief that only those who pursued truth could enter paradise; the funeral cult allowed in theory for the unjust to enter paradise. With this image of the netherworld in mind, it is not surprising that Gilgamesh, a great king and hero, sets out on an adventure to gain immortality, for death would render all his fame and fortune meaningless.

As the epic continues, after consulting with Utnapishtim, the mortal granted immortality after surviving the great flood, Gilgamesh learns how to become immortal: he must find and consume a specific plant at the bottom of the sea. He succeeds in finding it, but immediately after collapsing in exhaustion, a serpent eats the plant, robbing Gilgamesh of the reward of his great journey. Distraught and exhausted, Gilgamesh returns to his city of Ur, realizing the quest for immortality is pointless: everyone faces death and the humdrum existence in the netherworld.

Siduri, a tavern keeper who warned Gilgamesh of his futile endeavor, provides the answer to what the meaning of life is:

> When the gods created mankind, they established death for mankind, and withheld eternal life for themselves...As for you, Gilgamesh let your stomach be full, always be happy, night and day. Make every day a delight, night and day play and dance. Your clothes should be clean, your head should be washed, you should bathe in water, look proudly on the little one holding your hand, let your mate be always blissful in your loins, this, then, is the work of mankind.[28]

Sidur's point is very simply: death is inevitable and there is no pleasure in the afterlife, so stop wasting time and enjoy your life now to the fullest extent possible.

Life and the Netherworld

Albeit bland and gloomy, the netherworld was not necessarily a place for punishment like the Judeo-Christian Hell or the ancient Greek Tartarus. There were, in fact, moments of relief from the gloom of the underworld or netherworld. First and foremost, relief came in the form of the order and life of the netherworld. Moreover, the netherworld was a pale reflection of life on earth, in particular, their experience with rulers. The dead had some acquaintance about how things worked here. The gods and goddesses of the netherworld set up a royal court, and like any good ruler, they graced their subjects with a few pleasures including sunlight for a few moments on a daily basis, and even provided bread and clear water on occasion.[29] Most importantly, the inhabitants of the netherworld were permitted to visit their living relatives once a year and during festivals.

28. *The Epic of Gilgamesh*, 102.
29. Jo Ann Schurlock, "Death and the Afterlife in Ancient Mesopotamian Thought" in *The Civilizations of the Ancient Near East*, 1883-1893, vol. 3, ed. Jack M. Sasson (New York: Simon and Schuster Macmillan, 1995), 1887.

Similar to research on Egyptian afterlife there is ambiguity about Mesopotamian afterlife. What is certain is that the living's ability or inability to perform religious rituals on behalf of their dead determined how a loved one fared in the afterlife. Failure to perform the funeral offerings and participate in the cult of the dead made the ghost suffer and weep. Like the Egyptians, the goal for the dead was to become an ancestor spirit, a ghost that was continually remembered by the living by way of perpetual offerings and prayers on behalf of the dead. Some myths purported that after generations this ghost would become a member of the collective ancestor spirits. Eventually the ancestor would be recycled as a soul for a new life. Nevertheless, we have to be careful not to import alien ideas about reincarnation to the Mesopotamians, since it is not at all clear what is recycled: is it the human consciousness or simply the parts of that consciousness, which is tantamount to the destruction of the consciousness? The underlying cause for this evolution in the ghost's existence is the continual worship of ancestors and the existence of the corpse. Moreover, their belief in recycling is not a central part of their theological narrative, and it is unclear how it informs the funerary or bereavement customs.

FUNERARY AND MOURNING RITES

You may wonder why the Mesopotamians stressed the importance of funerary or memorial customs at all, given the depressing state that awaited their loved ones. This is because Mesopotamians believed that there was an alternative to the netherworld, wandering the world as sleepless ghosts. Existence as a wandering ghost for all eternity was the greatest punishment. Restless ghosts lacked any of the comforts that resulted from annual visits to living family, participation in festivities, and the remedial pleasures the gods offered that I mentioned above. Their existence consisted in tireless wandering and harassing the living.

The living took great lengths to ensure that their deceased family members were able to avoid the fate of a restless ghost. Like their Egyptian counterparts, the funeral customs functioned as a method for coping with death for the dying and living because it helped guarantee the best afterlife possible. Nevertheless, there was undoubtedly an element of self-preservation involved in funeral preparations in as much as failure to perform the proper funeral customs could result in hauntings. Restless ghosts were demonic figures that caused havoc in response to the lack of a proper funeral, resulting in violent death, or an inappropriate death for a Mesopotamian (e.g., death before marriage and death before giving birth to children). Unmarried dead persons joined a special class of demons that looked for victims to become the spouses that they never had. They would seduce the unsuspecting person that would lead to their early death and populate new generations of unmarried demons.[30] The living took various measures to ward off angry ghosts including wearing am-

---

30. Schurlock, 1890.

ulets, drinking elixirs, performing exorcisms, and burying figurines, representing the angry ghost, which helped to lay the ghost to rest.[31]

Needless to say, Mesopotamians were superstitious people. It was common practice for the living to contact good ghosts or ancestor ghosts and ask them to take evil with them when they returned to the underworld. Moreover, Mesopotamians practiced divinization, consulting their dead relatives for advice. This was a serious affair and in Mesopotamian society there were "professional ghost raisers" that would facilitate this communication and protect the family from welcoming angry ghosts into their homes.[32]

FUNERAL RITE AND BEREAVEMENT

Like the Egyptians, Mesopotamians had no universally accepted practice for coping with death for either the dying or the bereaved. Nevertheless, much like many Americans today, the ideal place to die was in the comfort of one's home in the presence of family.[33] When signs of death were evident, the dying would be moved to a special funerary bed and a chair would be placed at the left side of the dying. They believed that the spirit left the body and rested in this chair after a special incantation was recited. This allowed for the spirit to have a place to benefit from the first funeral offerings before its journey to the netherworld. Although the netherworld was thought to reside in the space directly below the earth, Mesopotamians believed that a ghost must undergo a dangerous journey to reach the netherworld. Funerals, therefore, provided necessities for the dead to successfully complete this journey. Archeologists discovered food, walking sandals, and even chariots in Mesopotamian tombs. Archeological evidence has also revealed that there were two main elements in this journey that included "the demon infested steppes," Khubur River, and finally entrance through the gates of the netherworld. The gates of the netherworld were guarded by Nergal and his wife Ereshkigal, the god and goddess of the netherworld.[34] Special provisions were given to these deities by the dead provided in the offerings to ensure that the dead entered the netherworld.

Nevertheless, immediately after death, the body was washed and perfumed and the mouth would then be closed. The corpse was dressed in clean clothes with as many personal items as the living could afford to part with. Relative to wealth and social prestige the funerals and burials would be lavish or modest. Like the Egyptian elite, the wealthy or rulers hired professional mourners to mourn the dead. With the family and friends, they lamented the dead with music, tore their clothes, shrieked, pulled out their hair, and eulogized the dead. Afterwards the dead were buried, and the

---

31. Ibid., 1891.
32. Ibid., 1889.
33. Ibid., 1883-1884.
34. Ibid., 1886.

burial occurred in a variety of places including the tomb, grave, or family crypt.[35] Corresponding to wealth and status the rich buried their dead in tombs; the poor had simple graves in the ground or even below their homes. Family crypts were not uncommon because they allowed the living to watch over their ancestors and provided the dead opportunities to more readily reconnect with their relatives.

The mourning for the dead began immediately after the burial and lasted up to seven days. Mourners dressed in shaggy clothes, sometimes sackcloth, and did not wash during this period.[36]

Mesopotamian Soul

Mesopotamians envisioned the human spirit as consisting of several elements including the ghost, life force, and spirit. While the life force left the body at the time of death, the ghost and spirit remained. The spirit is analogous to the modern concept of soul, as it clearly had an intellectual capacity. The ghost was the vehicle that the spirit used to travel to and from the netherworld. Thus the spirit descended into the netherworld by way of the ghost. The ghost was closely associated with the bones of the deceased, and the ghost existed only insofar as the bones existed. Thus, it was not an uncommon practice for kings to destroy the bones of the ancestors of the citizens in conquered cities so as to prevent the spirit from avenging their relations' defeat. By destroying the bones, the ghost became a harmless spirit.[37] Because the ghost is associated with material existence, it was to the ghost that the living made offerings and prayers.

Conclusion

Both the Egyptian and Mesopotamian religions provided their devotees with important answers to the question about their existence, meaning, death, and afterlife. These beliefs informed their practices and perspective on what is important in life and how to die well. Their stress on the correct performance of the funerary customs helped foster a continued connection with their dead and most likely helped them bereave their dead. Both religions addressed the four dimensions of the person to some extent: they defined the meaning of life (spiritual dimension); human relationships, especially in the solace that the dying had in the fact that their loved ones would provide a funeral and perpetual offerings on their behalf (social task); relative to their wealth, these religions allowed

---

35. Ibid., 1884.
36. Jerrold S. Cooper, "The fate of mankind: Death and afterlife in ancient Mesopotamian" in *Death and Afterlife: Perspective of World Religions*, 19-34, ed. Hiroshi Obayashi (New York: Praeger, 1992), 24.
37. Schurlock, 1892.

the dying to make decisions about their death and memorial (psychological task); and their religion informed their decisions about what happened to their body after death (physical task). In this way the ancient Egyptian and Mesopotamian persons were not that different from people in modern Western societies, who turn to religion to give their lives and the experience of death meaning. As we shall see many of the ideas about the afterlife that the ancients professed are appropriated by many of the world's religions that help their congregants die well.

CHAPTER FIVE

HINDUISM

Introduction

Originating around 2500 BCE, Hinduism is the oldest practiced world religion. Today it is the third largest religion in the world and the dominant religion in the countries of India and Nepal. Nearly 1 billion persons worldwide self-identify as Hindu, and nearly 2 million Hindus live in the United States.

Superficially, Hinduism may seem very similar to Egyptian and Mesopotamian religions inasmuch as there is no founder; it is a polytheistic religion that includes a pantheon of gods, goddesses, demons, and heavenly beings; and orthopraxy is stressed especially with respect to end-of-life rituals. However, the similarities end there, from the ancient religions; and, in fact, Hindus take great offense to the stereotype that they are polytheists. Hindus do not object that there are many gods but rather to the crude interpretation of their tradition that fails to understand that these deities are manifestations of the one god or sacred power.[1] Anyone familiar with writings of Mohandas Gandhi is aware that albeit a devout Hindu, he continually refers not to the gods but to the one God. His faith in the one God allowed him room to dialogue fruitfully with his Christian and Islamic counterparts. Professing his faith as a devout Hindu, Gandhi says: "I believe, along with every Hindu, in

---

1. Cf. Gavin Flood, *An introduction to Hinduism* (Cambridge: Cambridge University Press, 1996), 10-11.

God and His Oneness, in rebirth and salvation."[2] Hinduism does not fit neatly into Western categorizations of religion. This is due in part to the fact that religious Hindus are more concerned about correct practice as opposed to correct belief. Therefore, the practice of the Hindu religion is highly regulated and ritualistic, but the beliefs are inclusive inasmuch as there are very few dogmas that all Hindus agree upon.[3] Thus within the same community of Hindus you may find Hindus that believe in one God or those that believe that no personal God exists.

The closest example of a Hindu creedal statement is the Indian Supreme Court's 1995 ruling that defined seven basic tenets of Hinduism:

> (i) Acceptance of the Vedas with reverence as the highest authority in religious and philosophic matter and acceptance with reverence of vedas by Hindu thinkers and philosophers as the sole foundation of Hindu philosophy. (ii) Spirit of tolerance and willingness to understand and appreciate the opponent's point of view based on the realisation that truth was many-sided. (iii) Acceptance of great world rhythm, vast period of creation, maintenance and dissolution follow each other in endless succession, by all six systems of Hindu philosophy. (iv) Acceptance by all systems of Hindu philosophy or the belief in rebirth and pre-existence. (v) Recognition of the fact that the means or ways to salvation are many. (vi) Realisation of the truth that Gods to be worshipped may be large, yet there being Hindus who do not believe in the worshipping of idols. (vii) Unlike other religions or religious creeds Hindu religion not being tied-down to any definite set of philosophic concepts, as such. [sic][4]

Take note of the ambiguities and apparent contradictions between the various characteristics: while characteristic 4 states that Hindus believe in reincarnation and pre-existence, characteristic 7 states that "Unlike other religion or religious creeds Hindu religion not being tied-down to any definite set of philosophic concepts. [sic]" Characteristic 7 suggests that philosophical concepts like reincarnation could be rejected in the future since Hinduism is not "tied-down" to any set of concepts.

This lack of rigidity and inclusivity in belief are in part a result of Hinduism's history. The story of Hinduism is not a story of a single religious tradition or a particular prophet but rather of a variety of local religious traditions practiced by the inhabitants of India and Nepal that influenced and appropriated one another's traditions over several thousand years. As a result Hindus today, as characteristic 2 demonstrates, believe that truth is many-sided. It is not uncommon for Hindus to appropriate non-Indian gods into their belief system. However, we ought to be cautious of labeling

---

2. *The Gandhi reader: A sourcebook of his life and writings*, ed. Jack A. Homer (New York: Grove Press, 1956), 168.
3. Flood, 13.
4. "Bramchari Sidheswar Bhai & Ors. Etc Versus State Of West Bengal Etc. On 2 July, 1995," Supreme Court of India 1995, http://judis.nic.in/supremecourt/imgs1.aspx?filename=10725 (February 27, 2015).

Hinduism as relativistic or pluralistic, which would imply they do not make universal truth claims. To the contrary, Hindus make truth claims with respect to at least three aspects of their faith, namely their belief in reincarnation or *samsara, moksha*, and *dharma*. These terms will guide the first part of my discussion in this chapter, which will provide the background necessary for comprehending how Hindus approach end-of-life care, the second part of the discussion, and how health professionals in North America can effectively care for their Hindu patients, discussed in the last part of the chapter. This chapter ends with an interview with a Hindu priest, Dr. Vijayaraghavan Chakravarthy. His interview provides important insights on Hindu theology, rituals, and end-of-life care.

The Doctrine of Samsara

HINDUISM BEFORE SAMSARA AND THE CASTE SYSTEM

Hindu belief in reincarnation or *samsara* is a part of the narrative of the Hindu religion. However, reincarnation does not appear in the earliest books that comprise the *Vedas* or the Hindu holy texts: the Rig Veda (circa 1700 BCE), which is the oldest Hindu holy text, makes no mention of reincarnation. The first detailed account of reincarnation is the Chandogya Upanishad (circa 600 BCE). Note that this teaching arises during what I described in the introduction as the axial age. The Chandogya Upanishad is a part of the Hindu canon of scripture known as the *Vedanta* or the end of the Vedic corpus.

Early Hinduism or the Rig Veda was ritualistic and furtive. By this I mean that early Hindus believed that the gods and humankind lived in a symbiotic relationship. If humankind performed special rituals such as the fire sacrifice that provided sustenance for the gods, then the gods would bless the people with long life, peace, health, good harvest, among other things. Veda means knowledge, and the oldest Vedic texts provide readers the knowledge to facilitate this relationship: sacred hymns (Rig Veda), sacrificial formulas (Yajur-Veda), chants (Säma Veda), and magical spells (Atharva Veda) had a cosmic significance that kept order in the world.[5] The religious rituals associated with the Rig Veda continue to inform Hindus, and, in fact, this stress on correct performance of rituals and sacrifices influences the karma marga or the path of action that many Hindus practice today. Nevertheless, many particular rituals in the Vedas are no longer practiced, new rituals have developed, and many rituals that were practiced have changed in significance.

---

5. Dominic Goodall, "Introduction" in *Hindu Scriptures,* trans. and ed. Dominic Goodall (Los Angeles: University of California Press, 1996), x.

One of the most lasting and visible contributions that the Rig Veda has on contemporary Hinduism is the caste system. As illustrated in the Rig Veda's hymn "The Sacrifice of Primordial Man," the caste system reflects the cosmic order in creation. There are four main castes that derive their existence from the sacrifice of primordial man (Purusha): "His mouth was the brahmin, his arms were made into the nobles, his two thighs were the populace, and from his feet the servants were born."[6] Thus castes include the *brahmin* (priestly and intellectual caste), "[h]is mouth"; *kshatriyas* (ruling and military class), "his arms"; *vaishyas* (merchant caste), "two thighs"; and *shudras* (laborer caste), "his feet." Each caste's function in society is best explained in relation to the ancient fire sacrifice. While priests were the highest caste since they performed the fire sacrifice that ensured natural and cosmic order, the warriors and rulers kept order in society to allow the priests the leisure and security to perform the fire sacrifice, and while the merchant caste supported society with its economic activity, the laborer caste was the backbone of society, the workers or majority of people whose daily labor made society function.

My non-Hindu students generally have great difficulty understanding the caste system, as it seems not only outmoded but discriminatory and to contradict the basic tenet of American culture that all people are entitled to equal rights. To be fair, in India, discrimination on the basis of caste is illegal. Moreover, even though every Hindu is aware of their caste, especially in North America, caste does not confine their freedom to pursue the American dream. In India, albeit unlikely for a shudra or outcast (i.e., a person outside the caste system), every Indian has the potential to be the prime minister of India. Moreover, many Hindus internalize the caste system and reject the notion that the caste system is inherently patriarchal, based on a system of discrimination and superiority.

Interestingly, Mohandas Gandhi, the greatest advocate for social justice and human rights in India's history, was also a strong supporter of the caste system. Gandhi did not interpret his advocacy and defense of the caste system to be in contradiction with his commitment to social justice, and in fact, he rejected intermarriage or interdining with members outside one's caste. Gandhi not only justified the caste system as representative of the order in the cosmos, but more importantly argued that the caste system revealed the real person and the requisite self-restraint that persons need to better themselves. In other words, caste members were created with specific talents that should be cultivated. Relative to their caste obligations, the caste system with its requisite dharmas or duties that regulate a caste members' life do so in order to help that person restrain oneself so as to better serve the community and attain enlightenment.[7] Thus Gandhi's intention behind his prohibition of intermarriage or interdining was not discriminatory but self-effacing: to deprive oneself of the pleasure of being with these other persons so as to further cultivate one's personality and those of other members.

---

6. "Rig Veda: Book 10, Hymn XC," *Sacred texts,* http://www.sacred-texts.com/hin/rigveda/rv10090.htm (February 27, 2015).

7. Cf. *Gandhi reader,* 169.

Nevertheless the most visible influence of the caste today is in Hinduism's religious rites whereby the brahmin retains a central and mediating function between this world and the afterlife. This is particularly evident at the end of life when brahmin priest informs the dying, eldest son, and bereaved about the requisite Hindu rituals.

Jnana Marga: Samsara and the Upanishads

Among scholars there is no clear consensus how the teaching on reincarnation developed in Hinduism. While some scholars suggest that it was directly the result of the influence of Hindu ascetics or outside influences, others note that although the Rig Veda (circa 1700–1100 BCE) makes no mention of samsara, later Vedas such as Atharva Veda (circa 1000 BCE) contain verses that imply rebirth. They argue that this minor tradition over time becomes a major tradition. For our purpose reincarnation is not a dominant tradition in Hinduism until the axial age when the oldest texts of the Upanishads (circa 800–400 BCE) were composed and disseminated in the Indian peninsula.[8]

Whereas the early Vedas focus on the sacrificial ritual and afterlife that included a belief in an eternal paradise-like existence known as *svarga* or heaven, the Upanishads focus on an esoteric teaching about the attainment of liberation from *moksha*, the cycle of *samsara* or reincarnation, through concentration and meditation.[9] There is little doubt that this movement reacted to the ritualism that permeated Hindu society. Within the Upanishads, mystics criticize the path of action as a lower wisdom and argue that the Vedas has no use if you do not know the Spirit who is the author of the Vedas.[10] The authors of the early Upanishads establish the *jnana marga*, or path of knowledge, that many Hindus follow today. The path of knowledge stresses that liberation from the continual cycle of birth and rebirth is possible through contemplative practices. Followers of this path reject the world as we know it in order to pursue inner enlightenment through ascetical practices.

What follows from this path is the realization that your life is one life among many other lives that you have lived. Thus samsara is a continual cycle of life, death, and rebirth. Now the thought of endless lives may at first seem comforting, but for Hindus since all life eventually ends in death and death is suffering, endless time is suffering from which they desire liberation. To get an idea about what this means think about the losses in your life or the fact that everyone that you love will suffer and die. Endless rebirths mean endless loss of those persons whom you love. This cycle of continual life, loss, and suffering is the cycle of samsara (reincarnation). With this insight in mind, liberation from samsara or *moksha* is an appealing alternative.

---

8. There are over 100 Upanishads written between 800 BCE and 1400 CE.
9. Klaus K. Klostermaier, *A survey of Hinduism,* 2nd ed. (Albany: State University of New York Press: 1994), 193-194.
10. *The Upanishads,* 55-66, trans. Juan Mascarb (London: Penguin Books,1965), 75, 91.

To achieve liberation one must address the cause of reincarnation which is *karma*. Karma literally means action. Karma is not a thing onto itself, but refers to the process of cause and effect associated with action. In the context of samsara, karma fuels the cycle of birth, death, and rebirth because every action has a karmatic consequence that must be expiated or experienced. Karmatic consequences are evident in the fortunes and tragedies, but also our rebirths. Whereas good intentional actions affect our life in a positive manner, bad intentional actions affect our life in a negative manner. Good karma gives higher rebirth (e.g., rebirth as a brahmin or in the heavens); bad karma results in lower rebirth (e.g., rebirth as an animal). Thus karmatic energy is like glue that sticks us to the cycle of reincarnation. Sri Swami Viditatmananda, a Hindu guru, explains that there are three main types of karma: *kriyamäna-karma,* the karma that I perform now; *prärabdha-karma,* the karma that determined the location of my birth, caste, family, etc.; and *saïcita-karma,* the karma that I collected which I will see come to fruition in the future.[11] In order to achieve moksha, Hindus must not only atone for bad karma but stop the accumulation of these karmas.[12] Although there are various teachings on what and how to do this in the Upanishad corpus, the consensus is that we must achieve a habit whereby we act without desiring the effects of our actions, but also understand that the evil and good we experience in life are a result of karma. If this seems like a difficult task, you are not alone! Because it is difficult to do, the process of freeing oneself from samsara will take many lifetimes. For achieving moksha requires not only atoning for bad and good karma, but also a radical perception that the phenomenological world, the world that we experience with our senses, is an illusion. It is our desire for the things in this world (phenomenological world) that perpetuate our reincarnations. Only through intense training of the mind and meditation is liberation possible.

During this meditative training the *sadu* or religious ascetic/mystic will transcend the phenomenological world itself to come into contact with the neumenological world, a world of pure reality. This state of being defies objectification or description insofar as it is based on an ineffable experience. It is a mystical experience of reality as-it-is-itself that is beyond rational description. The Sanskrit term that is used to identify this state is *Turiya*. Turiya refers to reality beyond all that there is; "it is neither perception of external nor internal objects, neither knowledge nor ignorance. It is supreme consciousness of consciousness, a cessation of all movement and all multiplicity."[13] If Turiya seems illogical, you are on right track since rationale description cannot suffice because there is no analogy for this mystical experience. What usually results is that descriptions about this state are either illogical or overly negative, expressing what the state is not as opposed to what it is.

11. Sri Swami Viditatmananda, "Satsanga with Sri Swami Viditatmananda Saraswati
Arsha Vidya Gurukulam: Various types of *Karma*," *Avgsatsang* 2014, http://www.avgsatsang.org/hhsvs/pdf/Types_of_karmas.pdf (April 20, 2014).
12. Cf. Klostermaier, 198.
13. Ibid., 199.

DEATH & THE WORLD RELIGIONS

This experience of "reality as-it-is-itself" is the realization of Brahman, who is the single, all-encompassing reality behind the illusion of life. At the same time this experience is also the realization of our true self or atman. Moksha therefore entails the realization and experience that our true self (atman) is one with this reality (Brahman). Once this realization is acquired, karmatic action ceases (i.e., you cease to desire things that continue your illusionary existence).

Atman is sometimes referred to as the soul; however, atman is not the intellect or mind that enlivens the body because consciousness arises from differentiation (I and non-I) that is ultimately an illusion.[14] For my purpose this means that the human body and consciousness are shells for the atman. The goal for the sadu is to cut all ties with the illusion of the mind, body, soul, and the world. When the sadu has accomplished this, the sadu accomplishes moksha, and thereafter is free from samsara. Only after death will this sadu experience moksha completely: after death all the noneternal components of the soul, the non-atman, will dissolve all that will detach the atman from the phenomenological world and allow it to be fully immersed into Brahman.

To reiterate, liberation entails the realization that atman is Brahman and vice versa. Atman is therefore one true self or one's "heart of heart." It is the seed of eternity that everyone has within them. Atman is to Brahman what a ray of light is to the source of light. Just as the ray of light is the same as the source light in as much as it is composed of the same stuff that makes up the source of light, so the atman can be identified with Brahman. However, the source of light is greater than a particular ray of light, so Brahman is more than a single atman. The atman that is within every human being is our connection to the underlying reality of Brahman. Once this relationship is experienced and understood, the sadu experiences pure bliss. Part of this bliss is the recognition that to embrace Brahman-atman is to understand that all of our experiences have no true substance or reality. It is all an illusion. The experience of atman is the experience of oneness and wholesomeness, which is to say that everything is one and the same. It expresses an insight about the interconnectivity of existence, namely that there is a substantial and eternal reality underlying everything.

For many, confusion occurs on this point because they either import Judeo-Christian notions about God to Hinduism or confuse Brahman (the reality itself) with brahman (a personal God) or brahmin (the highest caste within the Hindu tradition). Note that Brahman as I described above is not a personal God,[15] but rather impersonal reality.

Although the authors of the Upanishads reject the notion that the gods and goddesses are eternal, they were not atheists. They accept that these gods and goddess exist; however, they are ultimately

---

14. Ibid., 215.
15. In one tradition Brahman is the creator God in the cosmic narrative. After he creates, Vishnu sustains his creation, and then Shiva destroys his creation. Brahmin then recreates creation. The cycle of creation-sustaining-destruction is perpetual.

an illusion. These deities are as real as you or me, but just like us, their existence is circumscribed within the illusion of existence.

Bhakti Movement

After reading about the *jana marga,* the path of wisdom, above, you may wonder if moksha is attainable for most Hindus who lack the education, training, time, and discipline to accomplish this pseudo-mystical-philosophical state. Interestingly, those who pursue this path are generally from the upper castes or a socioeconomic background that allows for this pursuit of mystical wisdom. The vast majority of Hindus today do not exclusively pursue this path toward liberation. Nevertheless, the core teachings of the Upanishads on samsara (e.g., moksha from samsara and Brahman-atman), are appropriated into the popular practice of the Hindu religion.

Most Hindus are primarily practitioners of the *bhakti marga,* or the path of devotion. Since the ancient Vedas, Hindus have expressed devotion to their gods or goddesses. What is unique to the bhakti movement is that devotion not ritual actions or ascetic/intellectual practice achieves liberation. In effect, the bhakti movement as represented by the *Bhagavad-Gita* or *Gita* (200 BCE to 100 CE) synthesizes the monism of the Upanishads with devotion to a personal God.[16] Particular verses from texts like Katha Upanishad provide the fodder for this synthesis. For example, the author of Katha Upanishad states, "Not through much learning is the atman reached, not through intellect and sacred teaching. It is reached by the chosen of him—because they choose him. To his chosen atman reveals his glory."[17] Picking up this tradition of divine election and that Brahman is a *purusa uttama* or supreme person, [18] which is beyond our understanding of personhood, the bhakti movement develops the Upanishad's esoteric teachings for the masses. God and liberation are accessible regardless of caste.

Impersonal Brahman in the Upanishads evolves into a personal God. The stress within this tradition is neither ritual action (*karma marga*) nor ascetic/philosophical action (*jnana marga*) but intense love for God. The one God is reality itself or Brahman. Today Hindus will most likely define the one God as a variety of deities including Vishnu, Shiva, or Devi. Each of these deities has their own schools of bhakti.

Even though we must be aware of the uniqueness of each school and bhakti tradition, we can make several generalizations about this marga: first, the goal of this movement is to acquire perfect love

---

16. In the *Bhagavad-Gita*, Krishna is not only Brahman that permeates all things, but a personal god that will liberate anyone that "Keep[s] me [Krishna] in your mind and devotion, sacrifice to me, bow to me, disciple yourself toward me." (*The Bhagavad-Gita: Krishna's counsel in time of war,* trans. Barbara Stoler Miller [New York: Bantam Books, 1986], 9:34.)

17. "Katha Upanishad" in *The Upanishads,* 55-66, trans. Juan Mascarb (London: Penguin Books, 1965), 60.

18. Ibid., 223.

that will permeate one's entire life. This is no simple task, as most schools teach that this is a lifelong process. Most schools speak about different degrees of *bhakti*, and the highest state is usually characterized by a complete immersion into the pure love of their god or goddess so that all desire, action, ritual, and knowledge is attached to their deity.[19] Ramakrishna (1836–1886), a popular Hindu saint known for his joy and devotion to Devi, provides a good example of what attaining the highest state of bhakti entails. Ramakrishna was so overwhelmed with his love for the goddess Devi that could no longer perform his duties as the local temple priest. He would spend hours in prayer and attained a mystical state known as samadhi, supraconsciousness, whereby his consciousness was totally absorbed by Devi.[20] Ramakrishna exhibited mystical signs such as the menstruation of his goddess!

Nevertheless, the Upanishad major tradition that Brahman is an impersonal reality is not reconciled with the bhakti stress on an all-inclusive, loving God. Within the bhakti tradition this tension is downplayed and there are at least three traditional responses to this issue. The first tradition simply synthesizes personal devotion with the impersonal reality: Brahman is God, and God is beyond personality as we understand personality. The result is that God albeit Vishnu, Shiva, or Devi is ultimately the impersonal reality. Sometimes this is called direct liberation. Once the soul is liberated it enters into God or Brahman. The second tradition is that Brahman is God, and that God is a personal being. Liberation remains an ineffable experience, but it is a reality that is experienced with a loving God.[21] The final tradition is known as indirect liberation. Once persons are liberated, they ascend into heaven with their god or goddess. However, this is the final step toward liberation. Harkening back to the *jnana marga*, liberation ultimately entails immersion into a nonpersonal reality of Brahman.[22]

With these insights mind, most Hindus characterize Hinduism as monotheistic. Belief in one god or goddess does not limit Hindu inclusivity since Hindus recognize that all the gods and goddesses, Hindu or not Hindu, are manifestations of their personal God.

Related to the *Gita* and the bhakti marga is the final marga, karma marga. Whereas in the Vedic period karma marga entailed exclusively acting out one's dharma and religious rituals, the *Gita* describes karma marga as acting without desire for the effects of that action. Hindus should act according to their dharma "without fear of punishment or hope of reward."[23] In the context of the bhakti tradition, Hindus embracing this marga dedicate all their actions to God, having no attachments to the fruits of their actions.

---

19. Klostermaier, 232.
20. Cf. Christopher Isherwood, *Ramakrishna and his disciples* (New York: Simon and Schuster, 1965).
21. Gavin Flood, "BBC religion: Hindu concepts," *BBC Religions* 2009, http://www.bbc.co.uk/religion/religions/hinduism/concepts/concepts_1.shtml (March 15, 2014).
22. Cf. "What is liberation," *Hinduism Today* (July/August/September 2007): 48-51.
23. Sumegi, 185.

Dharma and Hindu Identity

Thus far I have outlined the basic tenets of the Hindu belief system; however, as I mentioned above Hinduism stresses correct practice as opposed to correct belief. Therefore, to appreciate and understand Hinduism, especially how Hindus cope with death, we must also understand that Hindu praxis is related to the dharmas.

Dharma is perhaps one of the most difficult yet critical aspects of the Hindu religion for non-Hindus in the West to understand. First and foremost, dharma is the moral order of the universe. All existence is regulated by dharma; it reveals to Hindus how to accumulate good and avoid bad karma as it regulates ethical and religious behavior. Although it can be translated as "duty," dharma is an "all-encompassing reality,"[24] which refers to rules, rituals, and advice based on the "eternal laws of nature."[25] For many non-Hindus, dharma is a violation of personal freedom and autonomy since it is specific as to what constitutes meritorious behavior. To the contrary, dharmas are not intended to constrain the relative freedom that Hindus have in their beliefs, but rather regulate a Hindus' life in such a way that it creates good habits and leisure to pursue liberation or higher rebirth. Moreover, since dharma is based in the cosmic order of the universe, for Hindus it is a given and to avoid or reject one's dharma is to introduce disorder into the universe that is apparent in the effect of bad karma.

There are three basic groupings of dharma: *sadharana dharma*, *varna dharma*, and *asrama dharma*. *Sadharana dharma* refers to characteristics that Hindus should exhibit in order to live an ethical life. This dharma is a general list of attributes that all Hindus must cultivate throughout their life. There are various lists that elucidate this dharma, but most lists include at least nonharming (ahimsa), truthfulness (satya), and nonstealing (asteya).[26]

Varna Dharma

Varna dharma refers to the duties or way of life related to ones' caste. For instance the brahmins' duties correspond to fulfilling religious responsibilities (e.g., religious training, administering the sixteen main Hindu sacraments, and staffing the temple), but also intellectual activity.

---

24. Flood, 53.
25. Kamlesh Kapur, *Hindu dharma: A teaching guide* (Kamlesh Kupar: 2013), 43.
26. W. J. Johnson, *A dictionary of Hinduism* (Oxford: Oxford University Press, 2009), *Oxford Reference* 2014, http://www.oxfordreference.com/view/10.1093/acref/9780198610250.001.0001/acref-9780198610250-e-2124?rskey=GTFFtt&result=1 (April 28, 2014).

Asrama Dharma

Each of the three highest castes consists of twice-born people. "Twice-born" refers to those persons who are born into these higher classes and have undergone an initiation ceremony. Members of these castes have special duties that are relative to their requisite states of life. Thus asrama dharma consists of those duties relative to these four states of life: the student stage (Brahmacarya), householder stage (Grihastha), hermit stage (Vanaprastha), and renunciation stage (Samnyasa).

During the "student stage" young persons should be celibate and focus on their studies, in particular the study of the Vedas. The "householder stage" refers the time in life when persons marry and raise a family. Once householders have fulfilled their obligations, reaching retirement age, they enter into the "hermit stage." In this stage their obligation is first and foremost toward their religion. They may live as hermits in a forest or travel on a religious pilgrimage with their spouse. The final stage is the "renunciation stage." In this stage persons completely cut ties with the world as they have come to know it. In certain parts of India the renunciants must declare themselves legally dead to pursue moksha through the abovementioned margas. Renunciants in some parts of India are easily identifiable because they will only possess a few items such as a walking staff, a bowl for begging, and a saffron robe.

Afterlife

Because Hinduism does not stress orthodoxy there is not one universal tradition on the afterlife, yet some basic generalizations can be made. Within the context of reincarnation, there are at least 14 realms of existence. Each of these realms has various subdivisions. Thus in the material realm (i.e., the world as we know it) you may be reincarnated into various living things. Moreover after death the soul stays in the vicinity of its body and may become a ghost or a beneficial ancestor/pitr for an allotted amount of time determined by karma.

The 14 realms of reincarnated existence are demarcated by the material realm. The realms of hell are the realms lower than the material world. Realms of reincarnated existence above the material world are the realms of heaven. These heavens and hells are states of being relative to one's positive and negative karma. While good karma can lead to rebirth and enjoyment in heaven, bad karma leads to rebirth and suffering in hell. Souls in hell need to be expiated of their bad karma. In some traditions, the god Yama oversees Hell to certify that its inhabitants receive their requisite punishment for their bad karma.[27] Nevertheless heaven and hell are temporary and self-imposed realms. The only constant in the realms of heavens and hells is that they are inhabited by like-minded persons. Thus persons in both realms will be reincarnated after their reward or punishment is experienced.

---

27. Farnaz Masumian, *Life after death: A study of the afterlife in world religions* (Los Angeles: Kalimàt Press, 1995), 13.

However, heaven and hell are a part of the phenomenological world to which Hindus want to liberate themselves. Thus when bhakti followers speak about their God's heaven to which they want to be liberated, they do not refer to one of these heavens, but rather a state of pure and unmediated bliss beyond these realms of heavenly reincarnation.

DEATH, MOURNING, AND BEREAVEMENT

Although there are three paths toward liberation, most Hindus combine aspects of all three paths. This is nowhere more evident than in the sacrament of last rites that combines the karma, jnana, and bhakti paths. For many Hindus coping with dying and the preparation for death involves ancient rituals (karma marga), meditation and spiritual training (jnana marga), and the intercession of one's personal god or goddess (bhakti marga) that provide the best rebirth possible. Moreover, Hindus have dharmas associated with the dying, their funeral, and bereavement.

Dying and Death

From the Hindu perspective, with the exception of persons who have reached a venerable age, ninety-years of age or above, death is seen as a sad event.[28] Yet, dying is one of the most important events in life because it provides an important opportunity to atone for bad karma so as to prepare for a good rebirth. For this reason while sudden and traumatic deaths are considered bad deaths in Hinduism, good deaths include little mental or physical trauma, allowing time for the family to say goodbye and prepare for the death.[29] Thus a good death is a death after ample time has been provided to say goodbyes and to amend relationships with relatives and friends. Good deaths not only result in good karma for the deceased but also the family, as the family has the duty to help their loved one prepare for death. Recalling Corr's thesis on how to cope with dying, because the Hindu religion regulates the dying process, it naturally addresses the social, psychological, physical, and spiritual dimensions of the dying person.

Nevertheless, preparing for a good rebirth or the spiritual task is clearly the priority that is the context for how the dying addresses the other tasks. Thus once death is imminent, energies and actions are directed toward facilitating a good rebirth or liberation for the dying.

---

28. Rashi Gupta, "Death beliefs and practices from an Asian Indian American Hindu perspective," *Death Studies* 35 (2011): 244-266), 253.
29. Ibid., 252.

To further facilitate a good rebirth, the dying or dead Hindu will undergo the sacrament of death or last rites. What the last rites entails will vary within the Hindu community. For instance, although cremation is the most widely practiced means of disposal of the body, it is not universally practiced, as many Hindus practice burial. Moreover, burial is normative for young children and for renouncers, for they have liberated themselves of rebirth.[30]

The last rite of Hinduism is a highly ritualized sacrament that includes ancient prayers and actions that originated in the Vedic period. For my purpose the last rites consist of at least nine main stages: preparation for death; the moment of death; preparation of the body; procession to the cremation grounds; cremation; disposal of the ashes; *shraddha* rituals; *sapindikarana*, and annual *shraddha* rituals.[31] As explained in the interview below, Hindus in western New York generally conflate these rituals together or simply ignore some of them. How a Hindu prepares for death is relative to some extent to their state in life; however, Hindus will use these last moments to atone for bad karma and misdeeds, but also grow closer to their God and achieve liberation. It is believed that rebirth is directly influenced by the state of your mind as you die, so participating in this sacrament and making amends is very important because the dying Hindu will be less stressed about death and therefore be able to better focus on detachment from the karmatic cycle of life and death.[32]

With respect to the final sacrament, only male members of the family are allowed to perform it. Ideally the eldest son or adult male family member performs these rituals. (For the purpose of clarity, I will refer to the eldest son as I explain the elements of the last rite ritual.) Because death is associated with defilement, brahmins do not generally directly participate in the last rites. Nevertheless, the brahmin has a crucial role inasmuch as he informs the son how and when to properly perform the rituals. Because the Hindu priesthood is hereditary, many Hindu families, especially in India, have been associated with a family of priests for centuries. Hindu priests are trained from childhood how to minister to the gods and temple members; they are highly equipped to deal with death and make immediate arrangements to help positively facilitate the soul of the dead's transition into the afterlife. The brahmin informs the son regarding what texts to read as well as the timing of various rituals based on his astrological calculations to provide the dead with the best rebirth possible.

The preparation for death not only includes times for meditation and atonement for bad deeds but also to perform good actions that result in good karma, such as giving a gift of a silver cow to the brahmin or donating money to a local charity.[33] For a Hindu, death is a familial experience, and thus family is expected to console and comfort the dying, but also to perform these acts of charity on behalf of the dying if the dying is unable to do so.

30. Klostermaier, 189. For more information on this topic see the interview below.
31. Angela Sumegi, *Understanding death: An introduction to ideas of self and the afterlife in world religions* (Oxford, Wiley Blackwell: 2014), 187.
32. Gupta, 253.
33. Sumegi, 188.

At the moment of death, the eldest son places a *tulsi* or basil leaf and water from the Ganges in the mouth of the deceased. This ritual helps to further purify the soul and allow for an opportunity for liberation. There are various myths surrounding the Ganges; however, for Hindus it is a heavenly river that can purify the soul. At this point the intercession of the dead's god or goddess is invoked, and a symbol will be placed on the body to honor that deity.

Immediately after death, the deceased is placed on the floor with the head facing south, and the legs are bound together. Usually, hymns are sung or played on a stereo from chapter two of the *Bhavaghad-Gita* or other holy texts that help the soul rest. The name of the deceased's favorite god or goddess is then chanted. The body is then anointed with various oils, washed, dressed, and wrapped in a new piece of cloth by members of the same gender.

Interestingly, the last rite rituals also begin the bereavement period. Depending upon the caste, social status, and location the mourning period may entail twelve full days of prayers, rituals, intense crying, feasts, and entertainment of family and people in the community. Although these rituals can be exhausting for the bereaved and financially draining, they offer the bereaved comfort and support because this period brings people together for one purpose to collectively mourn the dead.[34] Some of the rituals that are included in this period are the ritual shaving of the hair on the heads of all sons and grandsons of the deceased and the determination of the time of burial by the brahmin priest.

Once the time of cremation is determined—usually within twenty-four hours after death—the body is brought to the cremation site and sacred hymns from various holy texts, including the Upanishads' "hymns of the dead"[35] or the name of deceased's favorite god, are chanted continually. At the crematorium, the family will place the body into the casket with the corpse's feet facing the south. The south in Hinduism has a special significance because Yama, the lord of the underworld and the god who is responsible for transitioning the soul into the afterlife, is thought to take residence in the south. Yama is the Hindu equivalent of Anubis in ancient Egypt.

The eldest son will then circumambulate the body, and after each counterclockwise circumambulation, he places seeds, grains, coins, and/or flowers into the mouth of the dead. Final prayers or hymns are recited before the body is cremated. In India, where open cremation is permissible, the eldest son will carry a pot of water on his shoulder and then circumambulate the crematory fire three times with another male. Each time the son passes the head of the corpse, a hole is made in the pot. Finally the pot is crushed. Ideally the pot is filled with water from the Ganges, which increases the benefit of this ritual for the deceased. Nevertheless the goal of this ritual is to purify the

34. Pattu Languani, "Death in a Hindu family" in *Death and bereavement across cultures,* 52-72, ed. Colin Murray Parkes (London: Routledge, 2004), 63-64.
35. Klostermaier, 190.

DEATH & THE WORLD RELIGIONS

cremation site, so as to deter demonic presences from interfering with their loved one's transition into the next life. Moreover, it helps to facilitate the departure of the soul from the body and from the mourners because the water creates a boundary that helps the soul of the deceased depart from the body. [36] Although Hindus may recognize death as brain death, they generally believe that the soul of the dead remains in or with the body until the body is destroyed. For this reason, cremation is preferred to burial because it destroys the soul's connection to this world that would otherwise result in bad karma for the soul since staying with the body is an attachment.

As the body burns, the family remains silent. Family members wait at the crematory until someone hears a cracking sound, which signifies the cracking of the skull and the release of the soul from the body. Family members may choose to wait until the body has been cremated and is ready for pick up.[37] When family members leave the cremation site, they do so in an orderly fashion: the family members turn their backs to the dead as they exit. This action also helps the soul of the dead to depart into the next life, as otherwise it may be tempted to follow the living home. If this occurs, the soul of the dead will have a bad rebirth.

After the cremation, the eldest son will return to the crematory to collect the ashes and shatter any remaining bone fragments. In the West, the eldest son will pick up the ashes from the crematory and after performing various rituals will dispose of ashes and bones in the nearest running river or sea. Sometimes this ritual is called the "bone-gathering ritual."[38]

Since all river water returns to the Ganges, using a local river is acceptable for Hindus living outside India. It is not uncommon for family members to fly to India in order to deposit these ashes into the sacred Ganges.

Between the tenth and thirteenth day after the cremation, the eldest son performs the *shraddha* ritual. The eldest son and his family will contact the local Hindu temple and schedule a time for this ritual to be performed. The eldest son at the funeral offers a small ball of rice called a *pinda* in honor of the *preta* or spirit of his deceased family member and says: "May this *pinda* benefit the *preta* of [insert name of the deceased]_____ of this family so that his/her ghost may not feel hunger and thirst."[39] The period between death and the soul's or *preta's* transition into a new life is a dangerous period. Many Hindus believe that failure to perform these rituals will result in their ancestor's transformation into an evil ghost.[40] Some Hindus, in fact, look for signs that their loved one shall have a positive rebirth. This is evident when crows peck at the *pinda*. If they do not, this is a problematic sign.

---

36. Sumegi, 189.
37. Languani, 61.
38. "Rites of transition," *Hinduism Today* 29.1 (March-Jan 2007): 66-67), 67.
39. Klostermaier, 191.
40. Ibid., 191.

The *shraddha* ritual culminates with the *sapindikarana* ritual, which is usually preformed on the twelfth day after cremation. Traditionally this ritual was celebrated twelve months after cremation. This is still the norm in certain parts of India. The goal of the ritual is to transform the *preta* into a *pitrs* or ancestral spirit that watches over the family. On the annual anniversary of death, the *shraddha* ritual is performed.

You may be wondering how these last rites that seem to transform souls into ancestral spirits can be integrated with the *bhakti* and *jnana* movements mentioned above whose goal is either liberation or to be in a paradise-like state with God. In reality there is no definitive answer, but again it is the practice not the answer that is most important. This is not to deny that some identify the transformation of a *pitr* with the soul spending eternity with God. Nevertheless, especially for followers of *jnana marga*, this state is only temporary, as the ultimate goal is union of atman with Brahman.

Nevertheless, I cannot overly stress the importance of these rituals for bereavement and for dying Hindus who want to be assured that their tradition and practices will be respected. For these reasons, living in the Western world can pose problems for Hindus. Not only are open cremations, which are preferred, generally not permissible but, more importantly, if a Hindu dies in a hospital setting the body may be moved to the morgue before the family is able to perform the necessary rituals (e.g., placing the *tulsi* leaf and pouring water from the Ganges into the mouth of the deceased). Unfortunately, there have been cases where bereaved family members were not allowed to see the body in the morgue when they arrived at the hospital. The result was that they were unable to perform this ritual and felt that they had failed their loved one. They believed that they incurred bad karma and would have to atone for this misdeed for seven generations.[41] Thus these rituals that normally provide solace may in turn cause great anxiety!

End-of-Life Care

Based on the above there should be little doubt healthcare professionals who want to provide effective care need to be sensitive to the unique needs of religious Hindu patients. Moreover, they must be aware that the spiritual task, attaining a good rebirth, dictates their end-of-life decisions from their social interactions (social dimension) to decisions about medical care (physical dimension). Anything that a healthcare provider can do that will help a Hindu patient address their spiritual task, in particular, will help the patient cope with death.

---

41. Sumegi, 188.

Helping Hindus atone for bad karma, by helping them finish any unfinished business (e.g., putting them in touch with family members/counselors to find closure in relationships or the local Brahmin) will greatly benefit the dying, as well as directly addressing their social, psychological, and spiritual dimensions.[42] Atoning for karma also informs a Hindu's decisions about the use medications, especially palliative medications.

SUFFERING AND MEDICAL CARE

Accepting death and the suffering associated with that death is an element of Hindu philosophy. Suffering is traditionally understood as a negative effect of past bad decisions and actions; this means that Hindus are willing to accept physical suffering. In this instance the spiritual task (liberation) clearly influences the physical task (relief of pain). It is not uncommon for a Hindu to fast from food and water and medications when death is immediate.[43] Thus atoning for one's karma will influence decisions regarding the physical dimension of care (e.g., the use of palliative medication). Treatments deemed as interfering with one's duty to atone for their karma will be rejected. Hindus want to prepare for death by intense prayer and meditation and have an unclouded mind at the moment of death[44]; therefore many Hindus will prefer to use palliative drugs sparingly. Palliative drugs are not viewed as objectively bad, but they should only be used insofar as they allow the sick to be pain-free enough to prepare for death. Moreover, aggressive treatments such as "intubation, artificial feeding" as well as traditions that "mutilate" the body are not congruent with Hindu teaching.[45] Therefore Hindus are willing to forego what other religions define as "ordinary means."

Hindus believe that they have died many times, and thus they view death as a necessary part of existence and strive to face death without fear. With respect to PAS, religious Hindus will not accept this option. Suicide results in bad karma and rebirth. In exceptional circumstances, where the dying has attained a state of spiritual insight, the dying may choose to starve to death, but this is not interpreted as euthanasia. For Hindus, PAS is a selfish action. On the other hand, spiritual masters that choose to die are not choosing death to escape suffering. To the contrary, they have fully embraced death and are prepared to die.[46] Thus the master's intention proceeds from an enlightened will, whereas the intention for PAS proceeds from an unenlightened will.

---

42. "Death and dying," *Hinduism Today* 29.1 (March-Jan 2007): 64-65), 65.
43. Shirley Firth, "End-of-life: A Hindu view," *The Lancet* (August 20, 2005): 682-686), 684.
44. Firth, 684.
45. Cf. Susan Thrane, "Hindu end of life: Death, dying, suffering, and karma," *Journal of Hospice and Palliative Nursing* **12.6 (2010): 337-342.**
46. Sharma Himanshu, Jagdish Vankar, Anusha Prabhakaran, and Bharti Sharma, "End-of-life care: Indian perspective," *Indian Journal of Psychiatry* 55.6 (January 2013): 293), 293.

Making the Dying Comfortable

As mentioned, a good death for a Hindu is to die in the company of loved one (e.g., family and friends). For this reason dying at home or at a facility that allows for groups of visitors is preferable to dying in a traditional hospital setting. Unless noted by the dying Hindu, providing the dying with ample space for multiple visitors is important, as it will help the dying to feel respected and more comfortable. Communicating with the patient about their needs and that these needs will be respected to the greatest possible extent addresses the patient's psychological and spiritual dimension.

Regarding the importance of family and their obligation within the Hindu religion to prepare the dead for a good rebirth, healthcare professionals should contact family immediately if they are not present when the patient dies. Unless otherwise noted by the patient or proxy, keeping the body undisturbed until the funerary rituals can be performed is very important. Moreover, healthcare professionals should be aware that the eldest male is usually designated as the healthcare proxy. In situations where the father is dying, the eldest male becomes the head of the family and proxy. It is likely that he will be under immense stress due to this new responsibility and coping with the death of his loved one. Once the patient is incapable of making decisions for him/herself, questions should be directed to the proxy. Note that especially when the proxy is from India, it may be seen as a sign of disrespect to make eye contact with him. Because there is a designated proxy, Hindus do not generally stipulate advance directives or living will.[47]

Although the body is simply seen as a shell for the soul, Hindus generally reject organ donation and autopsy. The rationale is that a connection remains between the soul and the body. Actions that disturb the body may also disturb the soul. Precisely for this reason, cremation is normative.

Conclusion

The Hindu religion is an inclusive religious tradition that includes a profundity of rituals and customs that guide all aspects of a Hindu's life from birth to end-of-life decisions. The goal in the Hindu religion is to gain the best rebirth possible or liberation from samsara. Hindu dharma regulates life in such a way as to provide Hindus, especially in the upper classes, the opportunity and time to accomplish this task. There are a variety of paths or margas to achieve liberation; however, most Hindus integrate aspects of the three major paths to do so. This is evident in the Hindu sacrament of the last rites.

---

47. Cf. Thrane, 340-342.

Liberation from the cycle of birth and rebirth is the mediating principle that helps Hindus make end-of-life decisions. Healthcare professionals who desire to offer holistic and effective care (e.g., care that addresses the four dimensions of a person) should aid Hindus in the pursuit for a good death and afterlife to the extent that they are comfortable. My interview with Dr. Vijayaraghavan Chakravarthy will help elucidate how dying Hindus, living in the United States, want to pursue a good death.

Nevertheless, the teachings on karma and liberation are not unique to the Hindu tradition, but are shared with our next major religion, Buddhism. Many of the challenges and values that Hindus have regarding end of life are appropriated by the Buddhist tradition.

Interview

Dr. Vijayaraghavan Chakravarthy (Vijay) is a Hindu priest serving the Hindu community of Greater Buffalo and other neighboring towns. He has served as the president and director of religious activities for the Hindu Temple and Cultural Society located in Getzville, New York. Vijay is also the past president of the Network of Religious Communities of Buffalo (New York). Vijay was raised as a Brahmin and was trained by his family to serve as a priest.

Q: In Hinduism there are a certain set of sacraments, one of which is the sacrament of last rites. Is it true that all Hindus receive these sacraments?

A: Yes, there are actually forty sacraments that are related to the various stages of life from birth until death. About sixteen of them are principal sacraments.

Q: Have you performed the last rites on many occasions?

A: I have not performed the last rites. It is not a very auspicious thing to do. Priests in India, especially the temple priests, stay away from performing last rites. This is because death is associated with defilement. When the dead body is there, the Hindus cannot even cook or eat in its presence. There is so much defilement attached to such occasions that they cannot give food to others, touch others. A traditionally trained Brahmin will know this and inform the family of the deceased about them. In fact, if the priest participates in the last rite, he is not supposed to enter the temple for three days. He has to ritually bathe, pray, and do *japa* before he can reenter the temple. Since I have a choice as a voluntary priest, I attend the funerals but I do not perform the last rites.

Q: My understanding is that the Hindu priest does not officiate at the rite, but rather informs the eldest son what to do. He is more or less a liaison?

A: Yes, but this is the case not only for last rites but all of the forty sacraments. The brahmin priest is the primary-intermediary between the worshipper and where the worship is supposed to reach. He plays a key role from the very start, the birth of the child. I do not see this in other religions. The Brahmin remains a key intermediary for the worshipper as he tells him what to do.

Q: What are/is the text/s used during the last rites?

A: They are called the Gruhya Sutras. The *Apastamba Sutra* is mostly followed. This has the last rites but also includes all of the sacraments.

A: So it is something like Jewish law?

Q: Yes, Jews and Hindus share many things. This Sutra regulates life. Like Judaism, Hinduism is based on culture. You cannot distinguish between culture and religion.

A: Given the fact that Hinduism is intertwined with Hindu culture in India, are there impediments to practicing Hinduism in western New York?

Q: The Hindu tradition is a lot more simplified here. I did my father's last rites in India. That includes ten days of mourning, creating a temporary shelter, washing in the river, having important meals on the tenth and eleventh day, etc. Some of the last rites are done when we are completely wet. Then we put a kind of temporary shelter outside the house. And then there is a lot of eating on the tenth, eleventh, and twelfth days. These things are completely gone from Hinduism here.

Q: Let's say that you are called in by a Hindu family who has a dying loved one. How would you prepare them for a good death?

A: Once you know that the person is in his final days, we try to maximize the spiritual and religious practices. We recite the gods' names all of the time. The person is immersed in the glory of God. There is constant praying. Hindus prefer to die in their home; at least this is true in India. Here they are most likely taken from the hospital directly to the funeral home. We prefer cremation. The body must be burned completely. There are only a few funeral homes that allow cremation in Buffalo. Here in the USA, once the body is there the family tells the priest, and the priest tells them when to cremate the body. It is usually in the afternoon. After the last rite, the body is placed in the casket and then placed in the furnace.

All living things are made of five basic elements, and these leave the body at death. But the human being is made up of twenty-four elements. The remaining elements stick to the soul. For ten days the soul hovers around the house visiting relatives. This is why Hindus make a shelter outside the home for the soul to stay. Then they place a stone in front of the home. This tells the soul it is time for the soul to leave. On the eleventh day they do the *sapindikarana*, this is when the soul rejoins the world of pitrs. On the thirteenth day, a ritual that symbolizes the return of auspiciousness is celebrated. We have mourned for thirteen days. The family goes to the temple to receive the Lord's blessings. Before this they are not allowed to enter the temple. All of these rituals are performed by the sons. Daughters do not perform these rituals.

Q: What happens if the deceased does not has a son? Will the daughter then perform the rituals?

A: The daughters do not have a role in last rites. The next best choice after an eldest son is a younger, male blood relative. It must be the paternal line. The son-in-law is always the last choice.

Q: Generally speaking, is it correct that these rituals are not performed in western New York?

A: Yes, they do the cremation on the first or second day. Then they take the ashes. You take the ashes to the local river. They may bring a handful of the ashes to India to deposit in the Ganges.

Q: I have read that young children and persons that have achieved moksha are buried not cremated. Is this true?

A: Yes, very young children, one or two years old, are buried. It is a consideration for the parents; they do not want to see their child burned.

For older people knowledge of their cremation is one way to develop detachment. If my body is going to burn, why should I care for it so much? A Hindu goes through the four stages of life. The fourth stage is renunciation. A true renunciant cannot stay in one place for more than a day. Now this is not followed today. Renunciants remain in ashrams today. The idea was that you cannot be attached to persons or places. There are renunciants who have taken *sannyasa*; they have formally given up their family relations. For this person the last rites are very different. They are buried. In order for liberation to take place, the soul must leave through the chakra in the center of the head. So what they do generally is create a small crack on the head with a coconut to symbolize the soul leaving from the head. At this point the eldest son comes back to do the last rites.

Q: We have spoken a lot about male renunciants, but do women also become sannyasas?

A: Yes, in the old days there were renunciant females. Nowadays after they marry, a woman's identity is completely submerged with her husband's identity. When the husband becomes a renunciant, the wife goes through widowhood. This widowhood is so painful; they voluntarily take this suffering. She is not allowed to actively take part in the forty sacraments. She becomes a spectator at these events. She is somebody that nobody wants because she brings bad luck. But there are a lot of social reform movements in India that are correcting this. To give you an idea about how much widowhood is hated in India, in parts of India, *sati* was practiced whereby the widow jumped on her husband's funeral fire, killing herself. But this is illegal today.

Even with my own mother, who is a widow, we respect her, but out of internal restriction, we do not include her in auspicious functions.

Q: With respect to the afterlife, you mentioned the realm of ancestors or pitrs. How do you reconcile this with the doctrine of reincarnation?

A: Karma itself is only an action. It is only a ripple. The law of karma deals with the effect of that ripple. The goal of karma yoga is to get rid of this karmic cycle. If you follow the Gita, karma yoga stresses having the correct attitude when you act. If you have not done this, then your karmas are carried with you. Just like the wind carries the fragrance with it, this karmic law, this bank account of good karmas and bad karmas is carried with your soul if you have not performed your karma yoga. Karma defines your next birth, timing of the birth, and who the parents of the birth will be. Your karma defines your future life.

Why then are there intermediate places like the world of pitrs, heaven, and hell? Some of the expiation of your karma is completed in these worlds. Instead of being reborn and expiating karma at that time, some of the effects of karma are expiated there. This depends upon the type of karma. For example, I can go to heaven to experience a good karma, but then I will be reincarnated on earth to expiate other karmas. This has all started from beginningless time. The initial condition is always filled with some karma. It goes in cycles. The only way to be delivered is to reach the world of the supreme Lord. You can return by choice, but not by force. This is the world of Brahman. Here you are the purest form. The passage of time is not there. You are constantly in bliss communing with the Supreme Lord. This is what all people desire!

Q: Based on the Upanishads it seemed to me that when you reach this realm you no longer exist. However, you speak about this realm as if we continue to exist with Brahman. Can you please explain this?

A: First is that it is an indiscernible existence, that which defies description and human comprehension. This is the state we all go to when we are liberated. There are three schools of philosophy that interpret this state differently. Advita school says you are always Brahman; it is just an illusion that made you feel that you are different from Brahman. This illusion ceases to exist at liberation. But this school of thought was forcefully challenged by two others, the Vishishtadvaita and Dvaita schools of philosophy. The Dvaita school is very close to Christianity. It argues that the soul and Brahman are different, so you are not one with Brahman when you are liberated. There is no merging there; the soul maintains its individuality. Vishishtadvaita school says you are a part of the Brahman, at least in terms of the existence of the soul. Just like our soul enjoys a relationship with our body, in the same way it enjoys a relationship with the Supreme Brahman. The body is only an instrument of the soul. In the same way our soul is a body for the Brahman that exists for His pleasure. He directs us. The soul is the instrument of Brahman.

Most people follow advita philosophy, because they are born in a family that adheres to this philosophy; however, in practice everyone is a dvaitin. So we believe that we are a part of God but never equal to God. We are always his servants, his instruments, and we exist for his pleasure. We do our actions not with the view to reap result, but only to please God. God should be pleased with what we do.

Q: What is a good death for a Hindu?

A: Hindus believe that a good death is when the body is in very good form. It should not be pricked by surgeries; it should be intact. When you die you should die healthy. A good death is also a death without suffering or very little suffering at the right age, generally above eighty years (after Satabhishekam).

Q: You mentioned that a good death is a death where the body is intact. Does this tradition influence healthcare decisions?

A: Here healthcare practices are not as much determined by the Hindu faith. Most Hindus do not have problems with modern healthcare. In India there would be problems. For instance, orthodox brahmins would not accept blood. My father in India refused bypass surgery. This is meaningless here.

Q: Is it true that Hindus in your community may be less open to palliative care since Hindus want to die with a clear mind to perform religious rituals as well as expiate bad karma through suffering?

A: Yes, this is a wonderful statement. But there is a way out of this. When you do the ultimate surrender to the Lord, and you can do this directly or through a teacher or a saint, all of your karmas are forgiven. So we await that final day when we will join God. So there is no doubt regarding that. For these people you can use whatever healthcare means to lessen suffering. This is because they know that they are going to the final reward of God irrespective of whatever happens!

But there are also various sects that may disagree with me. The school to which I belong says that liberation occurs after you have made the ultimate surrender to the Lord. But not all agree with this.

Q: What is the worst death for a Hindu?

A: The worst death would include a situation when the body is no longer present for the rituals to be performed.

Q: How do you respond to tragic deaths (e.g., death of child, parent)?

A: In my own family my sister lost her child. It is an irreconcilable loss. After thirty years she still mourns for her child. Now the way she consoles herself is that the soul of her child had some karma left from a past birth, and that the child came back to finish it off through suffering; the hope is that this child will have a better rebirth or be liberated and reach God. Liberation is possible if the family performs the ritual to send the child to the Lord.

Q: What advice do you have for health professionals caring for a Hindu at the end of life?

A: Kindness, compassion, and care are very well appreciated by any Hindu. Hindus are sometimes concerned with gender. For instance, it is not appropriate for a male doctor to touch a woman, especially to console her. This is especially true with older women. On the other hand, hospitals show respect by allowing relatives to bring food to their sick. Also respecting the dietary restrictions is very important, as many Hindus are vegetarians. Allowing the Hindu to play some devotional music may also be very important. These things are appreciated, and most hospitals allow for them.

Q: Suppose that the Hindu patient dies when the family is not present. What should a health professional who is caring for the patient do? Is there an issue if the body is moved to the morgue before the family arrives?

A: Yes, there definitely is an issue. The requirement is that the rites are done when the body is present. Even though these rituals are for the soul the body is very important. The body is washed before burning it, and great respect much be shown for it. It housed a great soul for many years. Respect the body and do your best not to move it. Let the family have time with it. Now if you have to move the body that is fine; but keep it in a proper place so that the relatives, the sons, the daughters can come and have a chance to do the final rites.

Q: Since the body is held in such regard, is organ donation permissible?

A: Traditional Hindus do not donate organs, but like the last rites this is more acceptable by Hindus that adopt American culture. My sister, for instance, has decided to donate her organs.

One of the requirements for the final rites is that the body is handed over to the Agni or the god of fire in as good a form as possible. It is an offering that the soul makes as the last karma. That is why the body needs to be burned completely.

Q: Let's say that a healthcare professional encounters a dying Hindu and there is no one else around. Is there any action that you recommend that the professional do?

A: Oh yes, say "Narayana." There is a story that goes with this: There was a very bad king. He had six children and all of his children left him except Narayana. Now when the final hour came, the king was approached by the messenger of the God of death, a very bad god who punishes people for bad deeds. The king out of fear shouted for his son, Narayana! Even though he called for his son, it was registered by the Lord Narayana, and his messengers came to take him. But the messenger of death said, "Why are you taking the king since he has done many bad deeds; it is my duty to punish him?" The messengers of Narayana said, "He uttered the name of my Lord so he will be delivered from all his sins!" That is the power of that name. It is important to say it as you die and to say the name in the right ear of the dying. Narayana is the name all Hindus use for Brahman or God. He is Vishnu, but also the formless Brahman. Just like all the water in all the rivers end up in ocean, the worship of gods in any form end up in Narayana.

CHAPTER SIX

BUDDHISM

Introduction

This chapter briefly introduces Buddhism; examines the two major forms of Buddhism, Theravada and Mahayana Buddhism; and looks at how Buddhists care for the dying and prepare for death. Because of its visibility and the fact that it is the largest Buddhist community in the world, the last sections focus on Chinese Buddhism. The chapter ends with my interview with Rev. Shaun Kaung, a Buddhist Master from Ten Thousand Buddhas Temple in Niagara Falls, Ontario.

The story of early Buddhism is a chapter within the narrative of Hinduism. The Buddha, Siddhartha Gautama, was a Hindu ascetic contemporaneous to the authors of early Upanishads. The Buddha appropriated much from the jnana marga tradition and the tenets of Hinduism, but he eventually broke with Hinduism by rejecting the Vedas, the caste system, and the theology of Brahman-atman.

Although Buddhism is indigenous to India, it quickly spreads the teachings of Buddha along the ancient silk trading routes into other parts of Asia. Today the majority of Buddhists are located in Southeast Asia (Cambodia, Laos, and Thailand) and East Asia (China, Korea, Japan, Vietnam, and Taiwan). There are over 350 million followers of the Buddha, making Buddhism the fourth largest religion in the world.

The Life and Dharma of Siddhartha Gautama Buddha

The search for the Buddha of history has perplexed historians for nearly a century. This search is frustrated by the fact that his life and teachings were not recorded until 600 years after his death. Although historians of Buddhism doubt the historicity of what the Buddha taught and said, there is little doubt that he did exist. Most historians agree that the Buddha lived between the sixth and fourth century before the Common Era in Northern India. This places Siddhartha within the above-mentioned axial period. The most popular biography of the Buddha is the *Buddhacarita,* a canon of Buddhist scripture in the Mahayana Buddhist tradition, written around the first century of the Common Era.[1] According to this text, Siddhartha began his life as an affluent prince in Nepal. He was a Hindu and member of the Kshatriya caste.

The *Buddhacarita* details the miraculous birth of the Buddha, who was in fact a heavenly being that entered into his mother's womb. After his birth a prophetic figure named Asita came to the palace, and prophesized that Siddhartha would either be a great king or mystic.[2] Wanting to ensure that his son would succeed him as king, Suddhodana, Siddhartha's father, carefully created a utopia conducive to this.[3] Sickness, old age, death, and suffering that might lead Siddhartha to question the meaning of life and pursue moksha were not allowed inside the palace walls. Siddhartha's father spoiled Siddhartha with finest luxuries and material pleasures.

For the first twenty-nine years of his life, Siddhartha was aloof to the tragedies and challenges of life. However, this false reality concocted by his father drastically changed when Siddhartha decided to accompany his servant outside the palace walls. He did this on four occasions, and on each occasion he encountered what he perceived as an anomaly: old age, suffering, death, and mysticism. After the third experience, he was overwhelmed by his new insight that everything is impermanent and will die or cease to exist in its current form. On his fourth visit outside the palace, however, he saw a sadu who was filled with joy and seemed to have insight about the meaninglessness of life. Attracted to this ascetical path, Siddhartha returned home and as his pregnant wife lay in bed, he experienced a "now or never" moment. He decided that he must leave to discover the meaning of life and embrace the jnana marga. He feared that if he did not leave before his child was born, he may become too attached, and therefore never leave. After leaving his home, he sent a message to his father regarding his choice. In a Hindu context, Siddhartha embraced the forest dwelling stage of his dharma.

---

1. Aśvaghoṣa, *The Buddha-Carita,* or *The life of Buddha*, trans. and eds. Edward B. Cowell, http://www.ancient-buddhist-texts.net/Texts-and-Translations/Buddhacarita/Buddhacarita.pdf, 4.

2. Frank E. Reynolds and Charles Hallisey, "Buddha" in *Encyclopedia of religion,* 2nd ed., 1059-1071, (Farmington Hills: MI, 2005), 1061-1062.

3. Darrell J. Fasching, Dell Dechant, and David M. Lantingua, *Comparative religious ethics: A narrative approach to global ethics,* 2nd ed. (Oxford: Wiley Blackwell: 2011), 168.

The legend continues that for six years he followed various gurus and groups of ascetics. Whereas in his childhood and young adulthood he experienced the greatest pleasures of life, now as an adult he experienced the greatest pains of poverty and asceticism, fasting to the point of emaciation. Even though he gains disciples and acclaim for his ascetical feats, he realizes that extremes in asceticism or hedonism do not lead to liberation from suffering and samsara. Siddhartha concludes that there must be a middle path between these extremes that leads to liberation, joy, and peace.

Pursuant of the middle path, Siddhartha committed himself to intense meditation to discover how to achieve liberation from suffering and the cycle of samsara. During his meditation he experiences what is described as the "four watches of the night" where he comes to four insights about his existence: first, he becomes aware of his past lives; second, he understands the law of karma and realizes that there is nothing substantial or eternal in the world of samsara; third, he realizes that there is no eternal self and that liberation is possible through the Four Nobel Truths and Eightfold Path; and fourth, he attains *nirvana* or liberation that brings him great joy. After seven days of basking in this state of nirvana, he dedicates the remainder of his life to helping others achieve nirvana.[4] Immediately, he sets out to find his former followers and teach them his new insights or his dharma. Together they found the first *sangha* or monastic community dedicated to living out and spreading the dharma of Siddhartha. Siddhartha from this point onwards is known as the Buddha, which in Sanskrit/Pali means "the enlightened one," and he becomes the master of this first sangha. The goal of Buddha's teaching is to awaken all his followers to their Buddha nature or Buddahood. Thus "Buddha" is not solely an appellation that designates Siddhartha since any person is able to attain nirvana or become a Buddha. For this reason the appellation of "Buddha" is used for any holy person who achieved nirvana in addition to the founder of Buddhism.

The Buddha himself, the Buddha's dharma, and the Buddha's sangha are known as the "Triple Jem." The importance of these central tenets of Buddhism is evident in the popular Buddhist mantra that Buddhists recite today: "I take refuge in the Buddha; I take refuge in the Dharma; I take refuge in the Sangha."

Buddha's Dharma

FOUR NOBLE TRUTHS

The core teachings of Buddha's dharma are the four noble truths: (1) the existence of suffering; (2) the causes of suffering; (3) the cessation of the causes of suffering; and (4) the path that leads to

---

4. *Buddhacarita,* ed. and trans. Edward Conze (London: Penguin Books, 1959), 54.

the cessation of the causes of suffering.[5] The first noble truth states emphatically that life is *dukha* or suffering, dissatisfaction, and anguish. Buddha was not a pessimist, but rather a realist. His point is that even the happiness that we experience in life is fleeting and will eventually give way to sadness and cause suffering. Thich Nhat Hanh writes:

> Your suffering is there because you have been feeding it. If violence, hate, despair, and fear are there, it is because you have been feeding them by your unmindful consumption. Therefore, if you know how to recognize the source of the nutrients of your suffering, and if you know how to cut off that source of nutrition, then the suffering will have to vanish.[6]

Thus knowledge of suffering leads to the second noble truth: desire is the cause of human suffering! Have you ever really wanted the newest phone? Remember how you felt when you finally received that phone. You will probably recall some form of happiness; however, almost immediately after you receive the object of your desire, you begin to desire something else. Perhaps you now want a newer version of your phone! Buddha's point is that desire for things, albeit material, spiritual, or emotional, is the cause of suffering. This leads to the third noble truth that since desire causes suffering, if we stop desiring we will cease suffering. If, for example, we no longer desire objects, then we will no longer suffer when we do not receive this object or when this object becomes outdated. Nirvana is the cessation of desire. It can literally be translated as "blowing out"!

Nirvana is the central but also the most difficult teaching of Buddhism for non-Buddhists to understand, and depending on the context, nirvana may have multiple meanings. First and foremost nirvana refers to the end of the cycle of reincarnation, due to a renunciant's lack of desire and retribution experienced for the karmatic effects of his/her actions. Yet nirvana also is the recognition that all things are interdependent inasmuch as they spring from the same source: the seemingly eternal karmatic cycle of cause and effect. I use the adverb "seemingly" to qualify the adjective "eternal" because nirvana is also the realization that everything we experience in the world is finite and mutable. Buddha and Buddhists who have experienced nirvana associate this experience with great joy. There are no words or concepts that can describe it. Buddhist masters are consistent in their stress that it cannot be understood until it is experienced. Thus the experience of nirvana precludes description as a state in-itself. What we know about nirvana is that it is an "unconditional state of liberation from suffering."[7] However, it is neither a heavenly place, nor nothing-annihilation.[8] It is beyond these extremes. Moreover, to further complicate matters, although nirvana can be experienced in

---

5. Gill Farrer-Halls, *The illustrated encyclopedia of Buddhist wisdom: A complete introduction to the principles and practices of Buddhism* (Wheaton, IL: Quest Books, 2000), 14. This text is a popular introduction to Buddhism in the English-speaking world.

6. "Extended Interview with Thich Nhat Hanh," PBS 2003, http://www.pbs.org/wnet/religionandethics/2003/09/19/september-19-2003-extended-interview-thich-nhat-hanh/2758/ (July 8, 2015).

7. Farrer-Halls, 16.

8. Ibid., 16.

this life, nirvana cannot be fully experienced until after death. In Buddhism a distinction is made between nirvana and parinirvana, final nirvana. Harkening back to Buddha's discovery that nothing is eternal, the body and existence as we know it are impermanent, and thus with death they will pass away. This means that after death the person who has experienced nirvana will no longer be a part of this impermanent world and enter into this state of utter emptiness from all attachments: this non-karmatic existence is an ineffable state. However, even the noun "state" which presumes existence is inadequate since nirvana is the cessation of existence. Yet it is not "nothing" because "nothing" presumes that there is a lack of something, which is precisely what Buddha rejects as substantially existing. These conditions finally disperse when nirvana and death are achieved. Nevertheless, Buddhists are not comfortable with the label nihilism, which Buddha himself rejected, or any label that would confine the ineffable experience of nirvana since nihilism is the negation of nothing and assumes that there is nothing behind something. Nirvana is beyond even the concepts we have when we think about nothing. Moreover consciousness as we know it ceases to exist, since consciousness is a product of this impermanent world.

Thus Buddhism neither advocates the Hindu belief in atman nor the Judeo-Christian belief in an immortal, created human spirit. Rather the human person for a Buddhist in his or her spiritual and material existence is an "unrepeatable matrix of conditions." Note that in the Buddhist tradition there is stress on a "store consciousness" or a soul-like substance, which is a constant condition, that is reborn. To complicate matters, within the Buddhist tradition there are schools of thought that stress the negative or positive aspects of nirvana. The "Nirvana school" of Chinese Buddhism, for instance, stressed that nirvana is an eternal and blissful condition.[9]

The fourth noble truth responds to the reality of suffering, cause of suffering, and cessation of suffering by offering the eightfold path. The eightfold path is a set of guidelines for livelihood that will allow the followers of Buddhism to achieve nirvana.

Eightfold Path

Buddhism is a pragmatic religious-philosophy or a religion that stresses orthopraxis. The fact that the Buddha, himself, avoided questions about the nature of reality (e.g., Why is there suffering? How did we get here?) is evidence of this. Buddha did not lack philosophical acumen, but rather recognized that answers to these questions would arise from desire. This is problematic since ending

---

9. John Bowker, "Nirvana" in *The concise Oxford dictionary of world religions* (Oxford: Oxford University Press, 2003), ebook: http://www.oxfordreference.com.libproxy2.dyc.edu/view/10.1093/acref/9780192800947.001.0001/acref-9780192800947-e-5249#

desire is a noble truth. Although later Buddhist theologians address these questions, and in fact, there are various answers to these topics within the Buddhist schools of thought, the answers to the meaning of existence and suffering are not major themes in the Buddhist narrative and ethos.

Buddha's pragmatism and stress on correct action is clearly evident in his dharma on the eightfold path. The eightfold path includes central tenets on wisdom (1–2), morality (2–5), and meditation (6–8) that Buddhist practitioners must strive to integrate into their life. The eightfold path should be viewed holistically, not in a linear progression, as each aspect is connected to one another.

The eightfold path includes:

1. Right understanding
2. Right thought
3. Right speech
4. Right action
5. Right livelihood
6. Right effort
7. Right mindfulness
8. Right concentration

Right understanding is the foundation of the spiritual path.[10] It refers to going beyond an intellectual understanding to an experiential understanding of Buddhist teachings. It also means creating habits that are conducive to living out Buddhist teaching. Right thought refers to renunciation, goodwill, and harmlessness, which means that we stop thinking about what makes us happy and start thinking about others. Buddha taught that whatever subject we reflect on is indicative of our habit of thought; thus we have to train our mind toward the habit of meditating on loving-kindness and compassion, producing right thoughts.[11] Right speech refers to being aware of what we say and how we speak. This means that we should avoid lying, false speech, gossip, and always be truthful, but also be aware of our mannerisms and nonverbal cues when we communicate. Eliminating false speech helps to dispel illusion for ourselves and others. Right action refers to living out these five precepts: nonkilling, nonstealing, nonmisuse of senses, nonlying, and nonintoxication. These precepts are character traits; thus not only should Buddhists not steal, they should not be tempted to take what does not belong to them. Right livelihood refers to choosing a career in accord with Buddhist philosophy. Based on the previous paths certain careers are prohibited for Buddhists (e.g., butcher, sniper, CEOs of businesses that exploit people for their work in order to maximize profits). The ideal livelihood is the life of a monk or nun (i.e., living a life similar to the Buddha, who was devoted to spiritual practices and teaching dharma). Right effort refers to finding a balance between

10. Farrer-Halls, 64.
11. Ibid., 67.

trying too hard and too little for nirvana. It refers to making every action a meditation so that you are "aware and awake in each moment."[12] In order to make each action a meditation one has to cultivate right mindfulness, which refers to being present to the task at hand or to the people around us. A person who cultivates mindfulness is able to focus on whatever he or she is doing. This entails "watching our thoughts without becoming involved with them…[we need to] concentrate on how a thought has disturbed us instead of staying disturbed [by our thought]."[13] Cultivating right mindfulness prepares the Buddhist for right concentration, which refers to meditating on those things that will help us achieve nirvana. Right concentration leads the practitioner back to the first path, right understanding, for through meditation one gains experiential insight on the emptiness of existence. This in turn fosters less attachment and desire that leads the practitioner closer to attaining the third noble truth, nirvana.

Buddhism in History

Like the major world religions discussed in this text, within the Buddhist religion there are many types and schools of Buddhism. Because Buddhism is first and foremost a pragmatic philosophy centered on the four noble truths, as it spread from the Indian Peninsula, it readily dialogues with and synthesizes indigenous religious traditions into itself. For example, within the largest Buddhist tradition, the Mahayana tradition, there are a variety of traditions that correspond to the cultures and indigenous religions of the peoples to whom Buddhism was preached. In China, Buddhism incorporates aspects of Daoism and Confucianism; while in Tibet Buddhism appropriates Tibetan shamanism. Moreover, within the same area there are various schools that stress different aspects of Buddhism. Even terms likes "Chinese Buddhism," "Tibetan Buddhism," and "Vietnamese Buddhism" are somewhat numinous since they can refer simply to various schools of Buddhism within the same country.

It is of interest to note, especially in the United States, many Buddhists do not perceive other forms of Buddhism as threats but rather as unique expressions of the same tradition. Thich Nhat Hanh, for instance, describes all forms of Buddhism as separate but equal expressions of the same faith.

For our purpose it is important to note that there are two main forms of Buddhism: Theravada Buddhism and Mahayana Buddhism.

---

12. Cf. Farrer-Hall, 75.
13. Ibid., 77.

Theravada Buddhism

Theravada Buddhism is the oldest form of Buddhism that is still practiced today. "Theravada" translates as "the teachings of the elders," and it is the dominant form of Buddhism in Southeast Asia and Sri Lanka. This branch of Buddhism traces its origin to the original community of monks taught by the Buddha. Their holy books retain the original language of Pali, which Buddha most likely spoke, and are known as the Pali Canon. The Pali Canon consists to three categories of collected teachings from the Buddha: (1) Vinayas, teachings regarding monastic practice; (2) Sutras, teachings of Buddha on various matters, including stories about the Buddha; and (3) Agamas, interpretations of the Vinayas and Sutras. In Theravada Buddhism there is generally a reticence to add to the original Pali canon.

One distinguishing feature of Theravada Buddhism is its teaching on *arhat*. An arhat is a person who has achieved nirvana. Buddha was the first arhat, or "worthy one," to attain enlightenment completely. The goal of Buddhism is to become an arhat like Buddha; however, the Buddha is a unique arhat—for this reason in Theravada Buddhism the appellation "Buddha" is generally reserved for the founder of Buddhism.[14] Although Theravada Buddhists strive to be an arhat, they do so only by the teachings and example of the Buddha. Once a Buddhist has achieved this state of enlightenment, upon death he or she will enter into the parinirvana. This tradition stresses the historical Buddha. Therefore, Buddhadasa Bhikkhu (1906–1993), a Theravada Master, argues that the Buddha was not a deity and rejects the personal devotion to the Buddha, and claims that the essence of Buddhism is to eliminate egocentric thinking, which is personal liberation.[15]

Mahayana Buddhism

Although Theravada Buddhism and Mahayana Buddhism share the central teachings outlined above, the Theravada doctrine of arhatship distinguishes these forms of Buddhism. As mentioned, Mahayana Buddhism is the largest form of Buddhism in the world, and the most popular form of Buddhism in the Asian continent. Mahayana Buddhists criticize the Theravada doctrine of arhathood as propounding an ideal of a self-interested recluse that lives a contradiction because of this

---

14. Theravada Buddhists recognize that there have been other Buddhas; however, each of these Buddhas' teachings was relative to their epoch. The Buddha as I have described above is the Buddha of our epoch.
15. Donald K. Swearer, "Buddhadasa" in *Encyclopedia of religion*, 2nd ed., 1071-1072, (Farmington Hills: MI, 2005), 1071-1072.

self-interest and lack of compassion and insight.[16] Similar to the Bhakti movement in Hinduism that develops ambiguities in the Upanishads, Mahayana Buddhism develops ambiguities in the Pali canon. Particularly it develops the idea that the Buddha had compassion for all beings, and that the person of Buddha is present in his dharma. New sutras are revealed further developing these ideas. For these reasons followers of this form of Buddhism identify themselves as Mahayana or "Great Vehicle" Buddhism as opposed to Theravada/Hinayana or "Lesser Vehicle" Buddhism.

What results is a form of Buddhism wherein the Buddha is not simply an important yogi that left us his dharma but a personal God-like being, personally present in his dharma. Buddha has not simply left reality but transcended and permeates reality. Thus the Buddha has three bodies or *Trikaya* that permeate reality as we know it. These are his bodies that exist simultaneously: (1) Truth Body, Buddha's nature is identical with the absolute reality; (2) Enjoyment Body, power to manifest in sublime forms in the heavens to educate the heavenly beings; and (3) Emanation Body, power to manifest himself to suffering beings out of compassion to help them.[17] The result is a more theistic Buddhism where the Buddha becomes the pinnacle of compassionate living without attachment and the object of devotion for the Buddhist masses.

For Mahayana Buddhists the goal of Buddhist practice is not an arhat but rather a *bodhisattva*. Note that the term "bodhisattva" is found in Theravada literature; however, within the Mahayana tradition it takes on a new meaning. A bodhisattva is an arhat that takes a vow not to enter final nirvana until all beings have reached nirvana in life. Out of compassion and joy for other human beings a bodhisattva takes this vow. For a Mahayana Buddhist, a bodhisattva is not a synonym for the Buddha. Rather a bodhisattva becomes a necessary stage to enter into nirvana and become a Buddha.

There are various stages of bodhisattvahood that a liberated person must progress through before she has realized her Buddha nature and becomes a Buddha. Note that there are at least two major distinctions between a Buddha and a bodhisattva. First, while Buddhas generally do not enter into the cycle of samsara, bodhisattvas enter samsara, albeit the bodhisattva does so out of compassion. In Chinese Buddhism there are various legends about the bodhisattva Guan Yam who frequently enters the world to teach Buddha's dharma or "Buddha dharma." Second, whereas the bodhisattva delivers the sentient being to nirvana by thought of that sentient being, Buddhas deliver sentient beings without thought of that sentient being. Once Buddhahood is achieved, the bodhisattva loses all sense of self or "I" and is identifiable with all other things. Thus the Buddha does not forsake the

16. Damien Keown, "Mahayana" in *A dictionary of Buddhism* (Oxford: Oxford University Press, 2004), ebook: http://www.oxfordreference.com.libproxy2.dyc.edu/view/10.1093/acref/9780198605607.001.0001/acref-9780198605607-e-1087#

17. Damien Keown, "Trikaya" in *A dictionary of Buddhism* (Oxford: Oxford University Press, 2004), ebook: http://www.oxfordreference.com.libproxy2.dyc.edu/view/10.1093/acref/9780198605607.001.0001/acref-9780198605607-e-1888?rskey=pVGeG9&result=1

vow to save all sentient life, but rather by virtue of being a Buddha, a fully enlightened being, saves sentient life by her existence as such.

Within Mahayana Buddhism, Gautama Siddhartha Buddha or Gautama Buddha has a cosmic significance. Moreover, since the path of Buddhahood is open to all, Mahayana Buddhists recognize Buddhas that have come before and after Gautama Buddha. What results is a lack of stress on Gautama Buddha and an addition of various sutras not included in the original Pali canon. Mahayana Buddhists recognize that Gautama Buddha did not teach the sutras central to their tradition, such as the *Prajnaparamita* or *Perfection of Wisdom* during his lifetime. But rather he revealed them to bodhisattvas that kept them secret until humanity was ready for them.

Moreover, within the Chinese Buddhist tradition, one of the most popular buddhas is Amitabha (Pure Light) Buddha. Amitabha (Amida) Buddha brings Buddhism to the masses. He is believed to be a king from a different world that encountered the teachings of Gautama Buddha and became a practicing Buddhist. When Amitabha attained Buddhahood, he created a pure land for meditation and contemplation. Followers of this tradition believe that Amitabha will intercede for any believer, allowing for them to be reborn in the Pure Land where they can attain nirvana, if they are determined to be reborn in it, or simply recite "Amitabha Buddha" and think of him with faith at the moment of death.[18] This is a particularly important idea when we examine the Chinese Buddhist view as to what a good death is and how to care for the dying.

MAHAYANA DOCTRINES

In the *Mahaparinirvana Sutta*, Buddha teaches enlightenment is blissful and pure: "it is the true self, present in the impermanent mind and body of sentient body."[19] The result is that nirvana is the realization of self, as a paradise-like state. The difference, however, from Judeo-Christian heaven is that nonduality does not persist. Thus although the true self exists, the true self is identified in all things and is everything. Even the dichotomy of nirvana and samsara does not hold since you become everything, yet you remain your "true self." What this means is difficult to ascertain because you have to rely on ordinary language in order to show that such ordinary language does not apply to the extraordinary experience of nirvana.

Another important doctrine for this study with respect to its influence on the end of life is the Mahayana teaching on merit. With regard to merit, Buddhists believe that not only does bad karma or demerit affect your rebirth negatively, but merit or good karma affects your rebirth positively. Like Hindus, Buddhists believe that one needs to get beyond desiring merit (e.g., act without any desire).

---

18. Reynolds, 1067.
19. Louis O. Gomez, "Buddhism: Buddhism in India" in *Encyclopedia of religion,* 2nd ed., 1101-1127, (Farmington Hills: MI, 2005), 1101-1127.

However, the Mahayana tradition makes a distinctive nuance to this tradition. First, merit does not simply lead to a good rebirth but rather liberation to the pure land. Second, you can transfer merit to other people. For the laity (i.e., nonmonks), gaining merit for a good rebirth or liberation is important.[20] The end of life provides important opportunities to do so. In the Chinese tradition Buddhists developed a distinctive prayer known as the "transference of merit" that allows for the transference of merit to the dead.

End of Life

COPING WITH DYING

As we turn to how Chinese Buddhists prepare for death, it is important note that a good death is dependent to some extent on how the Buddhist has cultivated detachment during his or her life. For a Buddhist death is evidence of the Buddha's teaching on the impermanence of reality. Death is therefore a central element of Buddhism, and, in fact, Buddhists claim that if you cultivate detachment and the teachings of the Buddha, you will have a peaceful and joyful death. This is because fear and anxiety associated with death are engendered by desire for attachment to transitory existence. We might rephrase this as, if people have addressed their spiritual dimension by appropriating the four noble truths, then they shall have little anxiety about their death.

For these reasons, as noted in the interview below, Master Shan Kwang argues that how well one has cultivated his or her detachment and living out the eightfold path is indicated by the level and frequency of fear and anxiety toward death. Before Master Kwang decides how he can best prepare the dying for death, he watches to see how they respond to their mortality. If they exhibit peace and tranquility, this is an indication that they will be reborn in the pure land or achieve Nirvana. If the terminally ill exhibit fear and anxiety, Master Shan Kwang fears the worst, namely that they will be reborn in one of the lower realms of existence. Therefore he will spend more time and energy preparing them for a good rebirth.

Within the Chinese tradition, there are six realms of life. These realms include:

1. The Realm of Hell
2. The Realm of Ghosts
3. The Realm of Animals

---

20. Gomez, 1113.

4. The Realm of Humans
5. The Realm of Jealous Gods
6. The Realm of Gods

Pure Land and Nirvana are outside these rebirth realms. There is not a proper category to describe it. Similar to the realms of rebirth in Hinduism, each of these realms has various sub-realms that correspond to particular merits or demerits. Moreover, especially in the realm of Hell, the time that a soul spends there is relative to the gravity and amount of misdeeds committed in the human realm. Thus the amount of time that Master Kaung or a group of lay Buddhist from his temple will spend with the dying will depend on how attached the dying person is to the world and life as well as other factors such as how much time the dying has left and the amount of pain the dying is in.[21] The goal of course is to prevent the dying from being reborn in the realm of Hell, in which they can spend almost an eternity suffering without relief.

The result is that the end of one's life, the moment of death, and the hours immediately following death are very important, as they provide ample opportunity to gain the best rebirth or nirvana. Cultivating detachment and a clear mental state is of paramount importance for a dying Buddhist. The stress in the Chinese Buddhist tradition corroborates Charles Corr's thesis that that spiritual dimension of a person dictates how a patient addresses the other dimensions of life. With this in mind, how Chinese Buddhists make decisions about palliative care (physical dimension), define their autonomy (psychological dimension), determine with whom they want to spend their last moments, and decide what relationships they want to strengthen (social dimension) are influenced by their religious tradition.

Preparation for Death

Although the preparation for death may involve long periods of meditation and silence for the dying to further cultivate detachment from the world, death, especially in the Buddhist community in western New York and southern Ontario, is a communal experience. What follows is that the spiritual dimension addresses the social dimension, particularly the Buddhists' relationship with the devoted members of the temple community. The terminally ill patient or the family of the patient will contact the local Buddhist community/temple. At the temple of the Ten Thousand Buddhas, either the master of the temple, Buddhist monk/s in residence, or active members of the Buddhist community will come to the bedside of the dying. If the situation permits, especially in the case of

21. Cf. Walter N. Sisto, "Buddhists and Dying: How to Effectively Care for Buddhists at the End of Life," *Journal of US-China Policy* 12.3 (March 2015): 233-238.

the laity, they will stay with the dying member of their community, teaching the dharma of Buddha, praying, and helping the dead to meditate. The goal is to help the dying overcome their fear of death and attachment. Two chants that are often used are the Triple Jem and the name "Amitabha Buddha." The community or monk will also encourage the dying or the family of the dying to do acts of charity. Again the goal is to gain as much merit as possible for the dying.

Because the focus is on gaining merit and detachment, all actions including eating and drinking are done with this in mind. Taking into account the gravity of the illness, the dying will be encouraged to live out the precepts of Buddhism radically. Patients will be encouraged to live as much as possible a monastic lifestyle that may include fasting from meals after noon, a strict vegetarian diet that harms no living beings, and avoidance of certain vegetables that have pungent aromas that may ward off good spirits, gods, and bodhisattvas, such as garlic and onions.

One of the main texts that the Buddhists use to prepare the dying as well as to help the bereaved cope with death is the *Sutra of the Past Vows of Earth Store Bodhisattva*. This sutra is extremely important because it contains insight on what happens after death and how to ensure that a good rebirth is possible for the departed. This discussion records some of the last teachings of Gautama Buddha before he entered nirvana. The text itself is a dialogue between various gods, bodhisattvas, ghosts, and Maya, Buddha's mother, with Gautama Buddha about the salvation and destination of the dead as well as how to attain the bliss of nirvana that can occur through devotion to Earth Store Bodhisattva. This sutra gives great insight into Mahayana stress on devotion and the importance of the bodhisattvas. Within the Chinese Buddhist tradition, devotion to Earth Store Bodhisattva, in particular, is seen as consistent with fostering a detached mind since detachment involves the abandonment of self-interest and the sacrificial love for others. Invoking Earth Store Bodisattva or Amitabha Buddha with faith is at the same time to enter further into their lifework and ministry to save souls, which is ultimately and important step in the achievement of nirvana. Earth Store Bodhisattva is the personification of self-sacrificial love requisite for Nirvana, since this bodhisattva has taken a vow not to enter into enlightenment until the realm of hell is empty. This bodhisattva saves souls from the effect of their lack of spiritual cultivation and bad karma. Earth Store Bodhisattva is a savior that is able to requite the dead of their necessary punishment caused by their bad karma if they approach this Bodhisattva in faith. Gautama Buddha teaches:

> If good men or good women make offerings to this Bodhisattva [Earth Store Bodhisattva], or recite *The sutra of the Past Vows of Earth Store Bodhisattva…* [t]hey shall naturally leave the sea of suffering and ultimately be certified as having attained the bliss of Nirvana.[22]

---

22. *Sutra of the Past vows of Earth Store Bodhisattva,* Free Distribution, 73.

Moreover in this text Gautama Buddha promises that the recitation of this sutra in the presence of the recently deceased or even saying the name of one of the Buddhas can transfer merit to the dead: "If, however, at the time of the offender's death, another person recited the name of the Buddhas on that person's behalf, that person's offense can be gradually wiped away."[23] This saying corroborates the popular tradition of reciting the name "Amitabha Buddha," especially as the person takes his or her last breath. Therefore the sutra is not simply a devotional to Earth Store Bodhisattva, but rather a guidebook to attaining a good rebirth/nirvana at the end of life. Thus it spends a great length describing various meritorious acts and the amount of merit that is transferred to the dead for performing these actions. The sutra offers the dying and the bereaved various manners in which they can gain a heavenly rebirth or Nirvana. The Earth Store Bodhisattva is also an archetype for the bereaved Buddhist. This is iterated in the legend that in a past life Earth Store Bodhisattva performed great acts of merit for her recently deceased mother, whom she feared was tormented in hell for her sins. In so doing Earth Store Bodhisattva saved her mother from the realm of hell. After experiencing this grace, once attaining Bodhisattvahood, Earth Store Bodhisattva vowed to help bereaved persons and the damned.

Funerary Cult

Within the Chinese Buddhist tradition, death is not clearly defined as brain death. Death is better described as the process between the last breath/brain death and the release of the soul from the body. As Master Shan Kwang iterates below, the soul remains in the body for eight hours. Although it is impossible to resuscitate the dead person, that person is very much alive since the soul or mind remains in the body. During this period it is very important that the family avoid crying and displays of emotion. This is not only because sorrow is a sign of attachment, thus it is not helpful for the family, but also because the soul can be led astray by this display and want to remain with the family, which again is a sign of attachment that will result in negative rebirth. The goal of the family is to prepare the dead for the best rebirth possible. Thus they will not only avoid disturbing the soul but also perform the transference of merit. This is a tradition that involves the recitation of Amitabha sutra, mantra, chants of the Buddha's name "Amitabha Buddha," and blessing of the dead. Family members, particularly the children of the deceased, are encouraged to take part in these prayers, as the closer the connection to the dead, the more the merit the dead will receive from these actions. Although most healthcare facilities do not allow the corpse to be undisturbed for this long period, the longer the body remains undisturbed the better. If the person dies at home, the family may wait until the allotted time has passed to contact authorities.

---

23. Ibid., IX: 65.

After this period, the body is washed by family members and then transported to the local funeral home. Once the soul has left the body, the body is seen as a husk. Although cremation of the body is preferred, Chinese Buddhists in the United States tend to adopt the local customs.

Buddhist funerals are very modest and tend to involve various chants, mantras, and recitations of sutras. This stress, especially in the Chinese community associated with the Temple of the Ten Thousand Buddhas, is not on the funeral but on the memorial services performed during the next forty-nine days.

Chinese Buddhists believe that if liberation is not accomplished during that eight-hour period, the soul enters into a forty-nine-day trial period. This is the Buddhist bereavement period. The bereaved have comfort in the fact that during this period they have the opportunity to gain merit for their loved one and thus provide their family member with a better rebirth. The *Sutra of the Earth Bodhisattva* in its entirety is recited at least weekly during this period at the local temple or at an approved shrine within the home in order to facilitate a good rebirth.

Afterwards, the bereaved will remember the dead throughout the year, especially at Buddhist all souls day.

End-of-Life Care

The Buddhist perspective on end-of-life care is similar to the Hindu perspective. The spiritual dimension, cultivating detachment, will influence their perspective on how they view their healthcare (physical dimension), autonomy (psychological dimension), and relationships (social dimension). Buddhists interpret suffering as an opportunity to atone for suffering and gain merit; therefore they reject euthanasia. Like Hindus, Buddhists recognize that some masters who sense that they are terminally ill will starve themselves to death, but do not understand this as euthanasia since there is no attachment. Because these are enlightened masters, some monasteries in China exhume, wrap, and lacquer the body for veneration. The master's body is known as a *jou-shen* or flesh Buddha.[24]

Buddhists stress that suffering is a result of karma, and that bad karma may be remitted through suffering but also by addressing the causes of bad karma. Thus there is no clear distinction between care for the body and care for the soul, as the latter influences the former. For this reason, to address bad karma, devout Buddhists will be encouraged not only to spend more time in meditation but also to live out the fullest extent possible the Buddhist lifestyle. Moreover, healthcare choices,

---

24. Judith A. Berling, "Chinese religions" in *Death and afterlife: Perspectives of world religions,* 187.

such as the usage and amount of palliative medications, will be limited in as much as the pain is bearable to allow the terminally ill to foster a sense of detachment and enlightenment. What is most important to a Buddhist is to cultivate a spirit of detachment and mindfulness that should manifest in the expression of calmness about their dying. It is very important that health professionals communicate exactly the prognosis of the illness, life expectancy, and the effects of palliative medication to help a Buddhist be as mindful as possible about death. This is important for two reasons: first, Chinese Buddhists want to be cognizant so as to be able to say the name "Amitabha Buddha" with faith at the moment of death that can result in liberation to the pure land; second, Buddhists may use this information to meditate on, so as to prepare themselves for their death. In this way, they can eliminate the fear or anxiety associated with the unknown that will affect their rebirth.

Moreover, health providers should be aware that their patient may begin a fasting regiment that may entail a certain kind of diet (vegetarian) and eating their meals at certain times of day.[25] This can complicate medical treatment plans, as medications that require that they be taken with food could only be administered at certain times of the day.

Probably the most important aspect of a Buddhist's preparation for death is the amount of time needed for meditation.[26] For this reason, a traditional hospital setting may be a cause of great anxiety for a Buddhist since the frequent stream of visitors, nurses, technicians, and doctors may make these final preparations that are important to a Buddhist problematic. For this reason, health providers that can effectively communicate to their patient that their time for meditation will be respected will greatly relieve the stress of the patient addressing his/her psychological dimension. Actions such as posting a schedule on the patient's door and alerting other health professionals to times when the patient does not want to be disturbed communicates respect for the patient and his/her autonomy. Respecting the family or the patient's visitors throughout the dying process and after death illustrate respect for the patient's social dimension.

As the patient dies, if family and/or religious leaders are present, it is best that the health providers do not disturb their final rites. Note again that death is not brain death for a Chinese Buddhist but rather when the soul leaves the body, which remains in the body for several hours after death. It is important for health providers to be aware of this. Although certain settings such as traditional hospitals do not allow for bodies to remain in beds for eight hours, anything that a health provider can do to respect this important time will be appreciated by the family of the deceased. Communicating this respect to patients before death will also help them be less anxious over what will happen to their body.

---

25. They will take their meals to correspond with the time that the Bodhisattvas eat their meals.
26. Cf. Ken Truitner and Nga Truitner, "Death and dying in Buddhism," in *Ethnic variations in dying, death, and grief,* ed. Donald P. Irish, Kathleen F. Lundquist, Vivian Jenkins Nelsen (Washington, DC: Taylor & Francis, 1993), 125-136; Cf. Dennis, "Death: Eastern perspectives," in *Death and spirituality,* ed. K. Doka (Amityville, NY: Baywood Publishing Company, Inc., 1993), 75-92.

If the Buddhist dies before the religious leaders or family arrives, anything that the health provider can do to respect the patient's tradition will be appreciated by the family. This could entail simply saying the name "Amitabha Buddha" into the ear of the dying as they expire or preventing the corpse being moved to the morgue before the family has an opportunity to see their loved one and perform their religious rituals.

Conclusion

This chapter has examined the core teaching and traditions of the Buddhist tradition. Although very close to Hinduism, Buddhism is a reform movement that stresses detachment and mindfulness. These teachings have a direct impact as to how Buddhists consider end-of-life treatments. Focusing on the Chinese Buddhist tradition, I have argued that the end of life is a very important event in a Buddhist's life, as the last moments of life have the greatest effect on one's afterlife. For this reason various rites are performed and precepts are followed in order to provide the Buddhist with the best rebirth possible. Following Charles Corr's four-task method, I have argued that it is precisely this stress on the state of one's mind at the end of life that is a key factor in holistic healthcare. Thus medications, visits from doctors and family, and diet are influenced by the spiritual aspect of a person. This is important to keep in mind as we turn to a growing and unique Buddhist tradition in North America, Tibetan Buddhism.

Interview

Rev. Shaun Kuang is the master or leader of the Cham Shan Temple or Temple of the Ten Thousand Buddhas that serves primarily the Chinese Buddhists in the Niagara Falls region. After raising a family and immigrating to Canada in 1989 to work as an engineer, Kaung started to realize that something was missing from his life. Interested in the afterlife and the meaning of life, Kuang began to read religious texts. This led him to Buddhism. In 1992 he decided to dedicate the remainder of his life to Buddhism and become a Buddhist monk. After qualifying as a junior master, in 1995 Kuang's master asked him to be the master of the new Cham Shan Temple in Niagara Falls, Ontario, where he has remained from that point until today.

Q: Rev. Shaun Kaung, what is your role at this temple?

A: I am the master of this temple. I look after the temple. I have people here to help me run the temple. We meet monthly to plan the future and day-to-day routine of the temple. The members of the community call me "cifu." It is like how your students call you "professor." But you may call me whatever you want.

Q: What is your role in the Buddhist community?

A: Actually I do not have much of a role in the community. The people of the Buddhist faith come here if they have any difficulties. They ask for a kind of blessing. People have different ways of looking at things. We get together and I explain the way to look at things. Followers of the Buddhist faith have certain rules. No one like rules! I teach them to be patient, and then what to do. I teach them the right way that produces positive results, and then I help them to look at their results.

Q: Many people reading this book are from a Judeo-Christian background and therefore have appropriated those ideas of the soul. The Buddhist idea of the soul is different. Can you please talk about what the soul is for Buddhists?

A: There is no soul, only spirit. The spirit is mind-made. That is why in the sutras it says mind is Buddha and Buddha is mind. It is as simple as that. There is no spirit; it is emptiness. It is an illusion. Your mind created the karma that makes you think that you exist. But there is nothing there. Your mind is a Buddha now and you can change it to emptiness. We have to eschew beliefs about spirit away. You need the teachings of Buddha to guide you.

You will learn that your consciousness or spirit has eight parts to it. Parts 1 to 6 are the senses related to action. The seventh sense is your hard drive or memory. The eighth sense is your consciousness or intellect. At death all seven are released. Only the eighth part remains and it alone allows for liberation.

Q: What advice do you give to a dying Buddhist? Is there a proper way to prepare for death?

A: Yes, there is a proper way:

Number One: How long do you have to live? Get a medical report from a doctor first. Have faith in your doctor and your medicine. This is the same as the Buddha. You must have faith in yourself first before you come and pray here. Your mind has all sorts of false thinking.

Number Two: You must vow to spread the teaching of Buddhism to others after you are cured.

Number Three: You have to practice the faith. Just like you have to take medicine to be cured, you must practice the Buddhist faith. By practicing the faith you improve self: more relaxation and positive energy in the body will grow to allow you to understand the truth about nature so that you have no discrimination. You accept the way things are, and you accept that this is the cause and effect from a past life. This is karma. Past actions result in the now! I try to help them slowly. As they grow in understanding/ interest I give them more information. We do not force. We give them time and do a little at a time and ask them "how did the teaching taste?" This also depends upon how much time they have left.

You can prepare your entrance into the next life. They can go to heaven. I tell them to keep their mind pure, do good and nothing bad.

Q: When you say "heaven," what do you mean?

A: For the general public the pure land is heaven. But heaven is not pure land. Heaven is a realm of rebirth. This is in the sky above you. This is a blessing. But there is no nirvana here. Pure land is forever. There is no life or death. In the pure land there are three sages: Amitabha Buddha, Avalokitesvara Bodhisattva, and Mahasthamaprapta Bodhisattva. They welcome you to the Pure Land. You must come here and study step-by-step to understand. Heaven is open to everyone; it is up to you to walk in.

Q: Why is Amitabha Buddha in the pure land since he attained Nirvana?

A: Yes, he is in the pure land teaching. Buddhas have transformation bodies. They do not have souls/ spirits; they are emptiness. They can transform themselves into anything to teach anything. He is anywhere. We all have Buddha nature: you can be Buddha. But you must practice the precepts of Buddhism to understand this.

Q: What is the pure land?

A: It exists in the other world. You will become a Buddha. But you cultivate in a lotus flower there. But this all depends on your cultivation here.

Q: My understanding is that the Bodisattvas in the pure land are waiting for humanity to enter the pure land. Afterwards they will enter Nirvana together with the three sages. Thus there is a final nirvana for them as well as for humankind. Is this correct?

A: Yes, this is correct.

Q: A student recently asked me if the Buddhist teaching to be liberated from desire is feasible. After all, even Buddhist masters must get hungry or cold and therefore they desire food and warmth. How would you respond to this student?

A: In order to cultivate my mind for nirvana I need this body. If you look at it this way, then you take care of your body, but you are also careful in what you do. You just use enough. You must always keep the precepts of Buddha in mind and only take from the environment what you need to cultivate nirvana. Thus you eat just enough and use just enough to survive. This is not an egotistical desire; you are not attached to it. This is a natural desire that you need to live. You need to eat, to sleep, etc. You do what is necessary.

Q: What are the signs that death is approaching in your tradition?

A: It depends upon the karma of every person. Generally speaking, there are three kinds of people who show different signs and require different activities on our part.

If the karma is good they are very relaxed, waiting for the time to go. This is the first kind of person or "stage 1 person." Every day he does nothing but recite the Buddha's name. He knows that the time is near and gives all his fortunes to the children, holding nothing back. He reads the sutras of the Buddha day-in day-out. He has the mind of the Buddha. This means no desire and false thinking. No more monkey mind!!

There is a middle type of person or "stage 2 person"; he has some good and some bad, 50/50, karma in him. Today he is very good, next day he is confused. He is restless when he goes. He needs for me or someone from the temple to go to their home quite often and lecture on the Buddha. And when it is time for him to go, we will be there to recite the Buddha name, so that he can relax. When the person dies you cannot touch the body, because the spirit feels pain. (This is true for everyone.) His mind is confused just as when he was alive. This is the time to recite the sutra. The closer you can recite the sutra before their dying breath, the better.

The third type or "stage 3 person" has bad karma and is therefore quarrelsome and cruel; he will do all kinds of funny things that normally one does not do. He does things like punching or hitting another person for no reason. He goes around the town talking nonsense. The body will shake before he passes away. There is terrible pain. In Buddhism when you are about to die, it is as if you are peeling the skin of a cow.

Especially for the middle and third type of person it is important to not disturb the body for eight hours. Afterwards you can do what you like, cremate or bury.

Q: After death, are there specific rituals performed?

A: Yes, it is like what a Christian priest does, but a different style.

Q: Can you walk me through the specifics of that process?

A: Yes, there is a ritual cleansing. You recite a sutra. In this country you have to go to a funeral home. In the east, the body stays in the home and you prepare the body for burial with the help of family members. Every country has its own way of doing things. We respect the way things are done in that country.

Q: It seems like the most important part of the dying process for Buddhists is the preparation for death and the eight-hour period after death. Is this correct?

A: Yes

Q: It is my understanding that the bereaved perform the "Transfer of Merit" in the presence of the deceased. Can you tell me about this tradition?

A: It is the Amitabha Sutra that we chant. This is for everyone to recite, the Buddha name. In the pure land the Buddha is Amitabha Buddha. At the end of this we read certain verses about the name, day of death, and age of the dead. More merits are transferred depending upon the closeness of the living to the dead. The transfer of merits from this prayer will affect a high rebirth if it is made by a close relative.

Q: Can you tell me about the mourning period for Buddhists? What particular rituals are performed?

A: Every week for seven weeks the family members or friends and relatives recite *The Sutra of the Past Vows of Earth Store Bodisattva*. Reincarnation occurs for people in stages 2 and 3 at the end of this period. For stage 1 people, you do not have to worry since at the time of death they go to the pure land.

Stage 2 and 3 people can be reborn as an animal, fish, or go to the hell realm. Thus it is very important to help them during this transitioning period. If it is a poor family who does not have access to this sutra, they can recite the Buddha name. At least the person will be reborn as a human being. The name also keeps the demons far away.

Q: There seems to be a forty-nine-day mourning process. Is this correct? Also should this ritual be performed in the temple?

A: Yes, and the best place to do this is in the temple. There is more blessing here. The merits here are much better since we have all of these things. They can pray in front of the Buddha statue. If this is performed at home then the family must face west, there must be a table, lit oil lamps, three cups of water, and flowers and fruits as offering.

Q: How do you respond to your followers who have lost their loved one in a traumatic death (i.e., suicide, car accident, sudden death), especially when there has not been an opportunity to prepare for death?

A: Cause and effect! What is yours is yours, what is not yours is not yours. Cause and effect is such that it is a result of your past karma. You have to face the situation. It will be much better for you if you can accept this. If you think of this trauma in a positive way, you will be okay. Before you and I achieve self-enlightenment, we have to suffer in this way. You need to achieve a certain level of cultivation or enlightenment to understand this. Before that you and I have to suffer in this world.

Q: Can you share your most difficult experience with the death of a loved one?

A: In my position there is no attachment. Birth and rebirth keep on recycling. You have to look at it this way. It is all cause and effect.

Q: Are there any end-of-life treatments that Buddhists should avoid (e.g., palliative care)?

A: The Buddha has advice for taking care of your body. First, do not eat meat. Second, do not eat onions and garlic. These are demon foods. If you eat them you will exhibit anger, sexual desire, bad smell that will make the heavenly beings run away, and this welcomes into your life ghosts and demons. Another one is respectfulness. You must respect parents, relatives, and friends. You have to take care of your health. No drinking alcohol, no drugs, no late-night parties. If you do not take care of your health, what is the point? Good results give you good merits.

Q: In terms of medication like morphine or other palliative drugs, what is the Buddhist position on this?

A: Extreme pain comes from eating too much meat, garlic, and onions. Look back at your lives and see what you have done, have you eaten meat, showed little respect for people, lied, cheated, stolen? It is related to cause and effect. If you accept the precepts of Buddhism your pain will decrease. Slowly your pain will go away. The five precepts are no killing, no sexual misconduct, no lying or cheating, restfulness for friends and relatives, and no drug taking.

Q: So in a sense, it is not that you reject morphine or other medications, but that they are not the answer. They just mask the real problems, the accumulation of bad karma and the welcoming of evil spirits into your life. Is this true?

A: This is right. There is also another way to live out the Buddha's teachings, a very strict way, fasting. You do not eat one to three days, or you eat only one meal a day. It is up to each individual if they want to eat or not. You have to try and practice this; only in doing so will you see results. It is like medicine; it will not cure you unless you practice it. There are extreme cases where the use of morphine may be necessary, but as time goes on they should observe the precepts of Buddha and cut down their use of the drug.

Q: What is the Buddhist position on organ donation and autopsy?

A: It is up to each individual. After eight hours, organ donation is acceptable.

Q: Is it correct to say that Buddhists in your community want their bodies to be left alone for eight hours?

A: Yes, the spirit is present when the body is there. It is important, especially for stage 2 and 3 people, during this time persons refrain from crying near the body. The dead person sees their loved ones crying, and he may feel bad and have pain. This results in attachment that effects rebirth. For persons in stage 1 it is okay to cry since they are already detached. There is no merit in crying; it is much better to recite the Buddha's name or the Sutra.

Q: Euthanasia is an important issue in the United States today. What is the Buddhist position on euthanasia? Would you ever say it is okay to end your life if you are in extreme pain?

A: Oh no, of course not. This has come up in the newspapers. If you terminate your life now, you will come back and face the same problems. If you do not, you can gain a better life. You have to repay past wrongs done. Now a person who commits suicide—it does not matter how they do it—will go to the hell realm. You have to suffer there. Then you will come back in the animal form, and then in the human form.

Q: I have read that some Buddhist monks fast themselves to death when death approaches. Is this correct and isn't this euthanasia?

A: No this is not euthanasia. This is for a high ranking master, an enlightened person, a person who has high ranking merits. He will let his disciples know at what time and date he will die. This can be done by you and me, if we have proper cultivation. These people are in stage 1 or the first type of person mentioned above. They have achieved self-enlightenment, not perfect enlightenment or nirvana. They can go to heaven and be reborn or cultivate in the pure land. He is in a lotus flower and after he has cultivated himself, he will be a Buddha.

Q: What should non-Buddhists do if they find a dying Buddhist?

A: Contact the temple and family members as soon as possible. Recite the Buddha name, Amitabha Buddha. It is appropriate for a non-Buddhist to say the Buddha's name.

Q: Many persons reading this book will be involved in healthcare for Buddhist patients. What advice do you have for them?

A: Be the best healthcare professional you can be! Do your work properly. It does not matter who it is in front of you. Then you can talk about religion. But Buddhism is not a religion but a way of life. There was an old song "Be the way you are." This is a good motto. Be natural; do not look down on persons.

CHAPTER SEVEN

TIBETAN BUDDHISM

Introduction

Although only 7 million people in the world identify as a Tibetan Buddhist, I have nonetheless opted to devote an entire chapter to this form of Buddhism due to its ubiquitous influence on American pop culture,[1] and the fact that Tibetan Buddhism provides perhaps one of the most extensive teachings on how to prepare for dying, widely used by Buddhists and non-Buddhists alike. Moreover, Tibetan Buddhism has attracted many Western converts because of its teachings and the influence of the Dalai Lama.[2]

---

1. This is evident not only in the large crowds that the Dalai Lama, the leader of a major sect of Tibetan Buddhists, can garner, but also in the visible influence of Tibetan Buddhism on popular culture. Take for instance popular films such as *Ace Ventura Pet Detective, Avatar: The Last Airbender,* and *GI Joe: Retaliation.* In these films, the search for meaning, truth, and/or healing involves locating a Tibetan Buddhist master.

2. Cf. "Reincarnation: Tibetan Buddhism," *NPR* 1998, http://www.npr.org/programs/death/980110.death.html (April 21, 2015).

Background of Tibetan Buddhism

THIRD VEHICLE

Although Tibetan Buddhism shares the core teachings and basic philosophies of Mahayana Buddhism as outlined in the previous chapter, it is distinct. Tibetan Buddhists identify their tradition as the Indestructible vehicle or Diamond path as opposed to the lesser (Theravada) and greater (Mahayana) vehicles of Buddhism. Closely resembling Mahayana Buddhism in as much it shares the same beliefs on bodhisattvas and Buddhas, Tibetan Buddhism has distinctive tantric practices and additional religious literature. Tantric practices involve "using symbols of the cosmos called *mandalas* and ritual implements like bells and drums with the hands held in special postures called mudras."[3] It may involve the repetition of various mantras and meditations including deity practice (visualizing oneself as a deity). The most popular mantra that many Western readers will be familiar with is "Om Mani Padme Hum." Commenting on this sacred mantra, the Dalai Lama argues that it precludes translation into the English language; however, it contains spiritual power that can transform impure body, speech, and mind into the pure body, speech, and mind of the Buddha.

These unique traditions and many others allow Tibetan Buddhist and scholar Robert A.F. Thurman to interpret Tibetan Buddhism as the fulfillment and extension rather than a negation of the Theravada and Mahayana traditions. Thurman, in fact, argues that there are three stages of Buddhism: the monastic Buddhism (500 BCE to 0 CE), Universalist and Messianic Buddhism (0 to 500 CE), and Apocalyptic, esoteric, and Magical Buddhism (500 to 1000 CE). The first two stages are also known as Theravada and Mahayana Buddhism, respectively. Tibetan Buddhism is the third stage of Buddhism that integrates and supersedes the first two stages. This is not to deny the validity of the first two paths, but rather stress that Tibetan Buddhism provides a vastly accelerated practice to attainment of complete Buddhahood, either in this life or in a few lives.[4]

Important differences between these three paths are evident in the ideals to be attained. Whereas the arhant and bodhisattva are ideals in Theravada or the Mahayana Buddhism, for a Tibetan Buddhist the mahasiddha is the ideal. Mahasiddha is a "female of male Great adept, the 'psychonaut' of Indian inner science, actual perfect Buddha maintaining ordinary human form in history, latent kingship of individual explicated ritually and artistically."[5] Psychonauts or 'inner-world adventurers" are explorers of the human psyche and spirit.[6] Tibetan Buddhists believe that they inherit and expand the

---

3. Farrer-Halls, 171.
4. Robert A.F. Thurman, *Essential Tibetan Buddhism* (New York: Harper Collins Publishing, 1995), 3.
5. Thurman, 17.
6 Cf. Robert A. F. Thurman, "Background" in *The Tibetan book of the dead: Liberation through understanding in the between* (New York: Bantam Books, 1994), 10.

tantric Indian traditions (e.g., yogic practices and chakras). Relevant to this study are a grouping of mahasiddhas known as *delogs*, Buddhist masters that remain dead for an extended amount of time and then return to life to tell us about their experiences.[7] Their experiences in conjunction with the *Tibetan Book of the Dead*, which was authored by the omniscient delog, Padmasambhava, charts what happens to the subtle consciousness or human personality between death and rebirth. Mahasiddha is not only synonymous with the achievement of Buddhahood or nirvana, but also someone who has intimate knowledge of the human psyche and spiritual existence.

Because Tibetan Buddhists teach that their tradition offers actualization of buddhahood or mahasidhahood at an accelerated rate, the Tibetan Buddhist tradition is easily misconstrued as a "short cut" to liberation (e.g., the path to achieve nirvana without the training of the arhant and the vows of the Bodhisattva). Tibetan Buddhists readily take offense to this caricature. For them the mahasiddha is not a negation of the arhant or the bodhisattva, but rather encompasses all of the attributes of the arhant (self-mastery) and bodhisattva (universal compassion): the mahasiddha not only must have the mastery of the arhant, but takes and fulfills the Bodhisattva's vow not to enter parinirvana for "three incalculable eons of lifetimes" to help liberate souls within their lifetime.[8] In so doing, many mahasiddhas are also known as lamas or teachers of the Buddhism. These lamas are able to bend the space time continuum to accomplish the impossible. Fulfilling the bodhisattva's vow in a single lifetime may seem impossible; however, Tibetan Buddhists retort that many persons like Milarepa accomplished buddhahood in a single lifetime.[9]

History

Although it is unclear when exactly Buddhism reached the Tibetan Plateau, most scholars agree that Buddhism was clearly an established religion in Tibet by the beginning of the first millennium of the Common Era. Nevertheless the Tibetan Buddhist tradition dates the arrival of Buddhism to Tibet to the fourth century of the Common Era when Buddhist scriptures arrived miraculously.[10] Only in the eighth century does a distinctive school of Buddhism arise in Tibet. Historically the spread of Buddhism in Tibet is linked to two Emperors of Tibet, Kri Srong Ide'u bstan (circa 742–797), who converted to Buddhism, and Trisong Detsen (circa 790–844), who became a great benefactor

---

7. Anyen Rinpoche, *Dying with confidence: A Tibetan Buddhist guide to preparing for death,* tans. Allison Graboski, ed. Eileen Cahoon (Boston: Wisdom Publications, 2010), 65.
8. Thurman, *Essential Tibetan Buddhism*, 27.
9. Ibid., 29.
10. Matthew P. Kapstein, "Buddhism: Buddhism in Tibet" in *Encyclopedia of religion,* 2nd ed. (Farmington Hills: MI, 2005), 1150-1159.

of Tibetan Buddhism. According to Tibetan tradition, Trisong Detsen not only established the first monastery in Tibet, commissioned the translation of Buddhist sutras into Tibetan,[11] but also was an avatar/incarnation of Manjushri, a Buddha from countless eons in the past.[12]

Nevertheless Tibetan Buddhism teaches that the main impetus for a distinctive form of Buddhism in Tibet was the Buddhist master, Padma Sambhava or Guru Rimpoche. The legend is that Padma Sambhava was a 1,200-year-old prince from Afghanistan; he had not only encountered the teachings of Gautama (Shakyamuni) Buddha, but became a perfect Buddha that practiced the monastic, messianic, and apocalyptic vehicles of Buddhism. At the invitation of Emperor Kri Srond Ide'u bstan, who had requested that Padma Sambhava come to Tibet to tame unruly gods and spirits, using his magical and tantric practices of Buddhism, Padma Sambhava tamed the savage gods and spirits in Tibet. Afterwards Padma Sambhava was an honored guest of the state and that allowed him the freedom and support to preach and convert the Tibetan people to Buddhism, founding a distinctive form of Buddhism that we know as Tibetan Buddhism. Before Padma Sambhava left Tibet, he hid various termas or teachings around Tibet and in the minds of his disciples that would be discovered when the time was appropriate. The most well-known terma that Padma Sambhava left was the *Bardo Thodol* or what is popularly known as *The Tibetan Book of the Dead*. Note that this text remained hidden until the fourteenth century.

Although Padma Sambhava formed the first order or school of Tibetan Buddhism, the Nyingma school, today there are four main schools of Tibetan Buddhist thought that include the Nyingma, the Sakya, the Kagyu, and the Geluk school.[13] The Geluk school is the largest school and includes the office of the Dalai Lama.

Dalai Lama and Guru Devotion

In the West, the Dalai Lama is often compared to the Pope of the Catholic Church. In as much as the Dalai Lama is the spiritual leader this is appropriate; however, the office of the Dalai Lama is unique insofar as Tibetan Buddhists believe that he is the Bodhisattva of Compassion and the authentic political leader of the people of Tibet,[14] who was exiled by the Chinese government in 1951. The Bodhisattva of Compassion has chosen to be reborn fourteen times as the Dalai Lama. The Dalai Lama is therefore a *tulku* or a being that has foregone Buddhahood in order to be reborn. The cur-

---

11. Kapstein, 1152.

12. Thurman, *Essential Tibetan Buddhism*, 5.

13. Thurman, *Essential Tibetan Buddhism*, 42.

14. "Significance," *His Holiness the 14th Dalai Lama of Tibet,* http://www.dalailama.com/biography/significance (August 13, 2014).

rent Dalai Lama, Sonam Gyatso, is the fourteenth Dalai Lama, and he is contemplating whether or not he will reincarnate after his death.[15]

The title Dali Lama translates as "oceanic wisdom." The Dalai Lama is one amongst many lamas or teachers of wisdom, albeit in the Geluk tradition, he is the authoritative interpreter of the Buddhist tradition. Although Tibetan Buddhists have a canon of scripture that includes "over three hundred volumes, each volume of which would translate into roughly two-thousand-page English text," the emphasis in this religion is less on reading these texts than finding a lama that can interpret and teach the wisdom contained in these texts. The necessity of finding a lama has led some to pejoratively label Tibetan Buddhism as "Lamaism." Putting aside this stereotype, Tibetan Buddhism is a religion of "Guru Devotion." The lama is viewed with respect not only for his teachings but for his dedication to living-out Buddha Dharma. Thus a Tibetan Buddhist needs to find a lama, who will then teach him or her Buddha Dharma. Only as they advance in spiritual development will the lama share the sacred texts and teachings of their tradition. Respecting this tradition, Robert Thurman in his classic introduction to Tibetan Buddhism, *Essential Tibetan Buddhism,* provides only excerpts of Tibetan scripture. This is his rationale: "I have left out enough detail so that a person who wanted to go beyond reading to actual meditation..would have to seek a teacher, accomplish the prerequisites, and receive initiation."[16] Thurman, who recognizes the problems associated with revealing these texts to non-Buddhists, justifies his publication of these texts in English with the authority of the Dalai Lama, who approved their publication.

Bardo Thodol

The Bardo Thodol or *The Tibetan Book of the Dead* is a popular and authoritative text within a genre of teachings about dying and rebirth. In Western society, we have the epithet "Knowledge is Power." This accurately expresses why Tibetan Buddhists focus on dying and the rebirth process. To know exactly what will happen when we die is to anticipate your death and the process of rebirth so that you will be less fearful and anxious when death occurs. This is consistent with the Chinese Buddhist views that fear and anxiety about death is indicative of a lack of spiritual cultivation. For these reasons, Tibetan Buddhists will not only spend time reading and meditating about *The Bardo Thodol* but meditate on the experience of dying.

In a recent interview, Thurman provides an example as to what it means to meditate on dying:

---

15. "Reincarnation," *His Holiness the 14th Dalai Lama of Tibet 2011,* http://www.dalailama.com/biography/reincarnation (April 21, 2015).
16. Thurman, *Essential Tibetan Buddhism*, 45.

Now imagine that you are dying and you are losing sight and memory of your town, your house or room, the people with you. Also your body starts to go numb, your breathing becomes labored and you lose track of who's drawing breath. You forget to breathe. And then you enter first the realm of hallucination. You feel like a sort of fainting, melting sensation. There's a visual swirl all around you but not in your eyes, you're not seeing. It's sort of in back of your eyes, in the center of your brain behind the eyes. It's a swirling visionary state which is mirage like and illusion like. And you feel kind of a melting. This is the earth element dissolving into water. Don't be frightened. Just let yourself go limp.[17]

This focus on death may be deemed as morbid or odd, but Tibetan Buddhists stress that focus on death helps to appreciate life; moreover, proper practice may prolong life and provide a positive rebirth. Nevertheless death is not welcomed, but rather accepted as our inevitable end. Thurman, in fact, argues that Tibetan Buddhists in Tibet are more afraid of death than Westerners, since death is seen as an enemy, a malevolent force that is personified in the God of Death, Yama, who is a ferocious, demonic force.[18] For these reasons it is all the more important to be prepared for death. This is where the *Bardo Thodol* is applicable.

Appropriating the Mahayana cosmology that includes the various realms of existence, Tibetan cosmology also includes several bardos or forms of living that a subtle consciousness will experience. There are at least five states of living or "in-between states" that include Life (birth to death), Dream (sleep and waking), Trance (dualistic and enlightened consciousness), Death Point (life and reality), and Existence (reality and rebirth).[19] The point of this schema is to stress that life as we experience it is constantly in-flux and transitory. This cycle of life states is superimposed on the cycle of rebirth into the various realms of existence that are continually perpetuated unless nirvana is achieved.

Within this context, the *Bardo Thodol* is concerned with the states of "Death Point" and "Existence," wherein the body dies and the subtle consciousness is disembodied and spends up to forty-nine days in a transition period; afterwards it is reborn or liberated from rebirth. The *Bardo Thodol* plays an important role during these periods, since it can give the newly dead subtle consciousness the ability to not only choose a beneficial rebirth but perhaps attain nirvana.

Buddhists are a part of the cadre of voices that are uncomfortable with the neurological criteria for death. For Tibetan Buddhists death is not associated with a nonfunctioning organ but rather when the soul leaves the body that may occur up to three days after brain waves are no longer visible. Since death is an extremely important event, Tibetan Buddhists look for various signs that death is

17. "Robert A.F. Thurman, Meditative exercises for the process of dissolution during death," *PBS*, http://www.pbs.org/witheyesopen/afterlife_counsel_thurman.html (April 22, 2015).
18. Thurman, "Background," 19.
19. Thurman, "The Tibetan science of death" in *The Tibetan book of the dead*, 34.

near. According to the Tibetan tradition, death is preceded by the dissolution of the senses and the dissolution of the elements. Note, however, that the two types of dissolutions need not occur in the respective sequence mentioned and may occur simultaneously.[20] Moreover, both sets of dissolutions can occur rapidly; therefore, the sooner that they are observed the better, as this will give the dying more time to make final preparations. For this reason, understanding and observing the signs that precede death are of utmost importance for helping the dead achieve nirvana or at least the best rebirth possible.

The dissolution of the senses consists of five dissolutions corresponding to the five senses that break down as a person dies. The first sense to dissolve is hearing. Thus the dying person and attendants to the dying are trained to look for signs that this is occurring, such as the inability of the dying person to understand what is being communicated to her. The second sense to dissolve is sight. The loss of the sight sense is usually preceded by complaints by the dying person that the faces of those around her are blurry. As death continues to approach the smell, taste, and touch senses dissolve.

The dissolution of the elements refers to the breakdown of the constituent parts of a person (e.g., the natural elements of which all things consist). The dissolution of elements is subdivided into eight stages. The first four stages refer to the breakdown of the natural elements of the body, the dissolution of the earth element into the water element (stage 1 and 2), the dissolution of the water element into the fire element (stage 2 to 3), the dissolution of the fire elements into the wind element (stage 3 to 4), and the dissolution of the wind element into the space element (stage 4 to 5).[21] There are visions and symptoms associated with the breakdown of each element. For example, associated with the breakdown of the water element are the symptoms of fatigue, the feeling of breaking into pieces, and clouded vision.

After these five stages of initial dissolution, the death process continues with the subtle stages, 6 through 8. If we superimpose the popular Western understanding of death as brain death, brain death occurs during the sixth stage. Nevertheless, for Tibetan Buddhists person is still alive even though the person is nonresponsive. The subtle consciousness of the dead person remains in the body and is subject to the subtle changes in the body that include the entrance of subtle winds through various channels in the body.[22] Death occurs during the eighth stage when the subtle consciousness has a vision of a clear light. Interestingly this vision corresponds to popular near-death observations of the light at the end of the tunnel. This state is known as the *Chikai Bardo* or moment of death. Depending on the cultivation of the person the subtle consciousness will stay here three days.

---

20. Rinpoche, 50.
21. Elisabeth Benard, "Tibetan Tantric religion" in *Death and afterlife: Perspectives of world religions,* 172.
22. Ibid., 173.

During the Chikai Bardo, it is now possible to achieve Buddhahood if the subtle consciousness recognizes that the clear light is the void of existence. Thus we find almost immediately a quite different interpretation of the light phenomena of near-death experiences, for although the clear light may be enticing it should not be embraced: Do not go into the light!

In order to help facilitate liberation or at least a positive rebirth, a Tibetan Buddhist may read the *Bardo Thodol* to the person during the subtle dying process. This may seem like a strange tradition, but for a Tibetan Buddhist this is reasonable because the subtle consciousness is present in the body and can hear what is being said. Also the subtle consciousness is a pure consciousness and intellect, and, therefore, it is adept to understanding higher truths than it was during its bodily existence. Nevertheless because most persons will not recognize this truth due to their lack of spiritual cultivation and egocentrism, they will proceed directly through the stages of dissolution of elements and senses in reverse order from the last to the first stage. However, instead of reentering her corporeal body, the subtle consciousness creates a new mental (spiritual) body that it will use to navigate the next stage of existence known as the *Chonyid Bardo*, or state between death and afterlife.

The Chonyid Bardo occupies a prominent place in the *Bardo Thodol*. This bardo contains some of the wildest imagery from outer body encounters with various Buddhas and horrific demons to displays of various soft and harsh lights. The *Bardo Thodol* speaks about the various temptations and signs of assurance that the subtle conscious will see on each day. Anyen Rinpoche, a Tibetan Buddhist master, notes that the depictions in the *Bardo Thodol* are relative to one's spiritual cultivation and vivid descriptions will only be witnessed by a properly cultivated consciousness. Less cultivated persons will witness less vivid and articulate visions.[23] For this reason it is more difficult for a subtle consciousness to attain liberation, since it will not be able to fully comprehend what is being read to it from the *Bardo Thodol* since it will not correlate with what is seen. This fact is, all the more reason why all Tibetan Buddhists are expected to cultivate their subtle consciousness through years of meditation on the dying process and the bardos. This is all the more important when we consider that liberation can occur at any time during the Chonyid Bardo that lasts about fourteen days.

Liberation entails what may seem to be a simple task: to recognize that these perceptions in this bardo are projections of the mind. They are ultimately not real! But this is much more difficult than it may seem, as the subtle consciousness is constantly tempted to embrace the pleasurable and comforting lights and perceptions; however, these are projections of negative karmatic tendencies that indubitably lead to a negative rebirth. Fear and attachment cause negative karma to accumulate.[24] Nevertheless, even the most feared emanations, including Yama, the Lord of Death himself, can be a cause for hope:

---

23. Rinpoche, 70.
24. Cf. Ibid., 69.

O nobly-born, when such thought-forms emanate, be thou not afraid, nor terrified; the body which now thou possessest being a mental-body of [*karmic*] propensities, though slain and chopped [to bits], cannot die. Because thy body is, in reality, one of voidness, thou needest not fear. The [bodies of the] Lord of Death, too, are emanations from the radiances of thine own intellect; they are not constituted of matter; voidness cannot injure voidness. Beyond the emanations of thine own intellectual faculties, externally, the Peaceful and the Wrathful Ones, the Blood-Drinking Ones, the Various-Headed Ones, the rainbow lights, the terrifying forms of the lord of Death, exist not in reality: of this, there is no doubt. Thus, knowing this, all the fear and terror is self-dissipated; and, merging in the state of at-one-ment, Buddhahood is obtained.[25]

This optimistic reading of the demonic encounters that await the dead is relative to the Chonyid Bardo. If liberation is not accomplished during its traverse through this bardo, then the subtle consciousness enters the *Sipai Bardo* or rebirth bardo. At this point liberation is no longer possible; however, choosing a good rebirth that will allow for the practice of Buddha Dharma in the next life is ideal. Accrued karma and habits make choosing a good rebirth difficult. Nevertheless, if the subtle consciousness has gained knowledge about the falsity of his perceptions and/or hears the recitation of the *Bardo Thodol* from a lama on earth, and then worships their personal deity, they may be transported to that deity's pure land. If this does not occur, as the *Bardo Thodol* illustrates, then they must focus on choosing compassionate parents conducive to practicing Buddha Dharma.[26] In fact, one of the last scenes that the subtle soul sees is its prospective parent copulating.

Dying, Death, and Bereavement Customs

Like Chinese Buddhists, for a Tibetan Buddhist preparation for death is of utmost importance, and thus it begins many years before dying. Anyen Rinpoche explains that because we will all die, we must reflect on death now: "[i]f we do not think about it now, it will be difficult to think about it when it is happening—as it inevitable will."[27] Returning to the eightfold path, the goal of a Tibetan Buddhist is to achieve mindfulness in death that can only be accomplished through achieving mindfulness about dying in life. In other words, by making mindfulness a habit, in particularly mindfulness about the dying and rebirth process, one will be able to achieve nirvana after death.

---

25. Bardo Thodol: Book One, Part Two: Fourteenth Day
26. Rinpoche, 72.
27. Ibid., 11.

For a Tibetan Buddhist a good death is a death without fear and attachment. Forewarning about death is also conducive to dying well as it allows Buddhists to maximize their time to prepare for death. Therefore sudden deaths or untimely deaths are a great misfortune. Although acts such as a phowa[28] can be performed on behalf of the dead to gain them merit, lack of time entails the lack of ability to prepare for death and perform efficacious rituals.

Moreover, the Tibetan tradition stresses that your last thought before you die affects your rebirth. Even if you have accumulated much bad karma, Anyen Rinpoche teaches that if your last thought is a good motivation, you will attain rebirth as a human in a few lifetimes.[29] Thus creating an environment that will help the dying have the correct state of mind is very important. This includes not only time to practice rituals and meditation but also space for an altar.

Settings conducive to Tibetan Buddhist practices are quiet and generally include a few people that belong to the Tibetan Buddhist community. This custom may be a great cause of tension for converts to Tibetan Buddhism that have family members who want to be at the bedside of their family member but are not practicing Buddhists. Here we find how the spiritual dimension of a person dictates the sociological dimensions (e.g., who is welcome during the last moments of the dying). The ideal persons to accompany the dying are other Buddhists who are familiar with the lama of the dying person and are able to assist in the spiritual practices.

Helping a Tibetan Buddhist cope with death involves respecting the Tibetan Buddhist's religious practices. Thus a good death entails not only how one dies but also that end-of-life and postmortem rituals are performed. For many Tibetan Buddhists this means that the *Bardo Thodol* will be read throughout the dying and rebirth process. Although in the popular Western imagination *Bardo Thodol* is synonymous with Tibetan Buddhism, the text is not a dominant scripture in all Buddhist schools. Depending on the Buddhist tradition with which the person is affiliated and the teachings of their lama, the *Bardo Thodol* may or may not play an important role. Tibetan Buddhism is an esoteric religion in as much as there are a variety of secret teachings and texts about dying, death, and rebirth that are only made available by lamas to practitioners as they advance in the religion.

Because these instructions can be complex and are meant only for a Tibetan Buddhist to read, Anyen Rinpoche instructs Tibetan Buddhists to create a Dharma Will. This is an example of what may be included in the will:

> It is very important to me on religious grounds that my body remain for three days, or as long as possible, without being moved. If this is impossible, I request that my family

28. Phowa will be explained below.
29. Rinpoche, 98.

and entrusted Dharma friends have as much time as they can to complete certain prayers before my body is moved.[30]

Because the rituals associated with death and the intermediate state are fairly detailed and individualized, Anyen Rinpoche encourages Tibetan Buddhists in the West to create a Dharma Box. A Dharma Box will include not only the Dharma Will, but also all of the following items: instructions from the lama, favorite prayer to be recited, photos of spiritual guides and deities to be used in a bedside altar, a photo of yourself praying for the phowa to be performed by the lama, blessed pills, recordings of prayers and/or mantras to be played for the dying and deceased, instructions for non-Buddhist family members, and a copy of all legal papers.[31] It also will designate an entrusted Dharma friend who will assist the dying Buddhist "through the dying process. And is like a spiritual contract with Dharma friends for special conduct to be carried out."[32] Moreover, it provides information about contacting a lama, purification rituals, prayers and phowa, sacred texts used during the forty-nine-day bereavement period, burial instructions, and how to distribute wealth to charitable organizations. Dharma friends are persons who not only practice Buddhism but are also devotees of the same lama as the terminally ill person.[33] Because it is unlikely that a lama will be present for the entirety of the dying process, they act in place of the lama and advocate for the patient when they can no longer advocate for themselves. A Dharma friend may be designated as the healthcare proxy, helping to determine that specific instructions of the Dharma Will is followed and that Western healthcare does not conflict with religious practice. Note that the Dharma friend may include a group of lay practitioners.

One of the most important instructions included in the Dharma Box is the phowa. Phowa is a means for transferring the consciousness of the deceased person to the pure land realm or liberation. Phowa can be performed by the dying as the five senses are dissolving or it can be performed on behalf of the dead. With respect to the terminally ill, the ideal time to perform phowa is "when the outer breath has ceased and the inner breathe is still visible."[34] Note that phowa can have negative effects if performed at the wrong time, and thus it is in the benefit of a practitioner to have a lama or Dharma friend perform it.

There are various forms of phowa that correspond to the level of cultivation of that person. In addition, the lama is the authoritative teacher of phowa and may have a phowa practice that is unique for his or her devotee. Some of the simplest practices of phowa involve looking upward at the moment of death and concentrating on the top of your head. Visualizations of deities, bodhisattvas, and orbs

---

30. Ibid., 144.
31. For a full list of what is included in the Dharma Box see pages 39-40 and Appendix III in *Dying with Confidence*.
32. Rinpoche, 34. Some of these rituals include leaving the body undisturbed for a period of three days after the last breath is taken, ritual cleansing of the body, dying with as clear a state of mind as possible.
33. Rinpoche, 124.
34. Ibid., 81.

of light leaving the body traveling into the heavens, dissolving in the Divine Presence, black clouds leaving the dying, symbolizing the bad karma leaving the dying, are all popular phowas.

The practice of phowa is important because it can liberate a person or result in positive rebirth in a pure land, avoiding the Chonyid Bardo and Sipai Bardo. Buddhist masters will look for signs that phowa has been successful, which include "an opening on the top of the head where the head touches the central channel or bump on the head in the same place; being able to stick a blade of grass in the wound, which oozes light-colored fluid."[35]

If there are no visible signs that transference of consciousness has occurred, then the further instructions of the lama in the dharma box will be carried out. This may of course include the reading of the *Bardo Thodol* directly into the ear of the dying person.

It is important to note that the fate of the body after the three-day period of dying after vitals are no longer present is inconsequential. For this reason, Tibetans in the West are free to bury or cremate their bodies after the three-day period is over. The body is seen as a husk. In Tibet we find one of the most interesting practices regarding the disposal of the body that is popularly known as sky burial. The corpse is brought to a ceremonial spot where it is slaughtered to attract vultures. It is given to the creatures of the sky. Sky burial is a final act of kindness, and therefore it merits good karma because the dead provide sustenance for another living being.

Caring for the Dying

Like Chinese Buddhists and Hindus, the spiritual dimension dictates to some extent perspectives on the medical, social, and psychological dimensions of care. Any effort to understand this tradition and respect the perspective of the dying person will increase the effectiveness of healthcare, since the patient will play an active role in his or her care, addressing the tasks relevant to the patient.

For a healthcare provider, the first conversation to have with a Tibetan Buddhist patient or the proxy is if there is a Dharma Box, Dharma Will, and/ or Dharma friend. If one or all of these are present, than one need simply to follow as best as possible the outlined plan of care in conjunction with medical responsibilities.

Having an environment conducive for prayer and meditation is important. This is a challenge in a traditional hospital setting for the same reasons mentioned in previous chapters. Nevertheless, for Tibetan Buddhists there are several generalizations that can be made.

---

35. Ibid., 81.

First, in the Tibetan tradition, there is stress placed on having a bedside altar that includes various mandalas, images, and personal pictures. The patient may also request a soundtrack playing of a mantra (such as OM MA NI PAD ME HUNG HRI), personal devotion, or the *Bardo Thodol*. Helping the patient set up this altar will be a great sign of support and kindness, as items on this altar are believed to help facilitate transference of consciousness, respecting the psychological, social, and spiritual dimensions.

Second, the environment may include only certain people in addition to the required medical professionals. As death approaches, Tibetan Buddhists want an environment that generates as little attachment or desire as possible. This can place healthcare professionals in precarious situations, since out of respect for the patient's social dimension, the healthcare professional may have to tell friends and family not to touch their loved one or that the patient does not want them to visit at the end of life.

It is of interest to note that the avoidance of loved ones during the dying process is not understood as an action of ill-will toward their loved ones by the Buddhist, but rather an action of love for them.[36] The patient may love her family so much that there is fear that having them present during those last moments may cause more attachment and desire, producing bad karma. Moreover, crying and unnecessary talking should be avoided, since these actions disturb the patient, making her more attached to this life. Remember that the moment of death is a central event for which a Tibetan Buddhist may have spent years preparing; great care with respect to the patient's wishes during their final moments alive must be taken seriously, since failure to respect the patient's wishes may interfere with a lifetime of religious practice. Generally speaking, the only touching that is encouraged is a gentle tap at the top of the head to remind the patient to keep focus as her consciousness dissolves nearing death. Healthcare workers are encouraged if the patient is dying, and there is no one present besides them, to tap on the forehead, as this is a form of phowa that is believed to help facilitate liberation since it helps the dying to focus on liberation.[37] Permission to do so should always be communicated to the patient.

Prohibition on unnecessary touching, strong signs of emotion, and unnecessary chatter will extend until the departure of the subtle consciousness to liberation or the intermediate bardo after three days. During this time it is not appropriate to move the body. How realistic the wish of the patient to have her body undisturbed for three days after vitals have stopped will depend on the setting in which they die. Nevertheless, making this wish known to administrators in the facility and documenting the time after the final breath that the corpse was moved will be greatly appreciated. This evidence will help the lama determine what course of action to take to positively influence the patient in the intermediate state.

---

36. Ibid., 119.
37. Cf. Marilyn Smith-Stoner, "End-of-life needs of patients who practice Tibetan Buddhism," *Journal of Hospice and Palliative Nursing* 7.4 (2005): 228-233.

Creating an environment conducive for a good death will also include scheduled times of silence for prayer and meditation, visits from Dharma friend and/or lama, and bodily posture. Again anything that a health provider can do to schedule medical appointments around these visits will be appreciated. With respect to bodily posture, the Tibetan tradition stresses that the ideal posture to die is the "lion's pose." This is the posture in which Gautama Buddha died. This involves lying on the right side with the head facing north. If this is not possible due to medical equipment, then the Dharma friend may help patients to visualize themselves in the Buddha's lion's pose.

With respect to the physical task to alleviate pain, the Tibetan perspective shares the Chinese Buddhist perspective. Pain management is seen as ethically indifferent, so long as it does not interfere with the mind (e.g., numbing the mind from the clarity it needs for liberation). Thus Tibetan Buddhists shall request that as little pain medication be given as necessary or that all pain medication cease once the dissolution of senses and elements begins to occur. This logic of taking medication until the signs of death appear applies to the position on life support in extraordinary circumstances. Nevertheless, although euthanasia is prohibited, when it is appropriate to let someone die, is relative to the appearance of the signs of death. Thus, removing life support before the signs of death are evident may be interpreted as euthanasia.

Regarding organ donation, the Tibetan Buddhist tradition has openness to it, even if it results in disturbing the body within the three-day period after the final breath is taken. It is considered a virtuous activity, but it is recommended only for advanced practitioners, since the taking of the organ disturbs the soul and can lead to attachment and a negative rebirth. Only advanced practitioners or those persons who have shown signs that the phowa has been successfully performed should donate their organs. For them it is a further meritorious act, benefitting another through death.

Conclusion

This chapter has surveyed one of the most detailed explanations of the dying, death, and rebirth process in the Eastern religions. We have also examined the unique challenges this tradition poses for health professionals, and given further credence to Corr's thesis that the spiritual dimension dictates the other dimensions of care. In the next chapter we move to Judaism, the oldest Western world religion practiced today.

CHAPTER EIGHT

JUDAISM

Introduction

Originating around the second millennium before the common era, Judaism is the second oldest practiced world religion and oldest Western religion. Today around 15 million people practice the Jewish religion worldwide, and nearly 6 million Jews live in the United States. The reformed Jewish community is the largest Jewish community in the United States.[1] Even though Judaism is the smallest Western world religion in terms of population of adherents, Judaism has a central place in the history of Western world religions because both Islam and Christianity purport to share Jewish patrimony and history. While Muslims claim to be descendants of the father of the Jewish people, Abraham, and reiterate much of the Torah in the Qur'an, the founder of Christianity was a religious Jew, and the Christian Bible contains Jewish sacred scripture. Thus it is not possible to accurately comprehend Christianity and to an extent Islam without understanding the Jewish faith.[2] For this

1. According to a 2013 Pew study, "[o]ne-third (35%) of all U.S. Jews identify as Reform, while 18% identify with Conservative Judaism, 10% with Orthodox Judaism and 6% with a different denomination, such as the Reconstructionist or Jewish Renewal movements" (http://www.pewforum.org/2013/10/01/a-portrait-of-jewish-americans/). In many areas of the country, such as Buffalo, New York, reconstructionist and reform congregations have merged due to their progressive interpretation of the Jewish tradition.
2. Within the Christian Church movements such as Marconianism were rejected as heresy because they attempted to present the Christian message and tradition without the Jewish context and scriptures.

reason, this chapter functions not only as an introduction to Judaism and end-of-life decisions, but also provides an introduction to Western religion.

For clarity this chapter is divided into four major sections. The first section provides a succinct introduction to the biblical history and sacred texts of Judaism. The second section briefly examines biblical views on the afterlife. I stress "views" and not "view" because the Hebrew Bible does not have one view on the afterlife, but several views. Nevertheless, this pluralism shall help explain the variety of beliefs about the afterlife in contemporary Judaism (Section Three). In the fourth section I examine the Jewish funerary and bereavement traditions. The chapter concludes with an interview with Rabbi Alex Lazarus-Klein.

Section One: History and Scripture

The central narrative in Judaism is the relationship between a personal and loving God (YHWH) and YHWH's people. What results from this narrative is a stress on personal relationships (between YHWH and people, but also between people) and the historical context in which these relationships occur: personality and history become the operative paradigms for understanding reality. This stress is unique to the Western world religions discussed in this text, but also serves to help differentiate Judaism and the Western religions from the Eastern religions. Albeit for a Buddhist or Hindu, personality and history are important, they are not operative paradigms because historical existence is ultimately transitory and our personality is not unique since atoning for karma requires multiple lives/personalities and historical existences. The result is a dualism that tends to emphasize the metaphysical reality (Brahmin-atman) or nothingness (parinirvana) while deemphasizing physical and historical existence, stressing renunciation of the world and personality. This is radically different from Judaism; in Judaism not only is the personality we create in history important and unique, but it determines our relationship with God and our existence in the afterlife.

Today the Western stress on history and personality is nowhere more evident than in the various quests for the historical and archeological basis for the events and persons of the Bible. Outside biblical scholarship, the Torah (i.e., the Jewish scripture that contains the biblical books of Genesis, Exodus, Numbers, Leviticus, and Deuteronomy) has been and continues to be the subject of scholarship from a variety of disciplines and popular entertainment.[3] Biblical scholars are divided as to whether or not the events (e.g., the exodus from Egypt and conquest of modern day Israel) and persons recorded—including Moses and Abraham—are legendary or historical. Like many ancient

---

3. Ridley Scott's *Exodus: Gods and Kings* (2014) and Darren Aronofsky's *Noah* (2014) are two recent examples as to how ancient biblical figures continue to occupy a space in popular culture.

persons (e.g., Buddha, Krishna, Alexander the Great) there is little evidence for their existence outside communities that say they existed. The historicity of the Torah and the biblical account of the Jewish people and religion are topics beyond the scope of this chapter.

Nonetheless, for Jews the events and persons in the Torah remain a vivid reality in their history, culture, and religious practice. The relationship between YHWH and the Jewish people began with Abraham (circa 2000 BCE), the founder of Judaism, and traditionally the first monotheist and believer in YHWH. YHWH asks Abraham to be the father of a new nation. YHWH and Abraham form the first covenant or agreement that is premised on the condition that God will bless Abraham with prosperity if he has faith in YHWH. A sign of this covenant is circumcision, which remains an important practice today. After various trials, Abraham and his wife Sarah are blessed in their old age with a son, Isaac. Isaac is also blessed and has two sons, Jacob and Esau. However, only Jacob receives YHWH's blessing to be the leader of YHWH's people. Jacob, who is called Israel, has twelve sons. Each son becomes the patriarch of his family and his name is associated with that family or tribe.[4]

Unfortunately, a great famine befell Jacob and his family that lead them to migrate to Egypt. After some time in Egypt they were enslaved, but finally freed by a prophet named Moses (circa 1300 BCE). Second to Abraham, Moses or "Moses Our Teacher" (*Moshe Rabbenu*) is the most important person in Jewish history. He is not only YHWH's prophet, but the greatest prophet in Jewish history. Not only does Moses, by YHWH's assistance, lead his people from Egypt to the land that YHWH gave to Abraham, but, more importantly, YHWH makes another covenant between Godself and the Israelite people (ancient Jewish people). Moses receives from YHWH the terms of this covenant known as the Ten Commandments on Mount Sinai. These commandments contain ten basic rules about how to relate to God and the members of their community. In return for living out theses commandments, YHWH promises to bless and protect the Israelites. The events of this exodus from Egypt remains enshrined in the Jewish culture, as Jews annually celebrate the release of the Jews from Egypt with the holiday of Passover. Moreover, during Sukkoth, a feast that is five days after Yom Kippur, Jews are reminded of the time that Moses and the early Jewish community spent traveling from Egypt to Israel. Yom Kippur, or the day of repentance for past sins, which is the holiest and most important day of the year for Jews, was itself instituted by YHWH's revelation to Moses (Leviticus 23: 26-28).

Even though the Israelites return to Israel, they are subjected to a series of calamities resulting from their unfaithfulness to YHWH. Eventually the Israelites split into two kingdoms (circa 920 BCE), Judah in the south that included the city of Jerusalem and the kingdom of Israel, which was comprised of the remaining tribes of Israel. Both kingdoms were sacked; however, in Judah most of the

---

4. With exception to Jews who associate themselves with the tribe of Levi or the Jewish priesthood, most Jews have lost their tribal identity.

survivors were exiled to Babylon (circa 600 BCE). After seventy years of exile, YHWH returns the Jews to their land and fortune. However, the Greek empire conquers Israel. By the edict of Antiochus IV, the Greeks attempt to Hellenize the Jews or forcibly impose Greek culture and religion in hopes of exterminating Jewish religion and culture. Revolt ensues and through the auspices of the Maccabees, Israel regains its freedom. This event is enshrined in the festival of Hanukah that celebrates the defeat of Antiochus IV, the cleansing of the Jewish Temple in Jerusalem, and the miracle of the candles. The tradition is that the candles in the Temple stayed lit for eight days on only one day of fuel (circa 164 BCE). During the final centuries of the biblical period we find a growing belief that the Messiah will return to fix the relationship between YHWH and YHWH's people, restoring and extending the greatness of YHWH's kingdom on earth. The biblical period or period in which the events of the Hebrew Bible (Old Testament) or Tankh that includes the Torah in addition to the writings of the prophets (e.g., Isaiah, Jeremiah), the historical texts (e.g., Chronicles), and the wisdom literature (e.g., Psalms)[5] ends with the defeat of Hellenism.

Section Two: Afterlife in the Bible

The afterlife is not a central theme in the Torah. The stress is on the gifts or graces received in this life. Nevertheless during biblical times (2000–100 BCE) Israelites or Jews believed in an afterlife; however, that belief becomes a more dominant and explicit theme in their tradition over time.

In the earliest texts of the Torah, for instance, the mediating narrative is YHWH's blessing. This is evident in the prophetic call of Abram (later known as Abraham) from YHWH.[6] YHWH says:

> Leave your country, your kindred and your father's house for a country, which I shall show you; and I shall make you a great nation, I shall bless you and make your name famous; you are to be a blessing! (Gen 12: 1-3)

Note that the blessing that YHWH offers Abram is a blessing that will come to fruition in this life. For Abraham, who is in his early seventies at the time of his prophetic call, he is promised prosperity and more importantly posterity: YHWH says, "Look up at the sky and count the stars if you can. Just

---

5. Note that the Tankh contains the same codex as the Protestant Bible but fewer books than the Catholic Bible. The Catholic Bible contains the Apocrypha (e.g., Tobit, Judith, chapters of Esther, 1 and 2 Maccabees, Wisdom, Sirach, Baruch, and chapters of the book of Daniel). The Tankh codex (list of books) is based on the Hebrew Bible codex that was codified in the first centuries of the Common Era. The Catholic codex is based on the Greek translation of the Hebrew holy texts known as the Septuagint (circa 200 BCE). Catholic apologists will note this was the codex that Jesus used.
6. YHWH is the personal name of God in the Tankh. It is also known as a tertragrammaton because it has four letters. Observant Jews are generally forbidden to pronounce this holy name and will use nouns such as "Adonai" or "Elohim" instead of the original pronunciation of YHWH.

so will your descendants be" (Gen 15:5). Given the fact that his wife, Sarah, is barren and the patriarchal and agrarian context that stresses the need for male heirs for survival, children and even more so descendants as numerous of the stars must have been perceived by Abraham as a great blessing to look forward to. No reference is made to the afterlife. In fact, as Rabbi Simcha Paull Raphael demonstrates, in the Torah there is no clear doctrine on the afterlife, but rather a this-world orientation.

It is not until the sixth century before the common era that a clear teaching on an afterlife is evident.[7] Among biblical scholars there is little doubt that the ancient Jewish community shared common conceptions about the death and the afterlife with the surrounding Mesopotamian and Near Eastern civilizations. After all, the biblical tradition places Abraham in Mesopotamia (cf. Joshua 24:3). Moreover the authors of the Torah are adamant that Jews should not take part in the Near Eastern practices such as feeding the dead by depositing food into the grave of the dead (Deut 26:14). Prohibitions are generally explicated when there is behavior in need of correction. Thus the prohibition indicates that this behavior occurred. Moreover, the facts that Hebrews buried their dead in ancestral tombs, much like their Mesopotamian counterparts, and refer to death as "to be gathered to one's kin" (Cf. Gen 25:8; Gen 35:29; Gen 49: 29) suggest that they also shared a view similar to the Mesopotamian underworld. In the Torah, in fact, *Sheol* is a close corollary to the Mesopotamian underworld.

One of the earliest references to Sheol is in the Book of Genesis where Joseph, the son of Jacob, says to his brother Reuben, "If any harm came to him [Benjamin], on the journey you undertake, you would send me down to Sheol with my white head bowed in grief" (Gen 42:38). "What is Sheol? What happens to the dead in Sheol? What does it mean to die?" are all important questions, but these question are not clearly answered in this period. Again the Torah is primarily concerned with life, not death. The fact that Joseph is a righteous man who would be sent "down to Sheol" with his head "bowed in grief" indicates Sheol was egalitarian, below in the ground, and a place of grief. Research on the Hebrew terms *nefesh hayyah* or living (Gen 2:7) and *nefesh met* or dead (Leviticus 21:11; Numbers 6:6) provide further insight about ancient Jewish afterlife beliefs: early Jews did not distinguish between body and soul, but rather viewed the person as a unity of body and spirit. When death occurred, what changed was the state of that *nefesh* (breathe, soul, life force, vital energy) that is evident in the qualifier *met*.[8] The dead in Sheol were "a depotentialized psychophysical entity."[9]

---

7. Cf. Simcha Paull Raphael, *Jewish views of the afterlife,* 2nd ed. (New York: Roman and Littlefield Publishing, 2009), 43.
8. In the Hebrew Bible there are three terms used for the soul: *nefesh, ruah,* and *nushamah.* They are used interchangeably without any discernible standard interpretation. These terms function as a standard when referring to the soul in Rabbinic and Kabbalistic circles. However, Kabbalah tradition incorporates them into a tripartite schema for the human soul. Thus *nefesh* is the life energy of the soul that comes with birth. Once that person begins to rise above mere vitalistic existence the *ruah* is awakened, which seems to refer to rational and pseudo-mystical aspects of the soul. Once this soul begins to study Torah and fulfill the commandments, the *neshamah* is awakened. This allows the person to contemplate the divine mysteries (Cf. Raphael, 276).
9. Raphael, 56.

This is similar to the Mesopotamian imagination of the dead as a shade lacking the vitality of their former self.

It is not until the pre-Exilic Period (1250–586 BCE) that Sheol's content is more explicitly revealed. The first book of Samuel provides evidence as to Jewish afterlife beliefs. In the excerpt below King Saul visits a female medium in Endor for purpose of conjuring the Prophet Samuel from the dead:

> The woman asked, "Whom shall I conjure up for you?" He replied, "Conjure up Samuel." The woman then saw Samuel and, giving a great cry, she said to Saul, "Why have you deceived me? You are Saul!" The king said, "Do not be afraid! What do you see?" The woman replied to Saul, "I see a ghost rising from the earth." "What is he like?" he asked. She replied, "It is an old man coming up; he is wrapped in a cloak." Saul then knew that it was Samuel and, bowing to the ground, prostrated himself. Samuel said to Saul, "Why have you disturbed my rest by conjuring me up?" Saul replied, "I am in great distress; the Philistines are waging war on me, and YHWH has abandoned me and no longer answers me either by prophet or by dream; and so I have summoned you to tell me what I ought to do." Samuel said, "Why consult me, when Yahweh has abandoned you and has become your enemy…What is more, Yahweh will deliver Israel and you too, into the power of the Philistines. Tomorrow you and your sons will be with me." (*1 Samuel 28:7-20*)

Interestingly, Samuel is depicted as a "ghost rising from the earth." If this passage is interpreted literally, it suggests that Samuel existed in a space underneath the crust of the earth, the underworld. Most importantly, however, is the fact that Samuel foretells Saul's death and future residence with himself. Take note that in the biblical tradition, Samuel is a great and righteous prophet and the final judge or leader of Israel, who elects the first and second kings of Israel. On the other hand, Saul is not a righteous man; at this point in time he had not only lost YHWH's blessing due to his disobedience, but also broke YHWH's commandment that prohibited necromancy; moreover, Saul commits suicide, which is a serious sin in Judaism. Yet, Samuel reveals that Saul will be with him tomorrow. If we assume that Samuel is in heaven and heaven is a reward for the righteous, then this scene is inconsistent, since Saul is undeservingly rewarded. However, if we understand Sheol as a corollary to Mesopotamian underworld, then no inconsistency ensues, since all the dead suffer the same fate.[10]

Nevertheless within the biblical literature the concept of Sheol evolves. Whereas in the Torah, Sheol is primarily an amoral and Godless space where the dead reside, in the prophetic and wisdom literature written during the post-Exilic Period (586–200 BCE), Sheol is primarily the realm for the wicked.[11] The exile of the tribe of Judah to Babylon (586 BCE) is an important event for this study,

---

10. Christians in fact argue that Sheol was a waiting place for the dead since entering heaven before Christ was impossible. The only exceptions to this are Enoch and Elijah who were assumed into heaven.
11. Raphael, 75.

because it forces Jews to consider more carefully how YHWH's justice functions in light of the fact that the just are persecuted and the unjust prosper. A doctrine of retribution is more clearly formulated in the books written during and after the exile to Babylon. In this period Sheol becomes a place of punishment for the enemies of Israel and YHWH.[12] Nevertheless those punished are the nations who assault the nation of Israel; the idea of individual punishment for sins is not yet a major theme. Gradually this changes, we find for instance in Proverbs a clear reference to individual salvation and damnation, "for an intelligent [righteous] man, the path of life leads upward, in order to avoid Sheol below" (Proverbs 15:24). Nonetheless it is not until final books of the Hebrew Bible (e.g., the Book of Daniel), that collective and individual judgment and reward are synthesized. The context for the synthesis is the doctrine of the resurrection of the body.

Resurrection of the dead becomes an important theme by the end of the biblical period. The resurrection is present in the books of Ezekiel (Ez 37:11-13), Isaiah (Is 26:19), and Daniel (12:1-2). Yet there is no consensus in the Bible or during the rabbinic and modern periods as to what resurrection entails beyond the observation that the soul will be reunited with the body for a final judgment. Resurrection is consistent with the ancient Jewish teaching on the *nefesh:* since the person is a body-soul composite, a disembodied soul is an incomplete existence. Resurrection from the dead reunites the soul to its body, affording that person the opportunity to experience the joys or sufferings of the afterlife in its totality.[13]

The book of Daniel is a watershed in the study of Jewish afterlife because it provides clarity as to how Sheol is synthesized with the resurrection of the dead:

> At that time there shall arise Michael, the great prince, guardian of your people; it shall be a time unsurpassed in distress since the nation began until that time. At that time your people shall escape, everyone who is found written in the book. *Many of those who sleep in the dust of the earth shall awake; Some to everlasting life, others to reproach and everlasting disgrace.* [Italics added] (Daniel 12: 1-2)

What follows is that Sheol is not necessarily a place of torment, but a waiting place for both the just and the unjust until the Resurrection of the dead. Note that in this account all humankind is resurrected, both just and unjust. Here we also find a more definite teaching on everlasting torment and life that will pave the way for Gahenna (Hell) and Gan Eden (Heaven).

---

12. Ibid., 60.
13. I am not suggesting that Jewish afterlife beliefs are solely the result of historical happenstance. For the believer, Jewish afterlife beliefs become more explicit as Jews are faced with new challenges and revelations from YHWH.

Section Three: Modern Judaism and Beliefs in the Afterlife

The end of the biblical period did not end discussion and speculation about the afterlife. After the destruction of Jerusalem by the Romans (70 CE) and execution and exile of the temple priests, the rabbi or teacher became the principal interpreters of the Jewish religious tradition. Their teachings on Jewish afterlife are found in a variety of texts including the Babylonian and Palestinian *Talmud* (circa 400 CE), which contains a variety of rabbinic discussions on various topics, and *Midrash* or rabbinic commentaries on the Torah. Although these texts provide further insight into Jewish afterlife, it is important to note the rabbinic penchant for debate and dialectics. Thus, these texts do not provide definitive answers on Jewish afterlife belief, but rather a variety of possible beliefs. What results is great comfort with a range, often conflicting ideas on important topics such as the afterlife. Today there are very few beliefs about the afterlife that are universally accepted by Jews. Contemporary Jews have a veritable cornucopia of rabbinic reflections from which to choose about the hereafter. Nevertheless belief in Heaven (Gan Eden), Hell (Gahenna),[14] and resurrection are dominant traditions among rabbinic authors of these texts. Today Jews who accept the afterlife generally accept the realities of Heaven, Hell, and the Resurrection. Note that according to a recent Pew study, four in ten Jews in the United States do not believe in an afterlife.[15] Rabbis and Jews that support this perspective note that Judaism stresses this life as opposed to the next life, as well as the fact that Judaism has no dogmas about the afterlife, and the lack of references to the afterlife in the Torah.[16] Nevertheless, as evident in the interview below, within Judaism today there is a growing discontent with this view and appropriation of Jewish afterlife traditions. Scholars such as Rabbi Simcha Paull Raphael are a part of this renaissance and demonstrate that the belief that there is no afterlife in Judaism is misinformed, and is representative of an overly rationalistic and reductionist interpretation of Judaism.[17] He argues that the secularizing rationalism of the enlightenment, negative reaction to Christian notions of the afterlife, and the Holocaust were all important factors in the perpetuation of this tradition.

HEAVEN AND HELL

If you have been raised in North America, when you hear "Heaven" and "Hell" you are likely to think about popular imagery of pearly gates, white angels, but also hellfire, pitchforks, and demonic

---

14. Gan Eden and Gahenna are by no means the exclusive biblical and rabbinic terms used to describe heaven and hell. However, over time they become the most popular terms for heaven and hell.

15. "Summary of Key Findings," *Pew Forum on Religion & Public Life 2007*, http://religions.pewforum.org/pdf/report2religious-landscape-study-key-findings.pdf (May19, 2015).

16. Herman Cohen (1842–1918), an important Jewish-philosopher, argued that Jews do not believe in the immortality of the soul, but rather "social immortality." The dead only live on in the works and memories of their loved ones (Cf. Raphael, 26-27).

17. Ibid., 13.

presences. Although some of this imagery is evident in the Jewish tradition, Jewish interpretations of heaven and hell are different. Hell, for instance, has much more of a punitive function in the Jewish tradition. The Talmud purports that hell lasts for twelve months.[18] The *Zorah,* the most important text of the Jewish mystical tradition known as Kabbalah, argues that during this period the sinner is purged of her sin by fire.[19] The Hasidic Jewish tradition teaches that the fires of hell are requited on the Sabbath and when a tzaddik[20] enters Gahenna. However, the Talmud also assigns eternal torment in Hell to those that deny the resurrection and reject the Torah.[21] There are attempts to reconcile these two views: Nahmanides (1194–1270), a medieval Jewish Rabbi and philosopher, for instance, argues that after twelve months of suffering, the soul does not enter heaven on par with the righteous but is rather placed at the feet of the righteous.[22]

Hell is the inversion of heaven: whereas hell is painful and filled with gradations of torments relative to the sins committed by various sinners, heaven includes gradations of bliss or joy relative to the fidelity and love expressed toward YHWH in life. Heaven or Gan Eden is based on the Garden of Eden depicted in the first book of the Torah, Genesis. In certain Midrash literature, the Garden of Eden is one of the seven realms of heaven. Certain Jewish traditions like Hasidism stress that heaven is a realm of spiritual and moral evolution.[23] In each realm one grows in consciousness about God as well as self-awareness.

Although descriptions of heaven and hell abound in the Jewish tradition there is a discernible pattern of events that occur in the Jewish tradition that include

> an encounter with celestial light, meeting of divine beings who show the way through the landscape of the beyond, a review of life experiences, a process of judgment, and individual realms of torment and bliss.[24]

Synthesizing this observation with the kabalistic sources and Jewish bereavement customs, Rabbi Simcha Paull Raphael argues that there are seven stages in the postmortem journey in the afterlife:

1. Death Process
2. *Hibbat ha-kever* (pangs of the grave)—when the Spirit goes through a three- to seven-day period that releases the soul from attachment to the body
3. Gahenna—Emotional Purification

---

18. *Shabbat* 33b in Raphael, 144.
19. Ibid., 302.
20. Tzaddik means "righteous one." It is usually a Hasidic rabbi that has attained a heightened level of spirituality.
21. Raphael, 145.
22. Ibid., 266.
23. Ibid., 351.
24. Ibid., 369.

4. Lower Gad Eden—Final completion of the Personality
5. Upper Gan Eden—Soul experiences paradise and consciousness continues to mature
6. *Tzor ha-hayyim* (Store house of souls)—the soul receives its directive for its next reincarnation
7. Preparation for Rebirth[25]

This seven-tiered outline of the afterlife provides a guideline for what Jews should expect after death. Throughout this process the soul is purified for an encounter with the living God; whereupon, it is given new directives to prepare it for its next rebirth. Although reincarnation may not be accepted by all Jews, it is within the purview of rabbinic and mystical Judaism. However, reincarnation in a Jewish context is not related to impersonal karma, but rather to YHWH's mission. Reincarnation affords the opportunity to complete the work that YHWH wills. Kabbalists refer to the cycle of reincarnation as the recycling of the souls, the *gilgul*. There are conflicting traditions within this mystical tradition as to the purpose of the gigul, especially, since the soul was purged of its sins in hell. In one tradition, each purging results in the purification of only one of the three parts of soul, the nefesh, ruah, or neshamah.[26] This of course means that every soul should only be reincarnated three times. But there is no consensus as to the amount of reincarnations. However, in the Hasidic Jewish tradition, after you die you are judged by the court of heaven. Reincarnation is one of two options offered to atone for sins. The second option is to be purified in hell.[27]

Nevertheless reincarnation occurs after the disembodied soul has experienced the various realms heaven and then enters *tzor ha-hayyim*. Here the righteous see the glory of YHWH and YHWH's angels, which prepares them for their new life on earth.

RESURRECTION

If the above seven stages provide a general overview of the literature on the afterlife in Judaism during the centuries after the destruction of Jerusalem (70 CE), the doctrine of the resurrection is the closest that Judaism comes to professing a dogma with respect to postmortem existence.[28] Resurrection of the dead is a tenet of Rabbinic Judaism that has dominated the Jewish tradition for almost two millennia.

Nevertheless, when Jews speak about the resurrection they do not mean resuscitation of the body or reanimation into a zombielike state, but a new corporeal-bodily existence that involves the original body.

---

25. Cf. Ibid., 370-394.
26. Ibid., 320.
27. Ibid., 346
28. Another important dogma in this tradition relevant to this study is that a life in pursuit of virtue and interpretation of the Torah results in a painless death and benefit in the afterlife (Cf. Raphael, 291).

In Jewish eschatology, resurrection refers to an event before the final judgment when souls shall re-animate their body. The impact of the dogma of the resurrection is evident in Jewish burial customs and great respect that Jews have toward the body of the deceased. For instance, many Jews buried outside of Israel are buried with "a small stick or dowel" or have earth from the Mount of Olives in Israel sprinkled on their caskets or placed in their mouths. Jewish tradition states that these items help the newly resurrected body travel more quickly to Jerusalem for the final judgment.[29]

Nevertheless how reincarnation coalesces with the Jewish teachings on resurrection and the importance of existence in history—if we have many lives, then one particular life loses its significance—is a matter of debate. This is evidence in the variegated responses by Jewish rabbis, who espouse reincarnation, to the question: which body will we have at the resurrection? Many rabbis see no conflict because they interpret resurrection as a metaphor or spiritual phenomenon that may involve none or all of our bodies. Some, however, teach that resurrection involves only the most recent bodily existence. Nevertheless reincarnation does not necessarily conflict with resurrection as reincarnation is circumscribed within time as we know it and does not continue after the resurrection; moreover, the resurrection occurs at the end of time or outside of time as we experience it.

Section Four: Dying Well and Care for the Dying

It is important to reiterate that many Jews are simply ignorant of wealth of images about the afterlife and theological meanings associated with their end-of-life customs that their tradition offers. This ignorance may contribute to an inability for these Jews to achieve peace regarding the spiritual dimension of their life.

Based on the Pew study mentioned above, the belief that Judaism is a religion that focuses on this life is a dominant idea in North American Jewish identity. Nevertheless, the Jewish tradition provides a wealth of rituals associated with dying and bereavement that have been collected in Jewish law (*Halakha* or *Halakhah*). With respect to the end of life, Jewish law addresses a variety of circumstances, from visiting the sick to directives on how to mourn for the dead.[30] Note that how strictly a Jew follows Jewish law is to an extent relative to Jewish communities: whereas Orthodox Jews strictly adhere to Jewish law, Reform, Reconstructionist and Conservative Jews may adhere to Jewish law strictly or interpret Jewish law as a reference point and guide.[31] Reformed and Reconstructionist

---

29. Ibid., 160.
30. *Mourning in Halachah* is the most comprehensive text regarding Jewish law on dying and bereavement available in English. (Rabbi Chaim Binyamin Goldberg, *Mourning in Halachah: The Laws and Customs of the Year or Mourning*, Brooklyn: Mesorah Publications, 2012) Note that work has wide appeal in Orthodox Jewish communities.
31. Cf. John Loike, Ph.D, Muriel Gillick, M.D., Stephan Mayer, M.D., Kenneth Prager, M.D., Jeremy R. Simon, M.D.,

Jews recognize that Jewish law is a mutable document that reflects a particular socio-historical context that may not be entirely relevant to contemporary life.[32]

Interestingly, Rabbi Simcha Raphael collocates these laws with Jewish teaching on the afterlife, arguing that each of the prescribed practices benefit the deceased as it travels through the seven stages of postmortem existence. Although Jewish patients may not be cognizant of this, these practices remain an important part of their religious and cultural identity. Therefore, anything that a healthcare worker can do to help facilitate these practices will be a great assistance to the deceased. As I will demonstrate below, how the body is treated after death is important for many Jews, and thus assuring the dying that their expectations will be respected shall help facilitate a positive death for them.

COPING WITH DEATH

Jewish law addresses three important aspects of coping with death: (1) visiting the sick, (2) the confession of the dying (*Viduy*), and (3) the threshold of Death (*Goses*).

It may seem odd to include visiting the sick as a key component of coping with death, but Judaism is a communal religion, and thus Judaism is attuned to the importance of addressing the social dimension of a person. Visiting the sick is a *mitzvah* or commandment, and thus the duty of every Jew. Close friends and relatives are therefore required to visit their loved ones who are seriously ill. The mitzvah consists of

> (a) Praying for him. (b) Cleaning and mopping the room, or making sure that his relatives do so, or seeing to any other material needs of the patient. (c) Speaking to him in an understanding manner, to encourage, strengthen, and calm him; sitting with him or watching him if he so requests.[33]

We might add that the mitzvah also requires that a group of people and not simply one individual meet with the dying person.

The psychological and sociological benefits are evident, as the visitors are required to not only confirm the dying in their faith but also attend to their basic material and individual needs. Interestingly, the Jewish tradition forbids mourning to begin until the person has died. This may seem un-

---

Ph.D., Avraham Steinberg, M.D., Moshe D. Tendler, Ph.D., Mordechai Willig, M.S., and Ruth L. Fischbach, Ph.D., "The critical role of religion: Caring for the dying patient from an Orthodox Jewish perspective," *Journal of Palliative Medicine* 13.10 (November 10, 2010): 1-5; see also Anita Diamant, *Saying Kaddish: How to comfort the dying, bury the dead, and mourn as a Jew* (New York: Schocken Books, 1998), 5-7. In addition to Halakha, local synagogues may have their own customs known as *minhagim*.

32. Diamant, 126.
33. Goldberg, 1:20.

necessary, but the point of this law is to prevent visitors from objectifying the dying as a "corpse in waiting."[34] Note that the goal for visiting the ill person is to benefit the dying, and the commandment to visit the sick is not fulfilled unless the visit provides benefit to the patient![35]

Rabbi Simcha Raphael offers some suggestions as to how visitors and caregivers can benefit dying patients. He argues that the goal is to help the dying realize they are spiritual beings. If they are unable to respond, at the very least visitors can create a sacred space at the deathbed with fragrances as well as music that can help evoke the spiritual dimension of a person.[36] If patients are conscious, Rabbi Simcha Raphael encourages visitors and caregivers to ask them about their life story and earliest memories. He offers a simple meditation that is facilitated by asking patients to visualize themselves in varied states of their life (e.g., as a child, teenager, newlywed). If the illness does not permit this, then simply placing family pictures nearby, at eye level, may be sufficient. This helps the dying prepare for death, not only to find closure at the emotional and psychological levels, but also to be better prepared for the life review that occurs after death.[37]

VIDY

Vidy is a prayer confessing to YHWH the wrongdoing of the dying. This should be recited in the presence of only persons learned in the Torah and when patients are near death. In each case, the patient, rabbi, relatives, and friends may recite it.[38] Usually the visiting rabbi from the patients' synagogue leads the recitation. With respect to the psychological and sociological dimension of the dying, the vidy is a way of saying farewell to those you love and amend relationships before one dies.[39]

One need only examine the short version of the prayer that is used for Jews unable to say the long prayer to see the merit gained:

> I acknowledge before You, Hashem, my God and God of my fathers, that my recovery or death is in Your hands. May it be Your will that You heal me completely, but if I die, may my death be atonement for all the mistakes, sins, and rebellions I have erred, sinned, and rebelled before You. May my portion be in Gan Eden, and may You allow me to be in the World to Come, which lies in store for the righteous.[40]

---

34. Diamant, 34.
35. Goldberg, 1:22.
36. Raphael, 408.
37. Cf. Zorah II, 222a in Raphael, 408.
38. For a succinct overview of the liberal Jewish perspective on dying, death, and bereavement see http://www.myjewishlearning.com/ix_author.php?aid=46486 that contains articles and excerpts from books by Anita Diamant.
39. Within in an Orthodox Jewish context, this prayer is reserved for only those persons near death. The rationale is that it could have adverse effects if it is recited hastily, breaking the spirit of the patient.
40. Goldberg, 2:5.

This prayer stresses YHWH's forgiveness and the soul's entrance into heaven. A sincere confession must accompany this prayer, asking forgiveness from anyone that the person has sinned against. Interestingly, the stress in this ritual is not ensuring a good place for the soul in the afterlife, but rather helping patients to be more at peace with death, providing for their spiritual and psychological dimensions.

GOSES

A *goses* is a person in the last hours of her life. When this is evident, visitors are required to stay with the person. Although not universally accepted, it is custom in many communities that the soul leaves the body after taking its last breath. The "last breath" is indicative of cardiopulmonary failure, not necessarily brain failure. For this reason some Jews, particularly from Orthodox communities, reject the neurological criteria for determining death.[41]

Nevertheless, ascertaining when the last moment of life occurs is important. Not unlike the Eastern traditions, a good death for a Jew is one that is peaceful with little anxiety. There are a variety of Jewish laws to help ensure this occurs by regulating behavior around a dying person. Generally speaking, a good death involves dying in the presence of loved ones and without unnecessary disturbances.

Dying affords final opportunities to enter into YHWH's presence. For this reason in addition to reciting Psalms 121, 130, and 92 that praise YHWH for YHWH's righteous and speak of the rewards YHWH has for those who are faithful to YHWH, at the moment of death the Shema should be recited:

> Hear, O Israel: The Lord is our God, the Lord alone. You shall love the Lord your God with all your heart, and with all your soul, and with all your might. Keep these words that I am commanding you today in your heart. Recite them to your children and talk about them when you are at home and when you are away, when you lie down and when you rise. Bind them as a sign on your hand, fix them as an emblemon your forehead, and write them on the doorposts of your house and on your gates. (Deut 6:4-9)

The Shema is less a prayer than a proclamation of YHWH's oneness. On the centrality of the Shema to the Vidy rite, Anita Diamant, author of *Mourning in Halachah*, writes, it is the "ultimate reconciliation of the soul with the Holy One of Blessing, *Echad*, whom Jews also call Adonai. In many ways, the Shema says 'Yes.' In its own way, the Shema says 'Amen.'"[42] Diamant stresses that the recitation of the Shema at the moment of death helps the dying accept and come to peace with YHWH's will.

---

41. Cf. Loike, 3.
42. Goldberg, 3:7.

Funeral Rights

Death begins a period of ritual preparation for burial. The wealth of laws and customs that Jews have regarding the preparation of the body, funeral, and mourning may seem odd to a non-Jew given the fact that Jews do not emphasize belief in the afterlife, or like Buddhists and Hindus teach that how the body is treated influences the soul. Note that in the upcoming interview Rabbi Lazarus-Klein makes little mention of merit gained by these traditions (i.e., rationale about how these customs influence the fate of the soul). Rather his emphasis is that Jews take special care to follow these laws and customs out of respect for the dead. In fact, the best-selling text on this topic, *Saying Kaddish: How to Comfort the Dying, Bury the Dead & Mourn as a Jew*, is bereft of any mention of the afterlife. Notwithstanding the traditional stress on respect for the dead, Simcha Paull Raphael, whose research has great appeal to a liberal Jewish audience, demonstrates that these customs are indeed linked to a theology of an afterlife and benefit the deceased.[43]

Nevertheless Jewish laws provide space, time, and support for the dying and bereaved. The community and ancient tradition guides mourners through some of the most difficult times in their life, directly addressing the social, psychological, and spiritual dimensions of the bereaved persons. Judaism provides a task-oriented approach to grief that involves mitzvot for the bereaved and Jewish community.

Depending upon the individual Jew and community, these tasks will be treated as simply guidelines or laws to be closely followed. Even in the most progressive communities, Jewish law on bereavement is important. This being the case, any conversation caregivers have with terminally ill patients and family on handling the patient's body after death will be beneficial.

Respect for the dead, like respect in life, involves avoiding actions that interfere with YHWH's natural processes, or can foster inappropriate treatment of the body. Because we come from the "dust and return onto dust," any action that expedites or slows decomposition, cremation, or embalmment are generally interpreted as inappropriate.

Dignity and equality are also two very important themes necessary to keep in mind to understand Jewish views on dying and death. Unlike the Eastern religions, the body is not seen as a husk for the soul. Following from the belief in the resurrection and lack of dualism that bifurcates the body from the soul, the body is an integral part of the person. Dignity and respect afforded the person in life are extended to the person in death. Death is likened to a state of intense vulnerability; thus just as we should respect the vulnerable and treat them with dignity, we should treat the dead with dignity. To

---

43. He superimposes the Kabalistic theology of the soul and postmortem existence over the seven main elements of Jewish mourning: Aninuat, Funeral, Shivah, Shloshim, Kaddish, Yarhrzeit, and Yizkor. (See chapter eleven in *Jewish Views of the Afterlife*.)

this end there are specific rules regarding conduct around the corpse such as the body is never left alone, genitals are always covered, and the body should not be mutilated. For these reasons medical activities such as autopsies and organ donations are not acceptable.[44] Because embalming the body is not the custom, burial occurs as soon as possible.

With respect to equality, death in the Jewish tradition is treated as the ultimate equalizer among people: we all come from YHWH and return to YHWH. Therefore, Jewish funerals are simple without ornament: the bodies are placed in a simple burial shroud (*tachrichin*) and casket (*aron*).

Equality and respect are particularly evident in the preparation of the body for burial. As not only do all Jews undergo the same process, but the associated customs emanate respect for the person. In Jewish law, once the patient dies, the preparation of the body for the burial begins immediately. The term for the bereaved relative in this state is an *onen*. Depending upon the community, the *Chevra Kaddisha*, or Jewish burial society, which includes members of the same sex from the local synagogue or Jewish community, prepare the body for burial. In many instances Jewish funeral home directors fulfill this duty. Often the *Chevra Kaddisha* and the funeral home directors work in tandem. During this period the bereaved loved ones are obliged to make burial arrangements, and they may fast from alcohol and meat; they are also relieved of all the positive commandments.

The funeral arrangements include meeting with the rabbi of the deceased's congregation and planning the funeral, eulogy, and mourning customs. Interestingly, Jewish funeral and bereavement customs reverse Christian and Western secular customs. In Western society, viewings and activities to support the family occur before the burial. However, in Judaism, there are no viewings, and support for the bereaved occurs during the seven-day mourning period immediately after burial. The goal is to give the bereaved time to care for their dead and then to set aside time to mourn their loved ones.

Chevra Kaddish has an important function to prepare the body for burial. They perform various rituals and prayers, including standing watch by the body.[45] One of the most important rituals is the *taharah* or purification of the body that entails a ritual washing (*mikvah*) within three hours of the funeral. Note that the rabbi does not have a role in the *Chevra Kaddish*; the rabbi's function is to plan and then officiate at the funeral and burial.

The funeral generally occurs within 24 to 48 hours after death. Nevertheless, Sabbath and holy days take precedence over funerals, and thus the funeral will be scheduled after these events. In a Reformed community, the funeral may occur in a synagogue or at the site of burial.

---

44. Although this is the normative tradition, many conservative and progressive Jews donate their organs because they believe that in accordance with Jewish law, saving a life is a great merit and outweighs the prohibition against mutilating the corpse.

45. The person that stands vigil near the body is known as a *shomer*; he or she reads the Psalms to the body.

The funeral consists of four parts: the eulogy, Ker'iah (tearing of the garments), readings from the Tankh, and a memorial prayer. Afterwards the family processes with the casket to gravesite. The procession stops seven times to show the difficulty of losing their loved one and then the casket is lowered into the ground. The Mourner's Kaddish, one of the most powerful prayers in the Jewish tradition, is recited:

> May His great Name grow exalted and sanctified in the world that He created as He willed. May He give reign to His kingship in your lifetimes and in your days, and in the lifetimes of the entire Family of Israel, swiftly and soon. (Mourners and Congregation: Amen. May His great Name be blessed forever and ever.) Blessed, praised, glorified, exalted, extolled, mighty, upraised, and lauded be the Name of the Holy One (Mourners and Congregation: Blessed is He, beyond any blessing and song, praise and consolation that are uttered in the world. Amen) May there be abundant peace from Heaven and life upon us and upon all Israel. (Mourners and Congregation: Amen) He Who makes peace in His heights, may He make peace, upon us and upon all Israel. (Mourners and Congregation) (Amen)

Oddly, this prayer neither mentions death nor petitions YHWH for mercy on behalf of the dead. It may seem out of sync with a funeral; however, this prayer celebrates life and is meant to reaffirm the Jewish faith in YHWH, the Lord of Life. It gives comfort to the mourners, helping to transition them to the official bereavement process.

Mourner's Kaddish, in fact, begins the *shivah* period or the requisite seven-day period of mourning. This is a formal period of mourning where immediate family members of the deceased suspend normal activity to bereave and accept YHWH's will. The home of the mourners, which is usually the home of the deceased, is transformed into a house of mourning. This extends beyond simply refraining from work and pleasurable activities, as the home of the mourners is transformed into a space conducive to mourning for the dead, which may include sitting close to the ground, covering mirrors, lighting memorial candles, and leaving doors open for mourners from the community to enter and leave freely without disturbing the family. Today many funeral homes offer "shiva kits" that may include benches for "sitting shivah," directions, yarmulkes, and a shivah candle.[46] The focus of this period is to reminisce and share experiences with the deceased and grief in a safe space.[47] This is such an intense period of mourning that it is not appropriate for mourners to read the Torah because the Torah affirms life.

---

46. Diamant, 115-116.f
47. Ibid., 120.

During the first evening of shivah, a "meal of consolation" or *seudat havra'ah* is provided by friends and family that consists of foods that are round, symbolizing the cyclical nature of life.[48] Psychological overtones are clear: death is as natural as life. Nevertheless, the mourners are not abandoned but continually visited by friends and family. In some communities it is custom for ten men from the synagogue (a *minyan*) to visit the home and recite morning, afternoon, and evening prayer. It is a commandment for Jews to console mourners, and this period is a time for prayerful reflection and a gradual reacclamation to life without their loved one.

During shivah it is a popular custom to study Mishnah. Interestingly the Hebrew sounds that form the work Mishnah, "M Sh N H" when shifted to "N Sh M H" form the word for the soul or neshamah.[49] The implication is that by reading these texts, one benefits the soul of the deceased.

Shivah ends on the seventh day when the mourners ceremoniously leave the home of the deceased and then reenter it. This tradition serves to symbolize the reentry into life without the loved one. This ends the most intense period of mourning.

The next period of mourning is *shloshim* that is a thirty-day transition period. During this period the family gradually reenters the daily routines of life. Albeit not as restrictive as the prohibitions during shivah, Jewish law stipulates various prohibitions against cutting hair and listening to music. The goal is to prevent those who mourn from rushing back into the routine of life.[50] Note that the thirty-day period of mourning is extended for children mourning the loss of a parent.[51]

The deceased are continually remembered in the liturgy or religious services. On the anniversary of the death or *yahrzeit* the family will honor the dead by visiting the synagogue to light a candle, praying the Kaddish, or simply taking time out of the day to pray for their loved one. Remembering the dead is also required on the holy days of Yom Kippur, the last day of Sukkoth, Passover, and Shavuot.[52]

CARING FOR THE DYING

Health professionals should be aware that being present during a Jew's last moments is considered a sacred privilege. Considering this fact, heath professionals need to do their best to be respectful of their patients' religious practices. The most important action is perhaps the most simple: to ask patients about their religious tradition and any special requests that they want. Depending on the religiosity of the Jewish patient as well as her interpretation of Jewish law, their end-of-life requests

---

48. Raphael, 430.
49. Ibid., 430.
50. Diamant, 137.
51. Refer to the interview below for more information on this topic.
52. Raphael, 445.

may include seeking confirmation that their tradition is kept, which may mean that the health professional ensures that the patients' religious tradition will be honored with respect to not leaving them alone during the final moments of life and after death, as well as disturbing the corpse as little as possible. With exception to Orthodox Jews, Jewish patients do not generally make requests that are discernibly different than the general public.

Regarding healthcare decisions, Judaism stresses that YHWH is the author of life; it forbids any activity that hastens death. Thus euthanasia is not acceptable. Some rabbis, especially in Orthodox communities, are disconcerted with opiates like morphine that hasten death; however, there is consensus that medication to relieve pain for the terminally ill is necessary.[53] Generally speaking, Jews, especially from the Reformed tradition, have little hesitation with using palliative drugs or undergoing treatments that will prolong their life. However, in addition to their stress on the sacredness of life, they also believe not to frustrate YHWH's will. Thus treatments that are considered burdensome may be rejected. Life is given and taken away by the Lord YHWH.

At the same time living wills and DNR orders may pose ethical issues to Jews because they can be interpreted as frustrating YHWH's will for life. Thus doing YHWH's will informs decisions addressing their physical task. Nevertheless, a distinction is made by many authorities on Jewish law regarding "continuous form of life-sustaining treatment" and "intermittent form of life-sustaining treatment." Whereas discontinuing the former (e.g., taking the patient off a ventilator, whose condition is improving) is interpreted as murder, morality of discontinuing the latter (e.g., chemotherapy) is relative to the situation. Thus Jewish views toward medical care are not unlike the Catholic emphasis on the distinction between ordinary and extraordinary means.

With respect to caring for terminally ill Jewish patients, caregivers who are sensitive to Jewish patients' needs mentioned above will provide the most effective care. This may include, if they choose, putting patients in touch with a local Jewish rabbi or Jewish chaplain. Also if they choose, talk with them about the afterlife, as this is not uncommon especially for secularized Jews, who do not know about their tradition's teachings on this matter, and you are comfortable with this conversation, it is appropriate to speak of the ideas mentioned above by Simcha Paull Raphael, or offer them resources to Jewish views on the afterlife. All of the following actions address patients' spiritual and psychological dimensions.

With regard to their social dimension, forming a schedule for treatments around religious services and visitors is very helpful. Judaism is a social religion that requires the rabbi, members of the synagogue, family, and friends to be present to the dying; thus expect frequent and many visitors. A rabbi's visits include not only pastoral care but prayer and confession; and thus minimizing inter-

---

53. Loike, 2.

ruption during this time will be helpful. Also if the visitor is a conservative or Orthodox Jew from out of town, and they visit on a Friday, they are most likely intending to spend the night with the patient, since the Sabbath begins at dusk and observant Jews are forbidden to travel during the Sabbath. If death is imminent, expect that the visitors will not want to leave the room. As mentioned, the dying and the dead should not be left unattended. If for some reason their family or friends are not present when the patient dies, if possible, stay with the body until family or members of their synagogue arrive. This communicates respect and compassion to the family.

Conclusion

This chapter examined the Jewish religion, beliefs, and practices and offered suggestions on effective healthcare, in addition to providing a foundation for the next chapters. Even though Judaism is a religion that stresses the blessing of this life to the point where many Jews reject the afterlife, nevertheless Jews, perhaps more so than the religions discussed thus far, take extraordinary care of the dying and the dead, as to do otherwise is to disrespect a life that God created. Although Christianity does not share that same stress, the beliefs in the afterlife and many practices are appropriated into its own.

Interview

Rabbi Alex Lazarus-Klein is a member of the Reformed and Reconstructionist movement. He currently serves as the sole rabbi at *Congregation Shir Shalom* in Williamsville, New York. This is a newly merged congregation of Reform and Reconstructionist traditions.

Q: What is your role when your congregant is dying?

A: Often we do not get the call until after the person has died. If someone is in hospice and I get called, we say traditional prayers of forgiveness. They are connected to King David asking for forgiveness after the Bathsheba incident. Before death there is a confession. But confession is not primary as you will find in other religious traditions. Many Jews are unaware of it. I will also attend to the needs of the family by gathering them together to pray, to be present to the person, and say goodbye to the person. The Shema is then prayed from Deuteronomy. The ideal death is to say the Shema as you die.

Q: You mentioned confession. Can you speak a little more about this?

A: There is something called *Teshuvah*, which is repentance. This is a part of everyday prayer and the liturgy. You are supposed to pretend that you die when you say it. The tradition is that you are allowed to say it up until the moment of your death. Since we do not know when this is going to happen, by saying it daily you have a regular cycle of repentance. The great thing about Judaism is that there is this cycle of purification. There is a kind of early preparation for death, so that you have had the opportunity to make amends with your loved one before you die.

There is also a modified prayer (*Tachanun*) that is about confessing things you have done wrong. Here you ask God for forgiveness.

Q: What do Jews believe about the afterlife?

A: The thing about Jews is that often liberal Jews or non-Orthodox Jews know very little about Jewish customs related to the afterlife. There is this feeling that the Christians took over the afterlife, so Jews only think about life. There has been a shying away about afterlife beliefs.

We do believe that the soul is present. During the first week after death it is more present when it is going through these birth pangs, as it moves into the afterlife. The soul returns at times. During the first year, I tell my congregants that you should expect some type of communication from their deceased loved one (e.g., appearance in a dream). In the scientific community that studies this phenomenon, they say that these experiences are healthy and good for the healing process. I concur with this research. My family has had an experience like this. After my wife's grandfather died, he visited my wife in a dream to suggest to her the name of our unborn child.

Q: Does Heaven exist?

A: Yes, we believe in *Gan Eden*, the Garden of Eden. There is this peaceful place where the souls collect. It is where we connect to God.

Q: Do you teach reincarnation?

A: It is a part of mainstream Judaism. As a liberal Jewish rabbi, I would say that we do not know about it. But it is in our tradition.

Q: I have noticed that especially with respect to Jewish afterlife beliefs there seems to be comfort with a variety of beliefs about the afterlife. The stress in Judaism seems to be on the discussion about the beliefs as opposed to the answers arising from the discussion. Is this an accurate interpretation?

A: This is Rabbinic Judaism. For instance, in the Talmud there are no answers, rather debates between varieties of opinion. The only reason why you know the answer is because one of those opinions became the established practice. Belief was allowed to have variation and debate. It is perfectly permissible to have different understanding about the afterlife. Nevertheless, there are certain parts of the story of Judaism that are unquestionable, such as the restoration of the dead and belief in the afterlife. Nevertheless how these beliefs are expressed is less dogmatic.

Q: You mentioned the restoration or resurrection of the dead. What is the resurrection of the dead?

A: Among liberal Jews this is a difficult teaching. There is a lot of discomfort with dead bodies coming back, but also today persons are brought back to life after being clinically dead. In certain communities the stress is simply on God's power to bring forth life. Personally, I do not like the idea of an afterlife where the body is so central. But our burial practices are very much connected to the resurrection. Nevertheless, even this is changing. Among Jews, 5 to 10 percent cremate their dead. Traditionally this would have been frowned upon because it goes against the Jewish narrative involving resurrection. This frustrates the resurrection. There is a broad spectrum, and Jewish burial homes accommodate whatever Jews are comfortable with.

Q: When does death occur?

A: There is a period where life has no longer any value. This is called *Goses*. This is an in-between state, and you are allowed to let the body die. In terms of the actual moment when death occurs, it is difficult to describe. You can tell when life has left. Jewish death is connected to medical death.

Q: What are your best and worst experiences with the dying?

A: Most deaths are very peaceful. Even in the case of tragedy, once the person accepts death, there is peace. I have not had a tragic experience. Nevertheless, sudden death is hardest on the family. It is hardest on the soul, too, if the soul is not ready. There is confusion for the soul.

Q: Is there anything you would do differently in the case of sudden death or the death of a child in terms of Jewish rituals and law?

A: This is the worst part of my profession. Thankfully I have not experienced this. However, there is something that you would do differently. You would spend a lot more time with the family.

Suicide is tricky. Pastorally, my goal is to get the family to talk about it as a mental disease, untreatable depression. If the family is able to do this, it helps them to the next stage of mourning. When I was a chaplain, there was a nun who taught that grief kills. This is true; it is important to help them avoid this.

Q: What is a good death?

A: A good death is a good life. Death is one of those things we do not fully understand. It depends on the person.

Q: After the congregant dies, what are the next steps?

A: The family first contacts the funeral home. I always tell the family to do their best to leave the body in the room as long as they can before it is moved to the morgue. Hopefully the funeral home can collect it quickly. When it is brought to the funeral home it is watched. There are people who are paid to read Psalms in the presence of the body until the funeral. Traditionally, the funeral happens within 24 hours. Today, due to the fact the immediate mourners may be out-of-town or the cemetery may be closed, we have to wait. Moreover, funerals are never performed on Jewish holidays and the Sabbath. In terms of the Chevra Kaddisha, the family contacts them. There are two Chevra Kaddisha groups in Buffalo. They clean the body in a particular manner, dress the body, and prepare it for the burial at the funeral home. Generally speaking there are no viewings in Judaism.

In terms of the family, I meet with family. They talk about their loved one, and I help them plan the funeral and eulogy. They arrive the hour before the funeral, where the family can greet friends and relatives, if they wish. I stress that this is their time to grieve, and thus they can forego the traditional greeting.

Before the funeral there is Kariah, or the tearing of the ribbon. This is a tiny black ribbon that goes on the right side of the mourners; however, it is placed on the left side of a child's chest near the heart. Then a blessing is said. The ribbon is ripped. We pray again and then we start the funeral. The funeral consists of psalms, a eulogy, and a prayer for the soul to find peace. From the funeral home, if it occurs there, we proceed to the cemetery. We make seven stops carrying the casket to the place of burial to symbolize the days of creation. Afterwards the casket is lowered and we begin to cover it with dirt. We start with the back of the shovel to symbolize the difficulty of losing a loved one and then turn it around to fill the grave with dirt. Conservative rabbis will fill the grave or at least cover the casket with dirt. Then we say the Mourner's Kaddish, which is the beginning of the next stage. In liberal Judaism men and women are equal, so both sexes participate in this holy prayer. This is one of our most powerful traditions that speak about death and life. It is recited slowly in a monotone voice.

After this there is a meal of consolation that is usually at a restaurant. Then we have Shivah. Shivah usually refers to the people staying in their homes to mourn. But today it more generally refers to the bereavement service. Usually the mourners spend one or two evenings in their home. The services are in the home. The services are about telling the person about the lives of their loved ones. Orthodox Jews spend seven days in mourning in their homes, and all of the services are performed in the home. However, holidays and Sabbath stop Shivah.

Q: What is the hardest death for a Jew?

A: The loss of a parent traditionally requires eleven months of mourning. It is the hardest death. Today we would say the death of a child, but unfortunately, especially before modern medicine, the loss of a child happened frequently.

Q: Why is the preparation of the body so important for Jews?

A: In Judaism this is the way to purify the difficult experience of losing a loved one. These rituals cleanse that experience. In some way, this is the way to prepare them for the afterlife. In the afterlife everything is simple.

Q: Is it incorrect to state that these rituals gain merit for the deceased in the afterlife?

A: No, but it is really the rituals after the funeral, such as the Mourner's Kaddish that accomplish this.

Q: What do you do when there is no corpse?

A: This is partially why cremation is allowed. During the Holocaust there were so many bodies that were burned and disfigured. A lot of the stigmas about cremation left: what are you saying about all of the children that were cremated by the Nazis if you prohibit cremation? Nevertheless, you still bury whatever you have. Unfortunately, if the body is not recovered it is a problem, especially if there is no confirmation of death. Our society is trapped in this, too.

Q: Are there any laws are customs that frustrate Jewish rituals?

A: The only issues have to do with the speed of burial. Not only do cemeteries close on U.S. holidays, but it is difficult to transfer bodies across state lines. This is often the case when trying to transport a body from Florida to New York.

Q: Are autopsies permissible?

A: It is discouraged. But sometimes you do not have a choice if police are involved. Judaism believes that the law of the state comes first, so long as the law is not unethical.

Q: What is the Jewish perspective on letting a person die versus euthanizing that person?

A: There is a story that illustrates this. There was a maid of a great rabbi. Rabbi was dying, but his life was being prolonged by the efforts of his students. She said to the students, "I hope your prayers keep him alive." Nevertheless she sees that he is suffering needlessly because of the students' efforts.

So she drops a pot off the roof to get the attention of the students away from the rabbi, so that he can die. It works, and the rabbi dies. Letting someone die is ethical.

Personally, I do not think we should keep people alive that are dying. But there is a fine line between killing and letting die. The latter is permitted in Judaism. We do not believe in keeping a person alive at all costs. I reject euthanasia, but if you consider the use of morphine euthanasia, then I accept it.

Q: Is there any specific advice that you would give to a health professional whose Jewish patient dies before the family, rabbi, or funeral home arrives?

A: They should try to keep the body from leaving the room. If they can remain with the body, so that it is not alone, this is important. But it is within their purview. Also leave everything in the body (feed tubes, etc.).

Q: What advice do you have for health professionals who care for Jewish patients?

A: Contact a rabbi if the patient is connected to a community. Jews in America, outside of Orthodox Jews, operate like any other American. I wish pastoral care was more prioritized in healthcare, but it isn't.

CHAPTER NINE

CHRISTIANITY

Introduction

The Christian religion professes a message of hope premised on the belief that every person despite wrongdoings or merits is worthy of love because they are redeemed by the Son of God, Jesus Christ. This message of hope, love and redemption continues to inspire more than 2.5 billion Christians to spread the "good news" of Christianity throughout the world. Despite declining numbers of Christians in Western nations, Christianity is not only the largest but the fastest growing world religion. Moreover, Jesus Christ continues to fascinate and occupy the attention of not only devout Christians, biblical scholars, theologians, and archeologists but also popular Western culture. This is nowhere more evident than in the staggering amount of literature published annually about Jesus and in films portraying Jesus that are among the highest grossing productions.[1]

For the purpose of clarity, this chapter will be divided into six sections. Section One briefly introduces Christian revelation, Jesus Christ, and Church history; Section Two briefly examines the central Christian doctrines; Section Three examines Christian afterlife belief. Because the Catholic

---

1. Mel Gibson's *The Passion of Christ* (2004) grossed over $370 million and remains one of the highest grossing films in U.S. box office history. Recently, *Son of God* (2014), an adaption of the Jesus scenes from the miniseries *The Bible: The Epic Ministries* (2013) was number two at the box office during its opening week.

Church is the largest Christian denomination, Section Four will examine dying, death, and burial traditions primarily from the Catholic perspective. Section Five examines effective end-of-life care for Catholics. The chapter's concluding interview is with Father Peter Drilling, Catholic theologian, priest, and rector at St. Joseph Cathedral in Buffalo, New York.

Section One: Christian Revelation

SACRED SCRIPTURE

Christians believe that Jesus Christ, the founder of Christianity, is the Jewish messiah foretold in the Hebrew Bible. They argue that he fulfills all of the messianic verses including these verses: Genesis 3:25; Deuteronomy 18:25; 2 Samuel 7:12-13; Isaiah 53: 1-12; Daniel 7:13-14; Micah 5:2; Psalm 22:2, 7-9, 12-19. For this reason Christians use the appellation "Christ" that means messiah to refer to Jesus. Thus "Christ" is not Jesus' surname but demonstrates his authority, and *Christ*ians are therefore followers of Christ. As the Christ, Jesus proclaims a new covenant with God that engenders a more intimate relationship between God and humankind. Whereas the mosaic covenant (the covenant between Moses and YHWH) was premised upon following God's commandments or laws, the new covenant is premised upon the love of God and neighbor (Matthew 22:37-40); it is a covenant written upon the heart as opposed to the rock of Mount Sinai (Cf. Jeremiah 31:33) and dependent upon Christ's ministry, salvific acts, and grace or assistance of God. Nevertheless, the new covenant fulfills as opposed to rejects the mosaic covenant; Christianity began as a messianic movement within Judaism, and therefore Christians accept the Jewish scriptures as revelation. The Jewish Tankh is the Christian Old Testament. Whereas the Catholic and Orthodox Christian traditions accept forty-six books of the Old Testament, Christians who identify with the Protestant tradition accept only thirty-nine books as the Old Testament. The different enumerations of the Old Testament books are related to the different Jewish codices that the Christian traditions use. Whereas Catholic and Orthodox Christians use the ancient Septuagint codex, Protestant Christians dropped this codex in the sixteenth century for the so-called Jamnia codex that Jews have used since at least the second century CE. Nevertheless, all Christian Churches accept the twenty-seven books that comprise the New Testament as Sacred Scripture or God's revelation about Godself.

The New Testament consists of these texts: the Gospels according to Matthew, Mark, Luke, and John that provide accounts of the life and mission of Jesus Christ; the Acts of the Apostles, a short history of the events in the Christian Church or community that followed Jesus after Jesus' death and resurrection; the Letters of Paul to the Romans, 1 and 2 Corinthians, Galatians, Ephesians, Philippians, Colossians, 1 and 2 Thessalonians, 1 and 2 Timothy, Titus, Philemon, Hebrews; letters of James;

1 and 2 Peter; 1, 2, and 3 John, and Jude that elucidate Christian doctrine, ethics, and practical matters; and Revelation that reveals the final events of history and Jesus' second coming. The four Gospels hold a special significance since they contain the teachings of Jesus and narrative of the events in Jesus' life.

Christians argue that these texts and those of the Old Testament are revelation or God's *inspired* word. Christians recognize that writers of the texts as well as the Church authorities that accept them as revelation were inspired by God to do so. Thus the Sacred Scriptures neither fell out of the heaven nor were dictated by God to human authors, but rather reflect the history, culture, literary genre, and modes of expression of the biblical authors. Interpreting the Scriptures correctly must involve not only a spiritual reading of the text (i.e., to discover how God is speaking to you through the text), but also a discovery of the author's intention.[2] Nevertheless, these texts provide the clearest revelation of Who God is, and thus Christians believe that the canon or official text of the Bible is without error in matters of faith and morals and it is fixed. New revelation is not possible.[3] All Christians stress that the Bible, or the Old and New Testaments, is "the living word" which means that the Sacred Scripture is not meant for memorization/recitation but rather to be lived out, preached, and appropriated to contemporary life so as to spread the good news of Jesus Christ for the salvation of the human race and creation.

JESUS THE CHRIST

In the gospels of Luke and Matthew, Jesus' story begins with an ignoble peasant girl, Miriam or Mary, from a small town called Nazareth. One day the archangel Gabriel visited Mary and announced that God chose her to be the mother of the Jewish Messiah and Son of God. Mary's response to Gabriel's news is known as her *fiat* or her perfect acceptance of God's will. Mary says: "[l]et it be done according to your will." In a Jewish context pregnancy outside marriage was a violation of Jewish law. To complicate matters, because Mary was betrothed or legally married to Joseph,[4] even though she did not yet live with her husband, this pregnancy could have been construed as adultery.

---

2. For a succinct overview of what biblical inspiration means and how to interpret the scriptures, especially from a Catholic perspective, see paragraphs 105-119 of Article III in the *Catechism of the Catholic Church*, 2nd ed. (Vatican: Libreria Editrice Vaticana, 2011).

3. Orthodox and Catholics also accept sacred Tradition or "living tradition." Note that sacred Tradition is understood not as a separate source of revelation but rather the living interpretive tradition of the message of Jesus that is perfectly expressed in the New Testament. Church Tradition produces the New Testament, as the authors were not only members of the Church and transcribing Traditions, but also it is the Church that ultimately accepts their writings as authoritatively inspired by the Holy Spirit.

4. Betrothal was the first stage of Jewish marriage that could take up to one year. (Elizabeth A. Johnson, *She who is: The mystery of God in feminist theological discourse* [New York: Crossroad, 1992], 191.)

To protect Mary from capital punishment, Joseph planned to quietly divorce Mary; however, after a miraculous intervention by an angel in a dream, Joseph believed Mary and embraced her as his wife.

The culminating event of these early events in the story of Jesus' life is the birth of Jesus. Consistent with YHWH's penchant for choosing underdogs, poor marginalized people to be YHWH's prophets and leaders, Jesus' birth was ignominious, as his parents were homeless and unable to find anyone who was willing to give them a room for Mary to give birth to her child in Bethlehem. Only a barn offered respite from the elements for the birth of Jesus. The birth of Jesus or the Nativity is the Christian feast day known as Christmas that Christians celebrate annually on either December 25 (nations influenced by Catholic Christianity), January 6 (Orthodox Church in Armenia), or January 7 (nations influenced by Orthodox Christianity).

Because the New Testament writers were concerned about the teachings and mission of Jesus Christ, there is little in the New Testament regarding the events between Jesus' birth and the beginning of his ministry around age thirty-three.

The next major event in Jesus' life that is recorded in all four Gospels was his baptism by what Christians consider the last and greatest prophet, the forerunner to Christ, John the Baptist, in the Jordan River. Jesus' baptism inaugurated his mission to the world. After forty days of prayer and fasting, Jesus begins his ministry to spread the Good News that the Kingdom of God is at hand, to forgive sins, and to preach that God loves us and is approachable and tender.

Jesus referred to God in radically intimate terms such as "abba" or "daddy" and invited his growing group of followers to do the same. It is precisely this radically personal approach to God that leads him to stress internalizing the laws of Moses, to place the law of Moses in one's heart. Therefore Jesus argued that all the laws are contained in these two commandments: "'Love the Lord your God with all your heart and with all your soul and with all your mind...and the second is like it: 'Love your neighbor as yourself'" (Matt 22: 37; 39). This commandment of love for God and neighbor is not unique to Jesus as it is the heart of the Shema, as well as rabbinic tradition contemporary to Jesus. What is unique is the method by which Jesus preaches and lives out this teaching. Jesus goes out specifically to meet sinners, the ritually impure, or those persons that were ostracized and excluded from Jewish society because of their state of life or poor decisions, and welcomes them back into God's community. In fact, he chooses a tax collector—which was one of the worst professions a Jew could have since tax collectors were considered Jews in league with the occupying Roman state—Levi (or Matthew) to be one of his twelve apostles or leaders of his new church. In opposition to the contemporary Jewish leaders and teachers, Jesus places people before the laws of Moses. Jesus therefore accuses the Pharisees or rabbis as a "brood of vipers" and "white-washed tombs" that teach the law of Moses but miss the entire point of the law: to lovingly encounter the living God and then to reflect this loving encounter in our thoughts, lives, and relationships to all people. Jesus' criticism of the Pharisees, Sadducees, or the Jewish social elite, and the Sanhedrin or the Jewish governing body comprised of Jewish priests, is summarized in his teaching "[t]he Sabbath was made for man, not man for the Sabbath" (Mark 2:22), The Sabbath or day of rest was not meant for humankind to simply appease God by worshipping God in exclusion to life's obligations, but rather the day of rest was a gift from God to enjoy not only God's relationship to humankind but also humankind's relationship to God and all of God's creation. Jesus rejects fundamentalist and legalistic interpretation of scripture and is concerned with people and their relationship with God.

One of the reasons why there is consensus amongst New Testament scholars with doctorates from reputable institutions that Jesus existed and that the New Testament offers credible evidence for Jesus' historical existence, teaching, and death is Jesus' penchant for forgiving sins and speaking from his own authority.[5] A modern reader may gloss over these actions, but for first-century rabbis this is extremely problematic, as only God can forgive sins and good rabbis do not make definitive claims on the basis of their own authority, but rather on the basis of other Jewish teachers. Within a Jewish context, Jesus' actions situate Jesus as either someone who does not understand the Jewish scriptures, an insane person that thinks he is God, or God in the world. The gospel writers and the earliest group of Jesus' disciples tell us that Jesus believed and taught that he was God in the world.

Nevertheless, Jesus' message was not simply to forgive sins and proclaim his divinity, but to teach that the kingdom of God is at hand. The kingdom of God has several aspects. First it is a gift from God.[6] We did not earn or merit it. It is the good news that our alienation from God because of our sins or rejection of God is over if we accept God's forgiveness. Second, entrance into the kingdom of God is predicated upon conversion. This means not only to ask to be forgiven of sin, but also to live radically for Christ: "to gain the kingdom, one must give everything."[7] Christians must continually seek to live out the will of God and repent of their failings. Third, the kingdom of God is also heaven, God's kingdom, which will come to earth soon. Fourth, it is an eschatological event but imminently experienced now. It is present now on earth in Jesus' teachings and his community or Church (Luke 17:20; 10:7, 11). Fifth, the kingdom of God belongs to "the poor and lowly"; this means that not only does God show preference for the poor and vulnerable in our society and that how we treat these "least" in the kingdom of God will be the measure by which we are judged by God (Matthew 25:40); but also to enter the kingdom of God you must be "poor in spirit" or humble and recognize your need for God in all things (Matthew 5:3). The kingdom of God is good news especially for the

5. Throughout the gospels, Jesus ends many of his teachings with the phrase "Amen, amen I say to you." The problem with this phrase for ancient and contemporary rabbis is that it indicates that Jesus presents his teaching as the final and authoritative teaching on that matter. Only God should do this.

6. Cf. "Encyclical Letter *Spe Salvi* of the Supreme Pontiff Benedict XVI to the Bishops Priests and Deacons Men and Women Religious and All the Lay Faithful on Christian Hope," *Vatican* 2007, http://w2.vatican.va/content/benedict-xvi/en/encyclicals/documents/hf_ben-xvi_enc_20071130_spe-salvi.html (June 9, 2015).

7. *Catechism of the Catholic Church*, para. 546.

oppressed because God in the person of Jesus has come to not only free every human being from sin but reveal a means for personal and social transformation.[8] Thus the kingdom of God is concerned with more than personal salvation but rather the salvation of all people. This concern for others prompts Christians to share the good news about the kingdom of God.

Jesus' preaching about this good news, criticism of the legalism of the Jewish leaders, but also his claims to have a divine origin led to his execution. The gospels inform Christians that Jesus was clandestinely sentenced to death by the Sanhedrin for blasphemy; however, because this sentence occurred during the celebration of Passover, ultimately the Jewish leaders handed Jesus over to the Roman authorities, who at this time controlled Israel. After scourging and then humiliating Jesus, under the order of the Roman governor Pontius Pilate, Jesus was crucified (i.e., nailed to a wooden cross), which was a horrific death sentence only given to those accused of capital offenses. What made this death sentence particularly painful was the fact that death was not a result of blood loss from being nailed to a wooden cross, but rather the result of asphyxiation. Exhaustion from breathing would occur, causing irregular heartbeat and then cardiac arrest.

Interestingly, Jesus' death lends further historical credence to his life, because this death was so gruesome and embarrassing, especially to a first-century Jewish followers of Jesus, it is unlikely that it was fabricated. Nevertheless, Christians not only believe that Jesus' death by crucifixion was historical but also that Jesus' death was a redemptive death. Christianity, especially the Catholic and Orthodox traditions, stress the social dimension of human existence. All human beings are connected by their humanity. We are one human family. Jesus, in particular his miraculous birth and death, are very important because in Jesus, God not only enters into our world but enters into what makes us human: all of the joy as well as the hardships and sufferings of the human experience. God did this because God loves humankind and desires to fix humankind's relationship with God, but did not want to violate God's greatest gift, our freedom. The problem is that humankind is marred by sin: we not only have wrong perceptions about what is good for us and what is truth but as individuals and as a society we continually perpetuate bad decisions or sin. Thus while we recognize that child poverty is an evil and have the funds to eradicate it, we do not do so, but rather spend this funding to create weapons that are more efficient at killing people. Some of these weapons are so efficient at killing people that we can never use them. Prioritizing weapons over children in poverty is a sin that many do not realize because as a society we misunderstand what truly is important and prioritize funding accordingly. Jesus offers us a lifeline; he offers us not only hope that things will get better but a way out of the mess of sin. For Christians, Jesus can do this because he is fully human, so he acts on behalf of the human race, yet as God, Jesus can make our salvation possible. Yet Jesus does more than simply reestablish a personal relationship with God. For as God and man, he assumes

8. Donald Senior, "Reign of God," in *The new dictionary of theology*, ed. Joseph A. Komonchak (Collegeville, MN: The Liturgical Press, 1987), 860.

every aspect of the human experience so as to redeem it. Now because of Christ, Christians believe that nothing can separate them from the love of God.

In Jesus Christ's death on the cross God enters willingly into the human experiences of injustice, rejection, suffering, and dying.[9] The most difficult human experiences of suffering and death now take on a new meaning since God not only experienced them, but as God, Who is beyond time and space, Christ's suffering embraces and redeems all human suffering. The image of the cross and suffering of Jesus offers consolation when Christians suffer and die. However, Jesus Christ overcomes death. On the third day, or the first Sunday after Jesus' death, Jesus rose from the dead. Thus suffering and death are also events that offer hope because Christians believe that just as Jesus overcame suffering and death, with Jesus they will overcome suffering and death.

Christians following the Jewish tradition profess belief in the resurrection of the dead at the end of time. However, Christians claim that Jesus was the first to be resurrected and that humankind will eventually be resurrected like Jesus at the final judgment.

After Jesus' resurrection he remains with his apostles (the leaders of Jesus' community, which Jesus calls his Church) and his disciples (other followers of Jesus) for forty days and then ascends into heaven. Before his *Ascension*, Jesus informs his apostles not to begin preaching until they receive the Holy Spirit, and thus to remain in prayer. On the tenth day after the Ascension, the Holy Spirit descends from heaven upon Jesus' apostles and those gathered with them in prayer. This even is known as the *Pentecost*. The Holy Spirit blesses them with gifts including the ability to speak in different languages and confidence to spread the Gospel of Jesus Christ. Afterwards the apostles go out from Jerusalem to spread the good news about Jesus to the entire world.

JESUS CHRIST OF HISTORY AND FAITH

I mentioned at the beginning of the book that the stress on history differentiates Western from Eastern religions. The Christian tradition is a case in point, as the historicity of Jesus and Jesus' church are important to Christians. This is nowhere more evident in the attention and energy that the so-called quest for the Jesus of history as opposed to the Jesus of faith has received. For over a century, beginning with Albert Schweitzer's *The Quest for the Historical Jesus,* there have been three so-called quests to recover the Jesus of history. Search for the historical Jesus is complicated and beyond the scope of this chapter. However it is important to note that the majority of New Testament scholars

---

9. The question, "Why did Jesus have to die for our sins?" is an important question that has occupied the attention of Christian theologians for nearly 2,000 years. The dominant tradition is that Jesus' death atoned for the sins of the human race so as to make salvation for the human race possible. For a good overview on the variety of perspectives offered to this question, see Francis Schussler Fiorenza, "Redemption," in *The new dictionary of theology,* ed. Joseph A. Komonchak, 836-851, Collegeville, Minnesota: The Liturgical Press, 1987.

agree that this search was misguided and idiosyncratic. Luke Timothy Johnson, a respected New Testament scholar, and author of *The Real Jesus: The Misguided Quest for the Historical Jesus and the Truth of the Traditional Gospels,* makes this point and argues that this quest merely reveals what the researchers want to find. Although the New Testament is not a history book it is based in these facts that the majority of respected scholars accept: Jesus was a historical person; he preached and was known for miracle-working, he was crucified, and the earliest followers of Jesus believed that he rose from the dead.[10] It is impossible to separate the Jesus of history from the Jesus of faith without misconstruing the historical Jesus.[11]

History of the Major Christian Churches

Christianity differs from the religions discussed in previous chapters inasmuch as orthodoxy as opposed to orthopraxy is stressed. Christianity is based on the relationship to a God Who is love. However it is without meaning to say that I love someone if I do not know the person I love. Love requires understanding who we love. In Christian tradition how to love God is less important than loving God. The relational nature of Christianity as well as Jesus' stress on his correct interpretation of Jewish law (i.e., what is important is not simply what you do but why you are doing it) have led to a continued stress on orthodoxy in the Christian tradition.

Debate over what constitutes orthodox teaching was the impetus for various divisions as well as reconciliations between several Christian communities that is evident in the myriad of Christian denominations today. Whereas in Judaism the stress is on the debate itself, in Christianity the stress is the synthesis or definitive conclusion.

The first major debate in the Christian tradition is recorded in the Acts of the Apostles. Peter, the leader of the Apostles, as well as James, Paul, and Barnabas gathered in Jerusalem to discuss whether or not Christians must embrace Jewish orthopraxis (Acts 15). Influenced by the declaration of Peter that Christians did not need to be Jews first, the leaders of the burgeoning Christian Church concluded that Gentile (non-Jewish) converts need not become Jews in order to become Christians. This decision paved the course for an eventual break with Judaism as well as much of Jewish orthopraxis. Eventually, especially after the great successes of the apostles in non-Jewish communities, the Jewish cultural identity of the original Church members was lost.

---

10. This does not mean that the gospels or New Testament are history books. Note that the four gospels are theological texts written primarily by early Jewish Christians for a specific purpose, to serve a specific Christian community.
11. For a succinct and accessible overview of the quest for the historical Jesus as well as contemporary methods for evaluating the historicity of the Bible, see Kenneth Atkinson, a "'Historical Jesus' Lesson Plan" at http://www.oxfordbiblicalstudies.com/resource/lessonplan_1.xhtml.

Nevertheless, this meeting in Jerusalem became the precedent for Church polity or governance. Meetings of the bishops, who are the leaders of the Church that the apostles ordained to lead in their absence, occurred frequently throughout Christian history to clarify orthodox teaching. When all bishops in the world were invited to attend, this meeting was called an ecumenical council. All Christians accept the authority of at least the first four ecumenical councils that defined that Jesus is not a lesser God, but God himself (Council of Nicaea, 325 CE); the Holy Spirit is God (Council of Constantinople, 381 CE); Mary is the Mother of God (Theotokos) because Jesus is the second person of the Trinity and a human being (Council of Ephesus, 431 CE), and Jesus' divine and human natures are untied but distinct without mixture (Council of Chalcedon, 451 CE). These teaching have been codified in an ancient prayer and creed known as the Nicene-Constantinopolitan Creed or Nicene Creed that many Christians profess every week during their Sabbath celebration on Sunday. Here is the Nicene Creed:

> I believe in one God, the Father almighty, maker of heaven and earth, of all things visible and invisible. I believe in one Lord Jesus Christ, the Only Begotten Son of God, born of the Father before all ages. God from God, Light from Light, true God from true God, begotten, not made, consubstantial with the Father; through him all things were made. For us men and for our salvation he came down from heaven, and by the Holy Spirit was incarnate of the Virgin Mary, and became man. For our sake he was crucified under Pontius Pilate, he suffered death and was buried, and rose again on the third day in accordance with the Scriptures. He ascended into heaven and is seated at the right hand of the Father. He will come again in glory to judge the living and the dead and his kingdom will have no end.

> I believe in the Holy Spirit, the Lord, the giver of life, who proceeds from the Father and the Son, who with the Father and the Son is adored and glorified, who has spoken through the prophets. I believe in one, holy, catholic and apostolic Church. I confess one Baptism for the forgiveness of sins and I look forward to the resurrection of the dead and the life of the world to come. Amen.[12]

Christian leaders and their followers who did not agree with conclusions of these councils no longer remained in communication with the majority of Christians. From the time of Jesus' life, when he was betrayed by one of his apostles, Judas Iscariot, there have been divisions in the Christian Church. However, there were two major splits within Christian history that remain visible today and are responsible for the variety of Christian denominations in North America.

The first major division occurred in 1054 where the bishop of Constantinople and the bishop of Rome or the Pope mutually broke relationship with one another. Those churches that remained

---

12. "Nicene Creed," *United States Catholic Conference of Bishops*, http://www.usccb.org/beliefs-and-teachings/what-we-believe/index.cfm (June 10, 2015).

in relationship with the bishop of Rome are known as Catholics, while those churches that broke communion with Rome and remained in communion with the bishop of Constantinople are known as Eastern Orthodox.

The second major break occurred during the sixteenth century, and it is known as the Protestant Reformation. "Protest" is the root word of "Protestant," and it refers to several Catholic priests and theologians that protested Catholic teachings and sought to reform Christianity by creating their own Christian communities. Martin Luther (1483–1546) was a leading figure in this protest. Today there are more than 30,000 different churches that trace their origin to the Protestant Reformation. Yet spurred by Protestant theologians who were ashamed of the disunity in the Christian Church, the ecumenical movement began in the early nineteenth century which sought to overcome this disunity. This movement continues today and now includes members of every major Christian tradition. Many of these dialogues have resulted in reunion of particular churches as well as the recognition that many of the original reasons for separation are no longer valid. Nevertheless, the ecumenical movement has of yet failed to reunite all of the Christian Churches.

Today with over 1 billion members, the Catholic Church tradition remains the largest Christian Church in the world. The second largest Church but third largest group of Christians is the Eastern Orthodox Church. Nearly 300 million Christians are a part of this tradition that is dominant in Eastern Europe as well as the Middle East. Protestant Church tradition has nearly 700 million members and is therefore the second largest Christian tradition; however, "Protestant" refers to a set of theological beliefs that a particular Church accepts. Thus in the United States, although the Catholic Church is the largest denomination or church group (23 percent), most Christians in America identify with one of these Protestant traditions: Evangelical Protestant tradition (26.3 percent), Mainline Protestant (18.3 percent), or Historically Black Churches (6.3 percent). After Catholicism, the second largest Christian denomination or church in the United States is the Southern Baptist Convention (6.7 percent).[13]

Section Two: Christian Doctrines

Beyond the life, death and resurrection of Jesus and the implications those actions have for the salvation of the human race, there are two central doctrines known as the Trinity and Incarnation. These teachings are a litmus test as to what constitutes orthodoxy. Thus church traditions like

---

13. *Pew Research: Religion and Public Life Project| Religious Landscape Survey,* Pew Research Project, May 8 to August 13, 2007, http://religions.pewforum.org/affiliations (December 10, 2014).

Jehovah's Witnesses and Mormons are not considered Christian by most Christians because they deny these teachings.

Incarnation refers to God becoming human. The technical terms for the incarnation is the hypostatic union; Jesus, the second person (hypostasis) of the Trinity, has within himself a human and divine nature. Jesus is not simply God in a flesh suit, but rather God who has fully embraced the human experience. The general idea is that every rational being has a personhood and nature. Thus while you are member of the human race (nature), you are a person or hypostasis with a definitive name and life experience (person). Personhood is what distinguishes you from me. Yet you and I are members of the same human race. Every human being therefore shares one human nature, but each human being also has a definitive personhood: therefore every human being contains one nature and one person. Together human beings form the human race or human family, which is united in our common nature but distinct in our personages. When God became human, when Mary conceived Jesus, God became a member of the human race, and thus in Jesus, God has a human nature. Yet when God becomes human, God does not stop being God, and therefore in Jesus, God retains God's divine nature. Therefore Jesus has both a human and divine nature. However Jesus is unique because he is a divine person. For it is the person of Godself that incarnates, not simply an aspect of God. The conclusion reached is that Jesus is one person with two natures, a human and a divine nature. This means of course that Jesus' personhood is unique since his personhood includes a consciousness of not only his human nature but also his divine nature.

The incarnation reveals a deeper insight about the YHWH, namely that God is a unique being Who has one divine nature but multiple persons. For Christians the Bible reveals that God is three divine persons: God the Father, God the Son (Jesus Christ), and God the Holy Spirit. The latter two persons are revealed clearly in the New Testament. God is a distinct entity because God is absolute unity amidst God's three persons. Thus Christians are monotheists. Like the incarnation, this teaching known as the Trinity is a mystery of faith that human rationality cannot fully explain.

One of the most popular analogies that I have had success with when teaching the Trinity is a modified form of Richard St. Victor's analogy. To better understand the Trinity, we have to understand that for Christians God is love or more precisely interpersonal love. As opposed to the other religions discussed in this book, love is not simply an aspect of God but rather love is Who God really is! Love as it used in the context of relationships is a verb that implies being in a relationship with another person. My love is always incomplete without a person to love. For this reason it would be awkward for me to say that I am a loving person if in reality I fail to love actual people. Moreover, if my love for another person is rejected by that person my love is somehow incomplete, and if I purport to experience that I am "in love" with that person, we may consider my love as unhealthy or even an obsession. The result is that human love entails the subject-Lover (the person who loves), the object-Beloved (the person that is loved), but also the experience of being "in love" or love itself. We might express human love as Lover-Love Itself-Beloved=Human Love.

Since God is Love, human love as understood relationally provides a good analogy to speak about the Trinity. However, caution is needed, as God is a unique being since God is the first cause, eternal and without beginning or end. Thus whereas human love, which is created and time contingent, needs to find other people to love, God's love is complete within Godself. Within God we find the perfect personification of the aforementioned human love. Scripture reveals that the Father is the lover, who created creation and humankind; the Son is the beloved, or object of the Father's love, who does the will of the Father; the Holy Spirit is the experience of the joy and consolation of loving between the Father and the Son. The result is that the Father is the Lover, the Son is the Beloved, and the Holy Spirit is the reality of this loving relationship or Love Itself between the love of the Father and Son. Thus God is love that is never rejected or requited. Moreover, God as a Trinity of loving persons reveals to Christians that not only is humankind created in the image of Divine Love, the Trinity, but that human beings were made to love and when they love, they reflect the life of God.

Section Three: Christian Afterlife

Albeit Christianity appropriates Jewish ideas about the afterlife, Christianity makes two important nuances to this tradition. First, the main narrative in Christianity on the afterlife stresses relationships as opposed to realms of punishment or bliss. Second, because Jesus offers definitive teachings on Gan Eden (heaven) and Gahanna (hell) these realms become dogmas or basic statements of faith that all major Christian denominations teach.

HELL AND HEAVEN

Following from Jesus' teachings and example, relational categories are central to Christian theology of the afterlife. What we find especially in the Catholic Christian tradition is a stress on heaven and hell as states of being. The realities of heaven or hell are relative to the choices we have made in life to love or reject God. With the importance of relationships in mind, hell is not a place populated by fire, brimstone, and demons with pitchforks, but a "definitive self-exclusion from communion with God and the blessed."[14] Within the context of relationships, the punishment of hell is the inability to love God and to receive God's love because of our selfishness and sin. Hell exists for those persons who have "totally destroyed their desire for truth and readiness to love, people for whom

---

14. *Catechism of the Catholic Church*, para. 1033.

everything has become a lie, people who have lived for hatred and have suppressed all love within themselves."[15] These persons are damned because they have definitively said "No" to God's offer of eternal life and Love. Only persons who have lived lives that have continually rejected God's offer of salvation and life are capable of receiving hell.[16] Hell is not simply a punishment for bad deeds but a demonstration of God's love, as God loves human beings so much that God will grant them their heart's desire, eternity without God. Hell is eternal isolation from not only our human family, but, more importantly, the God who made, sustains, and redeems us.

If hell is to be without relationship to God for all eternity, heaven is premised upon the ability to be in a relationship with God and the saints (all our brothers and sisters in heaven), and the angels for all eternity. Pope Benedict XVI, the former leader of the Catholic Church, wrote that heaven is populated by "people who are utterly pure, completely permeated by God, and thus fully open to their neighbours—people for whom communion with God even now gives direction to their entire being and whose journey towards God only brings to fulfillment what they already are."[17] Heaven is a state in which persons live out more fully their personal, loving relationship with God and neighbor. In heaven God, the object of a Christian's faith, hope, and love, is fully encountered. This intimate and loving encounter with God is called the beatific vision or deification, to "see God" (Matthew 5:8) or to be "face to face" with God (1 Corinthians 13:12). It is not a passive state of reception, but rather a transformative experience with Jesus Christ and the Blessed Trinity, as not only are all of our questions answered, but rather "[i]t is the completion of all that we are as human beings."[18] It is an ineffable experience beyond description that prompted Paul to write "no eye has seen, nor ear heard, nor the heart of man conceived, what God has prepared for those who love him" (1 Corinthians 2:9). Heaven is the kingdom of God: it is a blessing and surprise beyond anything we can imagine. Yet heaven is "not a reward for being good…it is the reward of having been delivered from any seeking for rewards."[19] Christian heaven is not a place of pleasure or satisfaction of egocentrism but the event in which we overflow with God's self-giving love for ourselves, humankind, and creation.

Purgatory

Nevertheless, Catholics recognize that the majority of humanity are not fully permeated by God and fully open to their neighbor, but have not rejected God's offer of salvation, as their "remains in the depths of their being an ultimate interior openness to truth, to love, to God."[20] Basing themselves on the ancient Christian and Jewish custom of praying for the dead (2 Maccabees 12:44, 46; Job 1:5) as

---

15. Pope Benedict XVI, *Spe Salvi.*
16. Cf. Richard P. McBrien, *Catholicism*, Volume II (Oak Grove, MN: Winston Press, 1980), 957.
17. Pope Benedict XVI, *Spe Salvi.*
18. McBrien, 1142.
19. John Macquarrie, *Principles of Christian Theology* in McBrien, 1142.
20. Pope Benedict XVI, *Spe Salvi.*

well as biblical reference to salvation by fire (1 Corinthians 3:15), Catholics and to an extent Orthodox Christians[21] teach that these souls enter an intermediate state. Catholics call this intermediate state purgatory. Purgatory is similar to the Bardo Thodol or Islamic Barzkah in as much as it is contingent on the person's preparation for the afterlife. However, for Catholics, purgatory is a state in preparation to enter eternal beatitude or heaven. Thus those persons that experience purgatory are on their way to heaven. The rationale is that we need a certain level of spiritual maturity to say "Yes" to God's offer of salvation. If for some reason we retain base attachments, or desire other things (e.g., money, power, pride), we are not prepared for the bliss of heaven.

As I mentioned in my chapter on NDEs, the experience of the life-review in NDErs provides a great analogy for purgatory, and in fact, the experiences of seeing your life flash before your eyes and re-experiencing not only your actions but the effects those actions had on others can be a cause of great suffering. NDErs, who have had negative flashbacks, point to this experience as not only painful but also transformative, prompting them to change their life for the better. Purgatory is similar in as much as your suffering is subjective (e.g., the result of your failure to love in life), and this experience transforms or purifies you after death. In purgatory you mature spiritually so as to be capable of definitively saying "Yes" to God's offer of love and salvation. In purgatory we are purged of any residual selfishness, and the result is that we are God-oriented or "totally oriented towards others."[22] Purgatory is an encounter with the risen Christ; it entails being overwhelmed with God's Love.[23] This love is painful because it purifies the evil we desire as well as the evil that we have voluntarily and involuntarily caused. The result is that our soul is able to enter heaven and fully receive and participate in God's love for us, creation, and the human race.[24]

DEATH AND RESURRECTION

Following the biblical tradition, Christians argue that there are two judgments. The first judgment is the "particular judgment."[25] This occurs immediately after you die, when the soul leaves the body. Most Christians accept the neurological criteria for determining death. Afterwards your soul enters purgatory (Catholics and some Orthodox accept this doctrine), heaven or hell (Catholics, Protestants, and Orthodox accept these doctrines) until the second judgment which is known also as the final judgment. Traditionally, these four major events precede the final judgment:

---

21. Cf. Timothy Ware, *The Orthodox Church* (London: Penguin Books, 1997), 255.
22. McBrien, 1145.
23. Pope Benedict XVI, *Salve Spes*.
24. Many Protestant traditions accept that there is a middle state after death, or that the dead sleep until the resurrection.
25. *Catechism of the Catholic Church*, paras 1021-1022.

(1) the full number of the Gentiles [non-Jews] come into the Church (2) the "full inclusion of the Jews in the Messiah's salvation, in the wake of the full number of the Gentiles" (3) a final trial of the Church "in the form of a religious deception offering men an apparent solution to their problems at the price of apostasy from the truth." The supreme deception is that of the Antichrist. (4) Christ's victory over this final unleashing of evil through a cosmic upheaval of this passing world and the Last Judgment.[26]

Although debate remains as to when the resurrection will occur, traditionally it is believed to accompany the last judgment. Reminiscent of Jesus' resurrection, the bodies of the dead will be resurrected. Christians following Jews recognize that the human person is not just a soul but a soul with a body and history that will be redeemed at the end of time. When this occurs Jesus returns to earth in his glory accompanied by the angels of heaven. Jesus will judge the living and the dead. The final judgment is not for Christians an event to be feared but an event of hope, as God wins and there will be no more injustice, fear, death, or suffering. Moreover the resurrection means that for eternity persons will experience the totality of either heaven or hell in body and soul.

Section Four: Catholic Funerary Cult

Because there is a strong stress in the Catholic tradition that how we live our life will indicate where we spend eternity, a good death is a death in which there are little or no regrets. The dying can honestly look back at their life and say that they have followed Jesus Christ to the best of their ability. Thomas Kempis in *The Imitation of Christ,* a popular spiritual text on Christian spirituality, writes:

> Every action of yours, every thought, should be those of one who expects to die before the day is out. Death would have no great terrors for you if you had a quiet conscience. . . . Then why not keep clear of sin instead of running away from death? If you aren't fit to face death today, it's very unlikely you will be tomorrow.[27]

Notice that in the Catholic tradition the stress is not on preparing for the dying experience, but rather on living a good and faithful life, so that when it is your time to die, you will have nothing to fear.

---

26. Cf. Colon B. Donovan, "Endtimes, Millennium, Rapture," *EWTN,* https://www.ewtn.com/expert/answers/endtimes.htm (December 22, 2014).
27. *The Imitation of Christ,* 1, 23, 1 quoted in *Catechism of the Catholic Church,* 1014.

Christ gives a new meaning to death because he not only experienced death but overcame death in the resurrection. Therefore fear of death is not appropriate because in baptism, the ritual in which water is poured over the head of a new believer and the words "I baptize you in the name of the Father, Son, and Holy Spirit" are said, they have died to their former sinful selves, and from that point on live with Christ. Physical death is interpreted as "dying with Christ"[28] or to enter into the mystery of Jesus' death and resurrection. Thus after death, Catholics believe that they will fully experience what God had prepared for them in heaven.

Nevertheless, Catholicism is a social religion and thus the dying are not left alone. Not only are family, friends, and members of the local Church expected to visit and pray for and with the dying, but there are several rituals associated with dying. For Catholics it is important that last rites are performed before death. Moreover, because some of the rites require consciousness on the part of the dying, it is important that the dying have these rights performed before consciousness is lost.

LAST RITES

Last rites in a Catholic context generally refer to the reception of these three sacraments when a Catholic is dying: Anointing of the sick, Confession, and Eucharist (Viaticum).[29] Catholics teach that sacraments are "masterworks of God," whereby the Holy Spirit further sanctifies believers, or brings them into a more intimate relationship with God.[30] Thus sacraments are not magical incantations but rather an extension of the Incarnation in as much as God uses ordinary objects to do extraordinary things. The goal of these sacraments is to encounter God, which is a foretaste of the unmediated encounter with God after death in heaven. Thus each of these three sacraments prepares the dying to meet God "face to face."

Anointing of the sick is known as the sacrament of healing because the priest, who is the official leader of the local Catholic parish,[31] anoints the dying Catholic with oil and prays for the person's

28. *Catechism of the Catholic Church,* para. 1010.
29. Our Sunday Visitor Staff, "What every Catholic needs to know about preparing for death. Preparing for death means, most importantly, making sure that we reconcile with God and live in a state of grace," *Our Sunday Visitor* 2009, https://www.osv.com/TheChurch/EternalLife/Article/TabId/738/ArtMID/13694/ArticleID/4412/What-every-Catholic-needs-to-know-about-preparing-for-eath.aspx#sthash.8IHGGpNh.dpuf (December 16, 2014).
30. Cf. *Catechism of the Catholic Church,* para. 1116.
31. In the Catholic tradition there are three holy orders: the bishop, the priest, and the deacon. The priest is a minister of the Gospel. His main work involves not only leading the local Catholic community in worship, preaching the Gospel, but also in celebrating the sacraments that include baptism, eucharist, reconciliation, marriage, confirmation, and anointing of the sick. The priest works on behalf of the local ordinary known as the bishop, who is a successor of the apostles and leader of the local church that includes the local Catholic community. The priest is assisted by deacons. Deacons are involved in ministering to the needs of the Catholic community as well as "baptize, lead the faithful in prayer, witness marriages, and conduct wake and funeral services." (Frequently Asked Questions About Deacons, *United States Catholic Conference of Bishops,* http://www.usccb.org/beliefs-and-teachings/vocations/diaconate/faqs.cfm [June 3,

healing of body and spirit. For this reason, God can use this sacrament to forgive sins, especially when the dying person is unable to speak. Confession or reconciliation is also the sacrament of healing whereby Christ forgives the sins or wrongdoing of the dying person. Note that for confession to be possible the patient must at least be conscious.

The Eucharist, which Catholics believe is the body and blood of Jesus Christ (John 6:53), is the most important aspect of the last rites. Eucharist is "the source and summit of the Christian life."[32] Consuming the Eucharist is a foretaste of heaven, since in so doing the Catholic encounters the resurrected and glorified Lord Jesus Christ. When the Eucharist is received near death it is called the *viaticum*, which can be translated as "provisions for journey."

In the Catholic tradition the last rites are celebrated by a priest or bishop. However, in emergency situations nonordained Catholics are permitted to perform last rite prayers.

In addition to the last rite sacraments, if time permits, the dying may meditate on the Bible; pray to Jesus, Mary, and the saints or people in heaven; ask forgiveness of sins; and pay off debts so as to better prepare to enter into heaven.

Once the Catholic dies, the family, priest, and congregation continue to pray for the deceased. The family and the priest from the parish or church of the deceased will make final arrangements for the funeral. There is no prohibition to embalming the body, organ transplant, or stress on immediate burial. Organ donation is highly encouraged because it is considered as an act of love consistent with Jesus' teaching to sacrifice oneself for another.[33] Although Catholics believe in the resurrection of the body, they stress that nothing humans can do can frustrate this miraculous event, and thus donation of organs or body and even cremation of the dead are permitted. Note that Catholics retain Jewish respect for the body and therefore although they permit cremation, the ashes of the dead should be treated with respect.

FUNERAL CULT

The Catholic funerary cult involves three parts: The Vigil, The Funeral Mass, and The Rite of Committal. The text that it used to guide the priest is known as the *Order of Christian Funerals*. This text combines readings from the Bible as well as prayers to offer as a guide for Catholic Christians during this difficult time. Note that not all Catholics will opt for all three parts of the funeral cult.

2015].)

32. *Catechism of the Catholic Church,* para . 1324.

33. Cf. "Benedict XVI on Organ Donation," *Zenit* 2008, http://www.zenit.org/en/articles/benedict-xvi-on-organ-dona-tion (June 3, 2015).

The vigil is celebrated the evening before the funeral or immediately before the funeral at the funeral home. After the prayers and readings from the Bible on behalf of the dead are recited, it is common to have a eulogy where a relative or family member memorializes the deceased.

The funeral occurs immediately before the burial of the body. Although the Church is ideal, funerals may be performed at other locations including homes, which are becoming more common. The funeral usually involves a mass or liturgical service that is said on behalf of the dead. This will include not only prayers and readings from the bible, preaching on these readings (known as the liturgy of the word), but also the celebration of the Eucharist (liturgy of the Eucharist), and then concluding prayers. The Gospel of John (11:17-27) is a common text used during the funeral because it reminds the congregation to have hope that Christ is the resurrection and the life, and that the dead is with Jesus in a better place.

Afterwards the family, friends, and priest take the body in casket to the burial grounds for the rite of committal. At this point the priest leads the family and friends in final prayers for the dead. The rite of committal ends with this final prayer:

> With faith and hope in eternal life, let us commend her to the loving mercy of our Father, and assist her with our prayers. She became God's daughter through baptism and was often fed at the table of our Lord. May the Lord now welcome her to the table of God's children in heaven, and, with all the saints, may she inherit the promise of eternal life. Let us also pray to the Lord for ourselves. May we who mourn be reunited one day with our sister. Together may we meet Christ Jesus when he, who is our life, shall appear in his glory.

Note that the prayer ends with the hope that those present will see their love one again.

Section Five: Coping with Death

For Catholics, suffering and death are opportunities to not only grow closer to Jesus Christ but also help save humankind by our example and suffering. Christ's invitation to live out his message is also an invitation to enter into the mystery of his suffering, and by doing so enter into the mystery of his salvation. In this way the enigmatic statement "we complete what is lacking in the afflictions of Christ" (Colossians 1:27) makes sense. Health providers should be aware of this and therefore understand that devout Catholics view their healthcare options in light of Christian meaning of life, suffering, and death. Catholics avoid the extremes of excessive or burdensome treatment and the extreme of intentionally seeking their death by withdrawing treatments because they view their suffering and dying as meaningless.[34] Christ redeemed all things and thus suffering can be an opportunity for redemption, but at the same time death is a part of the life experience, and thus Catholics accept that the removal or withholding of extraordinary treatments are ethical. Evident in the interview below, it is not always clear when a treatment is extraordinary; it is usually determined by the dying person, the family, in conjunction with the physicians; the family may also consult a priest and/or Catholic ethicist. Nevertheless, because life is God's greatest gift, it is a grave evil to destroy it. Intentional killing, even to alleviate suffering (e.g., euthanasia or withholding ordinary means), is a serious sin. In this respect the spiritual dimension clearly influences the physical dimension, as not only is euthanasia prohibited but depending on the circumstances removal of food and hydration may be considered euthanasia. Health providers should try to understand that Catholics have freedom to interpret when treatments are burdensome or frustrating God's will; however, treatments that offer a reasonable hope of success without excessive burden to family and patient are required.[35] For these reasons the Church allows for Catholics to have advance directives; in fact, Catholic hospitals accept the advance directives of its patients, so long as it does not violate Catholic teaching (e.g., PAS).

In terms of caring for the patient's spiritual and psychological dimension, health providers should ask the Catholic who is seriously ill if they want them to contact a priest, as this demonstrates not only respect for the person but also their tradition. Most hospitals have a chaplaincy service that includes a Catholic priest or a lay Catholic chaplain on staff. The Catholic Church recommends that this request is made as soon as possible. A good death is a death in which the patient feels prepared to die; this will usually involve the person's sins being forgiven through the sacraments of anointing of the sick and reconciliation. End of life should be a simple transition.

Because Catholicism considers family a great blessing, it is encouraged for family to be present during the last moments. Regarding the social dimension, health providers should be prepared for visitors from the patient's family, friends, and parish. Nonetheless Catholics are quite comfortable in hospitals as well as hospice facilities. There is little in the way of Catholic culture and practice that modern hospitals do that conflict with Catholic practice. Nevertheless, allowing for the privacy of the patient especially when the priest visits is important. The sacraments, especially the sacrament of reconciliation, require not only the focus of the patient, but also a privacy to allow the patient to confess his or her sins to the priest, which is a solemn and intimate occasion. Any accommodations that can be made will greatly help Catholics achieve their spiritual and psychological tasks. These actions communicate respect for such patients' autonomy and decisions.

---

34. Cf. "Ethical and religious directives for Catholic healthcare services (fifth edition)," *United Stated Conference of Catholic Bishops* 2009, http://www.usccb.org/issues-and-action/human-life-and-dignity/health-care/upload/Ethical-Religious-Directives-Catholic-Health-Care-Services-fifth-edition-2009.pdf (June 11, 2015).
35. Ibid.

Note that there is no specified bereavement period in Catholicism or the Christian tradition. Bereavement is influenced by the local culture. Nevertheless, with respect to the Catholic tradition, most local churches provide bereavement ministries. However, these are not required and bereaved Catholics have to seek them out.

Conclusion

With primary focus on Catholic Christianity, this chapter provided a brief overview of the Christian tradition and its end-of-life practices and care. Following from the teachings of Jesus who stressed correct belief as opposed to correct practice, Christians approach death and funeral with much less rigor as compared to other traditions discussed. The last rites and funerary cult is highly recommended but is not required in its entirety. Catholics who commit suicide or die suddenly receive the same rituals as Catholics who have died from old age. These rituals nevertheless do provide not only comfort for the bereaved but also assistance for the dead, especially for souls in purgatory.

In the next chapter we complete our study of the world religions and end-of-life practices with Islam. Although it is the youngest world religion and considers itself the final revelation of YHWH that contains the correct teaching of Jesus and the prophets, it is closer to Judaism inasmuch as correct practice is stressed over correct belief.

Interview

Peter Drilling is a Roman Catholic priest, ordained in 1967, who has served in six parishes either as associate pastor, administrator, or as pastor. Currently, he is the rector of St. Joseph Cathedral in Buffalo, New York. He is also professor of systematic theology and pastoral studies at Christ the King Seminary, East Aurora, New York, where he has been teaching for over thirty years. He has published two books, *Trinity and Ministry* (1991) and *Premodern Faith in a Postmodern Culture: A Contemporary Theology of the Trinity* (2006), as well as articles in a variety of theological and pastoral journals.

Q: What is your role with the dying at your parish?

A: A parish priest can be very engaged with the dying and those who have lost loved ones. For example, I recently presided at a funeral for a fifty-seven-year-old man. I have known his family for years. In fact, I presided at his wedding over thirty years ago, and I baptized the couple's three children. Last August this gentleman became ill. I spent time with him and his family at the hospital. When he came home from the hospital I was with him. We prayed together. Before he died I celebrated the sacrament of the sick. This is an important sacrament in a Catholic context because it is our way to ask God to assure the dying that God is with them, that Christ the divine physician is present to them. It does not mean that they will get better, but rather that they and their family have the strength to deal with the illness, and to recognize that we are called in our suffering to unite with Jesus, who died on the cross to save the world. His wife and I placed our hands on his head and prayed for him. A couple of days later he died. I sat down with his wife and family to plan the funeral. I presided at the funeral and then joined the family at a memorial luncheon. This experience is often the case with priests. We are with the dying in their last moments, and then we are with their families as we prepare for and celebrate their funerals.

Q: In other religions discussed in this text, rituals are performed to gain merit for the dead to have a better afterlife. Does anointing of the sick gain some sort of merit for the dead?

A: We do not think of it in terms of the merit received. Rather the person can join oneself more with Jesus. We understand the Christian life to be a joining of ourselves with Jesus in life, in death, and then in resurrection. That is the understanding of Christian baptism, that we enter into sharing Christ's dying and rising. One side of that is that we are freed from our sinfulness. The other side is that we can enter more intimately into communion with the Trinity: the Father, Son, and Holy Spirit.

We get our sense of the anointing from the sixth chapter of the gospel of Mark. Before Jesus goes to the towns he will visit, he sends out his disciples two by two ahead of him. He says: when you get to the sick lay your hands upon them and anoint them in my name to assure them that I am with them. We also know that at various times Jesus worked cures. He did not cure everyone everywhere, but a few people to give them some relief at that point, but more importantly as a sign that the kingdom of God has come. So, in the sacrament of anointing of the sick the issue is not being made well for this life, but being united with Christ in terms of the next world as the sick keep dealing with their illness.

Q: In terms of uniting with Christ, purgatory is an important Catholic teaching. Can you elaborate as to what purgatory is and how or if purgatory informs end-of-life practices?

A: Our sense is that when we die, whether suddenly or in the middle of our life or when we are old, we realize that we have fallen short. We have sinned; we have done things wrong, and there are repercussions for our sins. All sin is social; so, for example, even if I have an inordinate desire for another person's possessions that I do not act on, this sin has an influence in the world. This is because I act in the world with this desire or temptation, these underlying feelings. Catholics have a wonderful sacrament called reconciliation where we can acknowledge our sinfulness to a member of the Church, the priest, who represents at that moment both the triune God and the rest of the Church, and receive forgiveness. We receive forgiveness, and we trust that God forgives us. But there is still the fallout of my sinfulness. If I get angry at you and lash out and say all kinds of inordinate things, now it is out there; I have done it! You might forgive me, but you still have that hurt. Maybe I have hurt you and other people. When I die, there is always this fallout. Before I move into the glory of heaven, that fallout has to somehow be purified. This is the meaning of purgatory, "purification." How does that happen?

In 2007, Pope Benedict XVI wrote an encyclical on the virtue of hope. There is a wonderful passage in the encyclical on purgatory. He said we should think of purgatory relationally. When we die, we go before Jesus the judge, and as we stand before Jesus we realize how infinitely gracious God's love has been for us even after we have sinned. God never abandons us. At that moment we realize how totally God loves us and how miserable, half-hearted our love has been for God all our life. The pain of this experience is purgatory. This experience purifies us of the remnants of our sin. Imagine how ashamed we will feel that we did not measure up to God's love. We are all sinners.

Q: What was your hardest experience coping with death, and how did your faith tradition inform your response?

A: Over the years there have been a number of difficult experiences. They were difficult for different reasons. Many of the most difficult were because the experiences were compounded. Very often a parent will die leaving behind young children. These are particularly difficult.

However, probably the most difficult for me occurred within my own family. My nephew and his wife gave birth to twin boys. Almost as soon as the children were born, people could tell that something was wrong. The babies were diagnosed with spinal muscle atrophy. The doctors told us that they did not have very long to live. For fifteen weeks my nephew and his wife cared for these children beautifully, and then the twins died one after the other. That was very difficult. In between their baptism, in the hospital, and their death fifteen weeks later, family and friends gathered to celebrate the twins' confirmation and first communion. Shortly thereafter one died, and within a week, the other died. Doctors had predicted that it would happen that way. The twins developed a bond; they were always looking at one another. So when one died, the other followed.

Q: As a pastor and theologian how do you respond to these tragedies in light of the fact that Christianity teaches that God is Love.

A: I will answer this theologically and then I will talk about this pastorally. The solid Catholic tradition based in the early Church and brought to fruition with Thomas Aquinas is that God is the omnipotent, all-loving, all-knowing, all-wise Creator-cause of the universe. Yet these tragedies occur. Thomas Aquinas came up with the basic answer in the thirteenth century. We need to think of causality in different ways. There is primary causality: God is the cause; nothing happens without God. But at the same time God has created this world where each thing has its own causality. We call this the secondary causality. This is especially the case for human beings who have freedom. Our freedom is our own causality. God did not make us robots. God permits our freedom or causality. Likewise, other worldly things and events have their proportionate causality; they, too, are secondary causes. The weather patterns that result in tsunamis or genetic mutations that express themselves as life-threatening illness are secondary causes. God does not orchestrate all of these things, including evolution—Catholics are comfortable with evolution—but allows all of these things to express themselves. But Aquinas also spoke of God as the final cause. Everything has its fulfillment in God. Another theologian, Bernard Lonergan, said we ultimately live in a friendly universe because ultimately God brings all things to their fulfillment, and God is love. That fulfillment will be good. Scripture, particularly the letters of St. Paul and Revelation, expresses this in terms of the future in which there is a new heaven and a new earth, a transformed creation.

Now how do we explain this to people going through terrible sufferings? Our faith gives us hope. This does not mean that we do not grieve terribly or go through huge suffering, but we know that there is something more. We have to say this to people in a gracious way.

There was a married couple in a parish where I worked. They were faithful Catholics. The husband had a series of strokes. One day the husband came to me and said: "I have been a lifelong faithful Catholic; why is God punishing me like this?" I said: "God is not punishing you; as the ravages of your illness overtake you, do not think that God is abandoning you. You have to trust that this is happening because this is the way your body is constituted. The more important thing is that we are with you; the Church is with you; God is with you. Together you and we are going to get through this." As time went on he had peace and eventually died.

Q: In most world religions, suicide is the worst death. Do Catholics share this belief? If Catholics share this belief, do Catholics treat suicides differently in terms of funerary and bereavement customs/rituals/pastoral care?

A: We would not call suicide the worst form of death. It is certainly most unfortunate. And it does have to be dealt with in a particular way. The fifth commandment is: "You shall not kill." This, of course, includes killing yourself. It is up to God when it is time for us to die. Interestingly, as the study of psychology developed and became more sophisticated as a discipline—this only began in the nineteenth century—we came to realize that almost always when someone takes their own life there is something wrong. These people are not mentally or emotionally stable. Therefore we cannot blame them. This is a fairly recent development that became normative in the middle of the twentieth century. Before this time suicides would not have been granted a Catholic funeral because they broke the fifth commandment, presumably without repenting. Now we realize that when people commit suicide they are likely not as responsible as they should be. So now people who have committed suicide can be buried with a Catholic burial service. It gives the family some consolation that their loved one who committed suicide can have a Catholic funeral and be buried in a Catholic cemetery.

Q: On the flipside, what is the ideal good death for a Catholic?

A: This is up to each person. You want people to feel comfortable that death is a part of life. This is easier to do when people are older. I think of my parents who were ninety when they died. Their deaths were so beautiful. I did not grieve. My siblings and I had a wonderful family life from beginning to end. There were no regrets. I remember I got a call that my father collapsed and was taken to the hospital. When I arrived, he was unconscious. I anointed him and celebrated the sacrament of the sick. Whenever a person seems to be unconscious, I speak very loudly. People in medical care will tell you that you never know what they are hearing or not hearing. When I had finished celebrating the sacrament, I said to my dad: "Okay dad, we are finished here; whenever you and God are ready, you can go now." All of a sudden my dad lifted up his right hand, as if to say 'thank you and goodbye.' He was sent to a hospice care room, and he died that evening. It was beautiful. It does not mean that it was easy, especially for my mother. She died six years later.

I remember taking her to the emergency room because something was wrong. The doctors found cancer and told me that there was nothing more they could do. After relaying the news to my mother, I remember her saying to me bluntly: "I am ninety; your father was ninety; I have cancer; he had cancer; it is time to go." Before my mother died, she was with my sister and a woman religious. She opened her eyes one day and looked up at my sister and said, "I am alive; I thought that I had died. It felt so good." I think this is how we want to die. We need to appreciate that we will die. Especially when we have lived our lives doing the best we can do, we can go in peace, even eagerly.

Q: We have spoken a lot about death, but do Catholics accept the neurological criteria? Also death occurs when the soul leaves the body. When does the soul leave the body according to Catholics?

A: We do not have to do extraordinary things to keep people alive. Sometimes it is not so easy to figure out what to do. We do not agree with killing them. On the other hand, we want to be reasonable, and not do things that simply prolong the dying process. I would say death occurs when the person is brain dead. The soul leaves the body at the moment of death. When I celebrate funerals, I stress that this is just the body; the person has moved on. This does not mean we abuse the body. We reverence the body because it was the temple of the Holy Spirit; it was God's shrine in which the person lived out his/her life in this world. We allow cremation that can happen as soon as death is declared. The body may be embalmed. My body will go to the University of Buffalo for medical research.

Q: Christians believe in the resurrection of the body; however, Catholics not only allow cremation and embalming, but encourage Catholics to donate organs after they have died. How do Catholics reconcile belief in resurrection with these practices that mutilate or destroy the body?

A: One of the phrases we use often is: "You came from dust, and unto dust you will return." What we mean is that we are not only created from dust but that your body will decompose. Someday we will become someone else's tomatoes! Our body goes through cellular reconstruction every seven years. My body now is not the same body of my youth. The New Testament teaches that in the end there will be a new creation. Our souls will be re-embodied. We do not know what that means other than the fact that we will have a body. Moreover our bodies will not be subject to time and space. We will be eternal. In chapter fourteen of John's Gospel, Jesus says: "Trust in God and trust in me because I am going to prepare a place for you so that where I am you may also be." St. Paul, in his First Letter to the Corinthians, uses imagery to stress the transformation of ourselves. How our bodies will transform and when it will eventuate, we do not know. In the meanwhile, after death, we go with our selves, the spiritual personality, to join the communion of saints in glory. When we go to glory, we will share in the eternal life of Jesus. But at this point we are without our bodies in glory with the Lord.

Q: In terms of the funeral, is the *Order of Christian Funerals* the main text used?

A: Yes, but there is a range of scripture that may be used. We do this for any sacrament. People do not have to choose the selections in the book, but rather any scripture passage. When meeting with people to prepare for a funeral, I will suggest popular readings for the celebration of the funeral, but it is the family's decision. So it is the same order, but there are adjustments that can be made. The funeral most often includes the celebration of the Eucharist. But this is not required. Some families just want a simple service. Recently I met with a small family who only wanted a relaxed service at the cemetery. This is what we did. I used the *Order*; I blessed the coffin; we listened to scripture and prayed together; I gave a reflection. I never know what I will be asked to do. On another occasion I celebrated a prayer service in front of the cremains and with the family in the bedroom where the loved one died. They placed the cremains of the wife, who had died earlier, with the cremains of the now deceased husband. We said some prayers, I gave a reflection, and then we had lunch in the dining room. So the *Order* gives us regulations and guides, but it is not rigid.

Q: Do Catholics have traditions with respect to preparing the body for the funeral or grieving the deceased?

A: Wakes and embalming have become the custom, but this depends on where you are. I was a student in Italy in the 1960s. There was no embalming. The deceased had to be buried very quickly. This was because of the practicality of the decomposing body. This is true in many parts of the world. The Catholic sense for what you do after death is to reverently bury the body at some point. We normally do not recommend keeping Grandma on the mantle indefinitely. But we do not make a big issue about this.

Q: Are there laws or practices in our culture that make it difficult to practice Catholicism in terms of end-of-life rituals or bereavement practices?

A: No, nothing gets in the way. American culture pretty much leaves it up to the family and/or the person's instructions.

Q: Euthanasia is becoming more acceptable in the United States. If euthanasia is legalized in this state, how would you minister to a terminally ill congregant who desires euthanasia?

A: I have never had to deal with this. I would hope to communicate what is foremost in our instructions on final illness and the core teaching of the New Testament. This teaching is explicated in Colossians. St. Paul is imprisoned, and he is writing to the Colossians. He says: 'Do not worry about me; I am fine, because I am joining my sufferings with the suffering of Christ for the salvation of the world.' We believe Jesus' dying is salvific. It is a mediating death that overcomes our sinfulness and saves the world. Even Jesus in his suffering only suffers as one person. Everyone's suffering is distinct. St. Paul is saying by the grace of God, not because God needs us, our sufferings can be productive in saving the world. We need to learn how to suffer in love. You try to help people see that we are here with you and that there is a salvific quality to your sufferings. This is not an easy conviction to communicate. But to take your life is not a solution.

Q: By redemptive suffering, do you mean that you participate in the salvation of others or the salvation of yourself?

A: It is all of the above. I would highlight that your suffering is helpful for you to grow in your relationship with our loving God by joining with the love of Jesus. In the gospels, Jesus says that his followers must take up the cross and walk after him. Recognizing that does not mean that I replicate Jesus' suffering, but it affords the importance of the social dimension. All sin, all our lives, and all salvation are social. We are in this together. We have to try to learn how to enter into the different stages of life. Now we also need to consider the fact that technology is allowing us to keep people alive longer, but not necessarily improving the quality of life. We need to be attentive to this.

Q: You brought up a few times extraordinary means of care. As a pastor how do you help a dying congregant distinguish between ordinary means, which for Catholics are morally obligatory, and extraordinary means, which are not morally obligatory?

A: Here is where I would use the phrase "prudential judgment." You do not need to be doing a lot of different things if there is no benefit except to prolong suffering. There are times when it is difficult to be certain what is ordinary and what is extraordinary. You do not need to keep a feeding tube if there is no more quality of life or benefit to health. That is keeping someone alive artificially. Sometimes the survivors keep the dying alive for themselves, because they cannot accept the death of their loved one.

Q: What should healthcare professionals do if they encounter a dying Catholic?

A: If there is family around, then they should consult with the family first. They will know the background and wishes of the patient. If you are in a situation where you are looking on a chart and see that the patient is a Roman Catholic, and no family is around, and the patient is not conscious, then let it be known that the chart says the patient is Catholic. Please notify a priest.

Q: What if the person is dying and there is no one around?

A: I would have no problem with a non-Catholic praying for me in their tradition. If the nurse is a Catholic, he/she could say the Lord's Prayer, a Hail Mary, and commend the person to God.

Q: In closing, do you have any advice for health professionals who will care for dying Catholic patients?

A: My general sense, after spending more than forty-six years visiting hospitals, hospice care, nursing homes, and meeting with visiting nurses is that health professionals are very sensitive for the most part. These persons are well trained and mature in their responses to these situations. I would say if you are in a position to recognize that a patient would be helped by having a priest visit them, then I think it would be a good idea to arrange this in the context of what the family allows.

CHAPTER TEN

ISLAM

Introduction

Since the terrorist attack on the Twin Towers in New York City on September 11, 2001, U.S. media has inundated the public with negative images of Islam. Unfortunately, there are no shortages of injustices, terrorist activities, and human rights violations committed by jihadists and Islamist states[1] in the name of Islam to provide fodder for stereotypes that suggest that Islam is a religion of violence and that all Muslims support terrorism. Stereotypes of Islam must be avoided, as Islam is the second largest religion in the world, encompassing 1.6 billion people from a variety of cultures and nations.[2] Recent studies of terrorism and the Islamic community suggest that the majority of Muslims

1. Note that the Organization of Islamic Cooperation (OIC), which is an Islamic international organization representing fifty-seven countries and the "collective voice of the Muslim world and ensuring to safeguard and protect the interests of the Muslim world in the spirit of promoting international peace and harmony among various people of the world" rejects acts of terrorism. However, many fault this organization because it has failed to adopt the United Nations' Declaration of Human Rights (1948) and instead has ratified the Cairo *Statement on Human Rights* (1990). Human rights are limited by shar'ia or Islamic law. ("The Cairo Declaration on Human Rights in Islam," *OIC* 1990, http://www.oic-oci.org/english/article/human.htm [July 22, 2015].)

2. There is no clear consensus as to how many people profess Islam today. This in part due to inconsistent measuring tools and lack of agreement on criteria of what constitutes membership. (Frederick M. Denny, *Islam and The Muslim Community* [Long Grove, IL: Waveland Press, 1987], 13.) Nevertheless, based on an "analysis of more than 2,500 censuses, surveys and population registers," Pew estimates that there are 1.6 billion Muslims in the world, making Islam the second largest religion in the world.

in Muslim-dominated countries reject extremist and violent interpretations of Islam.[3] Moreover, a 2011 study of Muslims in America revealed that American Muslims share the same concerns that non-Muslim Americans have about Islamic extremism.[4]

 As the second largest religion in the world, and a representative community in North America that is growing, the Islamic perspectives on death, afterlife, and end-of-life care are very important. For the purpose of clarity this chapter provides a brief introduction to the history, religious texts, and practices of Muslims, as well as an overview of Muslim theology of the afterlife and how Muslims approach end-of-life care. The chapter ends with an interview with Imam Chawla who is the religious leader at Jaffarya Center of Buffalo in East Amherst, New York.

History

Originating in the seventh century of the common era, Islam is the youngest world religion discussed in this book. Islam appropriates the Judeo-Christian revelations about creation and the prophets. Thus Muslims believe that the first Muslims were the biblical progenitors of humanity, Adam and Hawwa (or Eve). Moreover, the *Qur'an* or the Islamic-revealed holy text follows the basic message and stories of the Old and New Testament, and thus the major events and persons in the Bible including Moses and Jesus appear in the Qur'an. Even Mecca, the holiest city in the Islamic religion, is revered because it is believed by Muslims to be the place where Abraham built an altar and worshiped Allah (God)[5] with his first son Ishmael. Nevertheless, Islam does not accept the Torah or Christian Bible as revelation because Muslims believe these texts perverted Allah's message; the Qur'an alone provides the unadulterated teaching of these prophets. This final and correct revelation was dictated in 114 sayings (Qurans) to the Prophet Muhammad (570–632).

3. "Muslim Publics Share Concerns about Extremism," Pew Research Center 2013, http://www.pewglobal.org/2013/09/10/muslim-publics-share-concerns-about-extremist-groups/ (July 22, 2015).
4. "Muslim Americans: No Signs of Growth in Alienation or Support for Extremism," Pew Research Center 2011, http://www.people-press.org/2011/08/30/muslim-americans-no-signs-of-growth-in-alienation-or-support-for-extremism/ (July 22, 2015).
5. Allah was one of the 360 different deities and spirits that pre-Islamic Arabs worshipped; however, Allah of pre-Islamic Arabia was significantly different from Allah of Islam. "Allah" is also an Arabic noun meaning "the God" that corresponds to the Judeo-Christian noun "God" (Denny, 24).

Prophet Muhammad

The story of Muhammad is about a remarkable young man who overcomes adversity to become not only a prophet but the leader of what will become a dominant political and religious power in the world for over a millennium.

Muhammad was born in Mecca around the year 570 CE. Islamic tradition purports that Muhammad's life began with tragedy. By the age of eight he was orphaned by the deaths of his parents and grandfather. Luckily his uncle raised him and provided the necessary tribal protection to thrive in the Arabian Peninsula.[6] Muhammad grew to be a successful merchant, well known for his ability as an arbitrator. Tribes would seek Muhammad's wisdom to find peaceful solutions to difficult situations.

Beyond his business and personal successes, Muhammad was a man of prayer who frequently went on retreat into the mountains outside Mecca. Muhammad was a *hanif* or person with monotheistic convictions like Abraham before he had received his revelations from God (Qur'an 3.67).[7] Nevertheless during one of these retreats, in the year 610 CE, the angel Gabriel appeared to Muhammad in Mount Hijra. The angel Gabriel stated:

> Proclaim in the name of thy Lord and Cherisher, Who created—Created man out of a (mere) clot of congealed blood. Proclaim! And thy Lord is Most Bountiful—He Who taught (The use of) the Pen—Taught man that Which he knew not. (96:1-5)

Muhammad continued to receive revelations from God by way of the angel Gabriel until the end of his life in 632 CE. Muhammad preached that the meaning of this message was submission to Allah. Hence "Islam" may be translated as submission and a "Muslim" is one who submits to Allah.

Muhammad's career as a prophet and preacher about Allah was not without adversity. As he begins to make converts to his faith that stresses that there is only one God, he is perceived as a threat by the authorities. Muhammad's radical monotheism that rejected the deities of the local tribes threatened the economic well-being, social importance, and hegemony of Mecca. Mecca was a religious center of the Arabian Peninsula; in Mecca was the Ka'ba or altar to the gods that were patrons for the tribes in the area. Rejection of the existence of these gods was construed as a rejection of the economic, religious, and cultural importance of the city of Mecca.

Providentially, Muhammad was offered respite by the leaders of the city of Yathrib. Aware of Muhammad's skill as an arbitrator, they welcomed Muhammad and his burgeoning community on the

---

6. Ibid., 25.
7. Ibid., 26.

condition that Muhammad would be willing to end the disputes threatening the peace in their city. This immigration to Yathrib (CE 622) is known at the Hijra, and it represents the first year of the Muslim calendar. Yathrib was later renamed *Al-Medina* or "the City" by Muhammad.[8]

During the first three years in Medina there were three major battles between Muhammad's community and the Meccans who sought to eliminate the Muslims. These are the battles: The Battle of Badr, March 624; The Battle of Uhud, March 625; and the Battle of the Trench and Siege of Medina, April 627.[9] With exception to the Battle of Badr, the other battles were not clear successes for the Muslims, but they nevertheless demonstrated that the *Umma* or Muslim brotherhood or community was an established military power in the area. In 630, Muhammad and the Umma sacked Mecca without bloodshed. Rather than enslaving and/or killing the population that was expected, Muhammad offered the Meccan people mercy if they converted to Islam. The citizens of Mecca converted to Islam, and Muhammad destroyed the idols around the Ka'ba, reinstating the Ka'ba as the altar to worship the God of Abraham, Allah. After a revelation in Medina, Mecca and the Ka'ba became the religious center of Islam. To this day, Muslims face Mecca when they pray. After conquering Mecca, Islam began to spread its message and empire to the remainder of the Arabian Peninsula and beyond. Remarkably, in less than a century the Umma was an empire that spread from the Arabian Peninsula to Europe and Indo-China.

Sunni and Shi'ite Muslims

There is no separation of church and state in Islam, and therefore the *caliph* or the person who succeeded the Prophet as the leader of the community, like the Prophet Muhammad, had both a religious and political function. The third Caliph, Uthman, for instance, in addition to ruling the burgeoning Islamic empire also ordered that the saying of the Prophet be collected into the Qur'an. However, the Caliph's religious function was circumscribed by the revelations of Muhammad and Muhammad's teachings. Thus the Caliph's primary role as a religious leader was to implement and enforce Islamic Law. Nevertheless, the succession of leadership after the prophet's death led to the first major split in the Islamic community. Ali, who was a close companion and son in-law of Muhammad, with support from the minority of the Umma known as the *Shi'a* or party, argued that Muhammad chose him as his successor. The majority of Muslims retorted that the person best suited for the office of the Caliph should be elected. Even though Ali was eventually elected as Caliph, he and later his son Husayn were assassinated. Their deaths led to an irrevocable split in the Muslim

---

8. Denny, 29.
9. "Muhammad: Legacy of a Prophet," *PBS* 2002, http://www.pbs.org/muhammad/timeline_html.shtml (July 22, 2015).

community between the Shi'a and the majority of Muslims known as the Sunni (or those who stress the Sunna [teaching] on the prophet of the basis of law) that is visible today.[10] Today Sunni and Shi'ites remain divided.

Despite this division the Islamic religion and empire continued to expand until the seventeenth century. During the first thousand years of Islam, the Islamic empires were centers of philosophy, art, and science.[11] Nevertheless by the twentieth century the Islamic empire ceased to exist.

In Islam today there is no universally accepted religious or political leader; however, in Shi'ite Islam the central religious and political authorities are the ayatollahs or experts in Islamic jurisprudence.[12] In Iran, which is a Shi'ite-dominated country, ayatollah Ali Khamenei is the supreme leader of Iran who oversees both the government and the Islamic religion. Sunni Islam, by and large, lacks these authoritative interpreters of the Islamic tradition, but rather relies on a consensus of Sunni Islamic scholars. Exceptions exist in the Sunni Islamic populations that are influenced by Sufism, or Islamic mysticism, that stress reverence of spiritual beings. These mystics and in some cases their successors are spiritual leaders that have an authority corollary to the ayatollah.[13] Nevertheless there have been recent attempts to reestablish the Sunni Caliphate and Islamic empire in Syria and Iraq (e.g., ISIS, 2014) and in Nigeria (e.g., Boko Harem, 2014). However, the majority of Sunni Muslims do not accept these caliphates as legitimate.

Sacred Text and Law

The belief that the Qur'an is the word of God without any human admixture is the most important tenet of Islam. For this reason the Qur'an is a central facet of Muslim life and worship. It is commonly believed by Muslims that the Qur'an recited in Arabic is the most beautiful sound on earth. Muslims, like Christians and Jews, stress the importance of history and claim that their revelation is based on historically verifiable events. The past three decades have witnessed an intense search for the Muhammad of history as well as a historical basis for the Qur'an. The historicity of the Qur'an and the events of the Prophet remain problematic for Islamic scholars due to the genre of the

---

10. Today Shi'ite Muslims memorialize the death of Husayn as a day of mourning.

11. Cf. *The World of Islam: Faith, People, Culture*, ed. Bernard Lewis (London: Thames and Hudson, Ltd.), 1992.

12. Ayatollahs play an important role in guiding Shi'ite Muslims end-of-life decision. (Cf. Iqbal H. Jaffer and Shabbir M. H. Alibhai, "The Permissibility of Organ Donation, End-of-Life Care, and Autopsy in Shiite Islam: A Case Study" in *Muslim Medical Ethics: From Theory to Practice,* ed. Johnathan E. Brockopp and Thomas Eich [Columbia: University of South Carolina Press, 2008], 167-182.)

13. The Marabouts are examples of Islamic spiritual leaders. In the Islamic community in Senegal they are the religious leaders and authoritative interpreters of the Qur'an.

Qur'an, conflicting Islamic traditions about the collecting of the Qur'an, and lack of archeological evidence for the Qur'an existing before the eighth century.[14] Moreover, there is little evidence for the traditions that speak about the life and teachings of the Prophet before the ninth century CE.

Among historians there are at least three competing theories about the historicity of Muhammad and the Qur'an. One theory accepts the narrative of Islamic origins as legitimate. Muhammad did exist; he lived in Mecca, preached revelation from Allah to the Arabs. There is clearly an imprint of later times, however, on the Qur'an and Muhammad's life and teachings. Another school of thought rejects the assumption that the Islamic story is historical. The late date of texts and the assumption that oral transmission of these texts was accurate, which the first groups of scholars grant, does not seem cogent. They concede that finding a historical basis for Muhammad and the Qur'an is not possible.[15] A third school of thought, representing a minority of scholars, argues that Islam was a sect of Christianity, and "Muhammad" was an appellation for Jesus Christ. Over time this Christian sect evolved into a different religion that we know as Islam.

Furthermore, discovering the historical Muhammad through exegesis of the Qur'an is complicated by the fact that the Qur'an does not present the events of Muhammad's life in chronological order. In fact, the text itself speaks very little about the life and person of Muhammad. Moreover the Qur'an includes a variety of genres and many of these genres exist in the same surah or chapter. These genres include history, poetry, hymns, warnings, and jurisprudence. Although to a non-Muslim the arrangement of the Qur'an may seem to lack a discernable method of ordering, for Muslims the arrangements of the surahs is nothing less than divine decree: the Qur'an is like a ladder to heaven. With each surah, starting from the first surah, the Muslim ascends closer to Allah, gradually appropriating the messages of Allah. Thus you cannot fully comprehend the first verse without ascending to and contemplating the last surah. The Qur'an itself alludes to this providence: "Why is not the Qur'an revealed to him all at once? Thus (it is revealed) that we may strengthen thy heart thereby, and we have rehearsed to thee in slow well-arranged stages" (25:32).

Interestingly, the 114 chapters of the Quran are traditionally divided into the Meccan and Medinan verses. The division is based on when the Prophet received the revelation. Tone and content distinguishes these verses. Generally speaking, while the Meccan verses, which are the earliest verses addressed to Muhammad, are denunciated by their brevity and prophetic and apocalyptic tone, the Medinan verses, or those verses that the Prophet receives in Mecca, are much longer and address practical matters.

---

14. Cf. Ibn Warraq, "Introduction" in *The origins of the Koran: Classic essays on Islam's holy book* (Amherst, NY: Prometheus, 1998), 2001, http://www.qcc.cuny.edu/socialSciences/ppecorino/INTRO_TEXT/Chapter%203%20Religion/Koran-Origins.htm (November 22, 2014).

15. Nerina Rostomji, *The garden and the fire: Heaven and hell in Islamic culture* (New York: Columbia University Press, 2009), xx.

Nevertheless for Muslims, the Qur'an is the word of God that continues to inspire them to submit to Allah. The Qur'an provides the basic tenets of Islamic theology but more importantly jurisprudence. In other words, Islamic tradition stresses what you should do (orthopraxy) as opposed to what you should believe (orthodoxy). For this reason, law experts or jurists, professional explicators of laws necessary to follow in order to live a good life, as opposed to theologians, occupy a prominent role in the Islamic tradition.

The five tenets or pillars of Islam confirm this stress on orthopraxis. The first pillar is the *shahadah*, "There is no God but God, and Muhammad is Allah's Prophet." This basic statement of faith or orthodoxy it welcomes converts to Islam, and orients converts to a new life as a practicing Muslim. The remaining four pillars inform the believer as to what is entailed in this new life. The shahadah leads to the second pillar of Islam, *salat* or the formalized ritual/canonical prayer that involves various prayers and prostrations. Muslims are required to perform salat facing Mecca five times a day. It is also performed on holy days, funerals, and other special occasions. In Islamic countries, and increasingly in mosques, or Islamic centers of worship, in Western countries, an *adhan*, or announcer of prayer, calls all Muslims to prayer five times a day with this proclamation: "God is Greatest of All…There is no god but God!"[16] In order to perform salat Muslims must be ritually pure, which usually entails washing parts of the body or major ablutions in the case of persons who have had intercourse or performed serious actions warranting impurity.[17]

The third pillar is a tithe or *zakat*. Zakat is considered a service to God[18] because it is a means for a Muslim to support and help expand Allah's chosen community, the Umma. Traditionally the zakat was a tax that included one-fortieth of a citizen's wealth that would be given to the Islamic state. However, today there are a variety of interpretations regarding the amount that the zakat should include. Thus within Islamist nations and nations with a Muslim majority there is a wide spectrum of practices; while some states directly levy the tax on its citizens, other states leave the zakat requirement to the private conscience of their citizens.[19] For many Muslims in the United States, the zakat functions like a Christian tithe, or a percentage of income that is given to the local religious community to support that community and its ministries/outreach.

Practicing Islam requires not only praising Allah and supporting Allah's community, but following a strict fast regarding certain items and during certain times of the year. All Muslims are required to fast from pork products and alcohol. Fasting is a pillar known as the *sawm*. Swam refers primarily to the prescribed time of fasting from food, drink, pleasures, and medicines from dawn until

---

16. Colin Turner, *Islam: The basics*, 2nd ed. (London: Routledge, 2011), 139.
17. Denny, 49.
18. Denny, 52.
19. Cf. Jonathan Benthall, "Financial worship: The Quranic injunction to almsgiving," *The Journal of the Royal Anthropological Institute* 5.1 (March 1999), 27-42), 29.

dusk during the holy month of *Ramadan*. Ramadan is an important time for reflection and prayer because Muslims believe that it is the month in which Muhammad first received his revelations from the angel Gabriel. The ill, the young, and elderly are excused from this requirement, but it is expected that all healthy Muslims to have one meal in the morning and then to fast until evening.

The final pillar of Islam is the *hajj*. This is probably the most visible of the five pillars to non-Muslims, as the hajj draws millions of Muslims from around the world to the holy cities of Mecca and Medina in Saudi Arabia annually. Surprisingly albeit a pillar of Islam, it is not absolutely obligatory; however, Muslims with the means are expected to make hajj once in a lifetime. Although Muslims are encouraged to make pilgrimages to Mecca frequently, hajj is a canonical pilgrimage that occurs during the first two weeks of the twelfth month of the Islamic lunar calendar. Muslims believe that the pilgrimage was first instituted by Abraham, and today the pilgrimage involves not only circumambulating the Ka'ba, the altar that Muslims believe that Abraham and Ishmael erected as well as the original setting of the Garden of Eden, but reenacting and visiting various events in the lives of Abraham and the Prophet Muhammad.[20] Pilgrims are in a state called the *ihram* that has various duties associated with it including dress and tonsure.

Although there are five accepted pillars in Islam, jihad has been proposed by many as the sixth pillar of faith due to the centrality for every Muslim to practice it. Jihad is popularly portrayed as religious war and violence. This is one aspect of jihad, known as the jihad of the sword. It was used to defend and expand the Umma, and unfortunately Islamic extremists today use it to justify the killing of innocent people. Jihad of the sword is the lesser jihad. The greater jihad is jihad of the heart/soul, which is war against self-centeredness. This is the battle that all Muslims must fight daily, to submit their entire self to the living God. The five pillars serve as the path for Muslims to more fully accept and grow closer to Allah. Muslims stress that prayer, even in performance of one's obligation, is ineffective if it is not performed with the right intention to worship God. True jihad enlivens the soul so as to purify it for worship and performance of good deeds and the five pillars.[21]

---

20. One of the most famous rituals is the "stoning of Satan" where pilgrims throw stones that symbolize their renunciation of Satan and Satan's works, as well as their solidarity with Abraham who resisted the Devil who tried to persuade him not to sacrifice Isma'il to Allah (Turner, 161).

21. For a succinct introduction to jihad see the sections on jihad in the "Open Letter Dr. Ibrahim Awwad Al-Badri" who is the self-proclaimed leader of the terrorist organization, ISIS. ("To Dr. Ibrahim Awwad Al-Badri, alias 'Abu Bakr Al-Baghdadi', To the fighters and followers of the self-declared 'Islamic State,'" *Open Letter to Al-Baghdadi* 2014, http://lettertobaghdadi.com/ [July 22, 2015].)

Sunna and Hadiths

In the late 1990s in the United States, it was popular for young Christians to wear wristbands that said "WWJD" or "What would Jesus do?" This acronym functioned as a reminder for Christians to stop and think about Jesus Christ and how Jesus would act in a given situation. Because the gospels provide only a snippet of Jesus' life—perhaps only the last three years—Christians, who seek to imitate Christ, have to adduce from the Gospels how to apply Jesus' teachings to contemporary challenges.

For Muslims, Muhammad occupies this role; however, Muslims do not need to extrapolate from the Qur'an what Muhammad would do in a given situation, because they have the *sunnah* or teachings of the prophet that tell them exactly what Muhammad did. The sunnah illustrates how to imitate Muhammad, because it describes in intricate detail what exactly Muhammad did in a variety of situations relevant to contemporary times.[22] These teachings were preserved two to four centuries after the death of the Prophet in what is known as the *hadiths* or reports of the Prophet.[23] Thus it is not uncommon to find Muslims quoting the hadiths of the Prophet as opposed to the Qur'an in response to contemporary challenges.

The widely accepted, authoritative collections of hadiths were those collected by Imam al-Bukhari (d. 870) and Imam Muslim ibn al-Hajjaj (d. 875). Both scholars are praised for their assiduous study of their hadiths that indicates how the saying was transmitted from the Prophet to them. Their respective collections are known as *sahih* or the authoritative collection that purports Muhammad's teachings.[24] Sahih al-Bukhari is interpreted by many Muslims as second tier of revelation after the Qur'an.[25] Together these hadiths include over 14,000 sayings of the Prophet. The Hadiths are akin to the Talmud as it represents a commentary on the Qur'an, but also speaks about a variety of topics from dress code to the interpretation of dreams and criminal justice.

Shar'ia

These hadiths form the basis of *shar'ia* or Islamic law that explicates the rules by which Muslims must live. The history and development of shar'ia as well as the different schools of shar'ia are beyond the

---

22. Charles le Gai Eaton, "Man" in *Islam Spirituality: Foundations in Routledge Library Editions: Islam*, Volume 48, ed. Seyyed Hossein Nasr (Routledge: London, 1987), 364. When faced with difficulty Muslims will not ask "what would Muhammad do?" but rather "what did Muhammad do?"
23. Denny, 64.
24. Turner, 9.
25. Ibid., 9.

scope of this chapter. For our purpose, shar'ia developed to address some of the ambiguities in the Qur'an related to orthopraxy. The earliest Islamic community could refer directly to Muhammad for guidance. However, once Muhammad died, Muslims, who desired to submit to Allah in every aspect of life, needed clarifications as to how exactly Muslims should act. In the history of Islamic jurisprudence the watershed event was when judges were elected in the Islamic empire to arbitrate disputes. The complexity of the disputes and application of Islamic sources (Qur'an and Sunna) as well as the use of inductive reasoning from these texts that included "reasoning by analogy (qiyas), consideration of the public good (maslaha), equity or consideration of the fairest outcome (is-tih-san), customary usage (urf), and independent legal reasoning (ijtihad),"[26] and scholarly consensus led to a complex body of literature by various legal experts and the school of jurists that followed their example. While in Sunni Islam there are four schools of jurisprudence known as the Hanafi, Maliki, Shafi'i, and Hanbali schools, in Shi'ite Islam the major school of law is Ja'fari school.[27] Today shar'ia plays an important role for Muslims, as "all things are under God's legislation."[28] However, there is wide recognition that not every aspect of life is relevant to the religion and thus shar'ia as-signs a scale from "forbidden" to "indifferent" and "obligatory" to various actions. Also Muslims de-bate whether or not the *"gate of ijthihad"* (the process of using reason to derive shar'ia) is possible.[29] For example, Muslims debate whether shar'ia has ossified. More progressive Muslims argue that the Islamic world needs to reclaim its heritage of open debate and the historical process by which the shar'ia of the aforementioned schools was formed. Today moderate Muslims stress that shar'ia can in fact justify not only democracy, women's rights, but also freedom of religion. Muslims, especially in the West, also debate the applicability of twelfth-century Islamic law to modern living, as well as shar'ias that do not have a strong basis in Islamic revelation. Thus they argue that controversial shar'ias such as the death sentence for Muslims that reject Islam (apostasy) or the sharia that en-courage domestic abuse against women for disobeying their husband should not be enforced since they were only applicable to a specific historical, sociocultural context.

Afterlife Beliefs

Similar to Judaism and Christianity, accountability for one's deed, resurrection, the final judgment, and afterlife are central beliefs in the Islamic religion, especially in the Meccan verses of the Qur'an and hadiths.[30] Nevertheless, accountability for our actions that result in eternal reward or punish-

---

26. Kareem Elbayar, "Reclaiming the tradition: Islamic law in a modern world," *International Affairs Review,* http://www.iar-gwu.org/node/23 (December 1, 2014).
27. Turner, 95.
28. Denny, 8.
29. Turner, 98.
30. Ibid., 18.

ment is the operative paradigm in Islamic beliefs about the afterlife that influences how a Muslim lives and worships, makes end-of-life decisions, dies and buries their dead.[31]

MODERN ISLAMIC INTERPRETATIONS OF THE AFTERLIFE

Muslims believe that death is the separation of the soul from the body. After death the soul goes through three stages in the afterlife: (1) the Barzakh or the realm in which the soul remains from death until the resurrection, (2) the day of Resurrection, and (3) Eternal Abode.[32] Before I discuss these ideas it is important to note that today there are a variety of interpretations about these states within the Islamic tradition. To complicate matters, with exception to the ayatollahs in Shi'ite Islam, for Sunni Muslims there is no authoritative body to meditate between various and at times conflicting accounts of the afterlife. Generally speaking, Islamic theology is a theology of consensus, which means that the Umma takes as authoritative what the majority of the religious experts have to say. Thus even though theologies of rebirth are present in the Islamic tradition, this tradition is not considered orthodox because it lacks the consensus of Islamic scholars. Nevertheless, as Yvonne Yazbeck Haddad's and Jane Idleman Smith's research reveal, in Islam today there are three main interpretations about Islamic teachings on the afterlife: the traditionalist, modernist, and spiritualist interpretation.[33] Note that these categories are not mutually exclusive, but rather exist as to allow intelligible conversation about seemingly conflicting accounts of the afterlife.

Traditionalists accept the classical delineation of Islamic afterlife as literally true. Following classical Islamic theology, the afterlife is filled with physical pleasures and torments relative to one's morality and inner jihad. Nerina Rustomji proposes that life after life is an "afterworld" as opposed to an "afterlife".[34] In contradistinction to Christianity, Islamic afterlife stresses the content of the afterlife as opposed to the relationships contained therein. Thus Catholic teaching on the afterlife employs relational language to describe what happens after death whereas Islam provides descriptive language with respect to the rewards or punishments. The modernists, however, downplay the traditional teachings on Islamic afterworld, and stress human accountability in life: since it is our actions

---

31. In Islam, especially in the Middle East, there is a strong stress on the end time events at the societal and institutional levels. (Cf. Jean-Pierre Filiu, *Apocalypse in Islam*, trans M.B. DeBevoise [Berkeley: University of California Press, 2011].)
32. Cf. William C. Chittick, "'Your sight today is piercing': The Muslim understanding of death and afterlife" in *Death and afterlife: Perspectives of world religions*, 136.
33. Jane Idleman Smith and Yvonne Yazbeck Haddad, *The Islamic understanding of death and resurrection* (Oxford: Oxford University Press, 2002), 100-101. Note that these labels have a didactic purpose insofar as they help a non-Muslim understand the variations in the interpretation of the Islamic tradition. However, Muslims may not be comfortable with them; moreover members of each group appropriate material from the other groups.
34. Rustomiji, xvii.

that determine our future; no attempt is made to distinguish the immediate after-death period and the eschaton, or events of the final resurrection. The afterlife is a continuum, albeit with respect to death, not life as we know it on earth. There is no denial of the classical tradition espoused by the traditionalists per se but stress is on their incomprehensibility of the afterworld inasmuch pleasures and pains contained therein are discontinuous with our experiences on earth. On the other hand, spiritualists stress a spiritual or symbolic explanation about the afterlife. Thus the afterworld is more properly an afterlife, which stresses relationships. Whereas the modernists drop the barzakh from discussion, the spiritualists stresses the barzakh and attempts to link Islamic belief in the barzakh with pseudo-scientific studies as well as NDE research about what happens after death, offering something like a scientific proof for Islamic afterlife beliefs.[35]

BARZAKH: FROM DEATH UNTIL RESURRECTION

Two of the most important messages in Qur'an are Allah's oneness and humankind's accountability before Allah. These teachings are not juxtaposed but rather integrated as it is incumbent upon Muslims to reflect Allah's unity in ethical and ritual actions so as to reflect Allah in their life,[36] ridding themselves of anything that appears as "his" or "hers" so that the Divine Will operates without impediment.[37]They will be judged to the extent that they reflected Allah's unity.[38]

There are two judgments in the Islamic afterlife. The first judgment or "lesser resurrection"[39]occurs immediately after death and determines how you will spend your time before the second judgment. To an extent the second judgment is *pro forma*, as what will happen to you in eternity is prefigured in the first judgment. After the first judgment the punishment of the wicked and blessings for the righteous begin. Nonetheless, the environment of the first judgment is the *barzakh,* or realm wherein the dead remain until the second judgment. Interestingly, although classical Islamic thought, the hadiths of the Prophet are replete with references to the barzakh, the barzakh is only mentioned once in the Qur'an: "Behind them is the barzakh until the day they are raised up" (23: 100).[40] Nevertheless, for traditionalist and spiritualist Muslims, it is an important part of their tradition that directly relates to our concern for healthcare considerations.

---

35. Cf. Jane I. Smith, "Reflections on aspects of Islamic immortality" *The Harvard Theological Review* 20.½ (Jan-April 1977): 85-98, 116-118.

36. Ibid., 86.

37. Eaton, 359.

38. To understand the importance of human action before Allah, draw a horizontal line and second line perpendicular to it. While the vertical line represents our relationship with God, the horizontal line represents our relationship with creation, human beings, animals, the environment, and etc. While God can forgive sins against God, God will not forgive sins against other people.

39. William C. Chittick, "Eschatology" in *Islam spirituality: Foundations* in *Routledge Library Editions: Islam,* Volume 48, ed. Seyyed Hossein Nasr (Routledge: London, 1987), 398.

40. Cf. Chittick, 380.

Entrance into the barzakh occurs by mediation of an angel. The Qur'an says: "the angel of death, who has been entrusted with you, makes you die" (32:11). The angel of death or Azrael separates the body from the soul. Depending on how a person lived life, death can be a difficult, painful process or a peaceful transition. Reminiscent of out-of-body experiences, after death the soul remains around the body and is able to observe the funeral. If the soul was righteous it is escorted by several angels to the highest heaven, where its name is inscribed in the heavenly registries,[41] and then returned to the body in the grave. If the soul was unrighteous, it is welcomed by the guardians of hell that prevent the soul from ascending to heaven and cast it into its grave.

During the first day in the grave, the dead are questioned by two angels, Munkar and Nakir.[42] In most accounts, they ask the soul three questions: Who do you worship as Lord? What religion do you identify with? and Who is the Prophet? Depending on whether or not the soul is able to answer these questions with fidelity to the Islamic faith, the grave will transform into a foretaste of heaven, a paradise-like garden, or hell that the soul will experience until the Resurrection.[43] Pain or pleasure as experienced in the grave or barzakh is relative to the virtues or vices that a person has acquired during life, and thus in hell the sinner is tormented by sins that are personified as attacking serpents and scorpions. [44] The Barzakh has distinct parallels to the Tibetan Bardo, because it reflects to an extent self-perceptions.[45] Muslim theologians and mystics therefore stress that the questioning of Munkar and Nakir is less legalistic than the revelation of one's true nature to oneself on the topic of existential importance—that is, who you really are before Allah. Of course the parallels between the barzakh and the Bardo Thodol are limited as the barzakh is a definitive place of judgment; it is the realm of dreams that is without escape until the resurrection. Perhaps for this reason it is more appropriate to compare it to purgatory.[46] This analogy is appropriate for righteous Muslims who are experiencing the foretaste of heaven because like purgatory the barzakh offers opportunity for spiritual growth.[47] Beyond the aforementioned aspects of barzakh, the barzakh also includes the ability of the soul or spirit[48] to communicate with the dead and living.[49]

---

41. Asma Afsaruddin, "Death, resurrection, and human destiny in the Islamic tradition" in *Death, resurrection and human destiny: Christian and Muslim perspectives: A record of the Eleventh Building Bridge Seminar convened by the Archbishop of Canterbury.* Kings College London and Canterbury Cathedral April 23-25, 2012, eds. David Marshall and Lucinda Mosher (Washington: Georgetown University Press, 2014), 45.
42. Chittick, 380.
43. Many Muslims believe the souls reside in location of the physical grave.
44. Chittick, 396.
45. Citied in Chittick, 397.
46. Afsaruddin, 46.
47. Cf. Ibid., 106.
48. Note that there is no clear doctrine regarding the difference between the spirit and soul in Islam. Like Christian theologians, Islamic authors do not consistently subscribe to a preestablished determination how the soul and spirit are distinct. At the very least both terms refer to the consciousness that remains after death.
49. Smith, 121.

Greater Resurrection and Final Judgment

Like the Christian and Jewish traditions, a series of events occur before the resurrection of the dead and final judgment. Albeit there is no clear consensus regarding the chronology of apocalyptic events, all Muslims share belief that these events will occur.[50]

Detailed discussion of the events of the apocalypse is beyond the scope of this chapter; however, it is of interest to note a few salient details of this tradition. First, a cataclysmic battle occurs between the infidels or "Byzantines" and a Muslim army from Medina that results in many causalities but the victory of the Muslims. Afterwards Allah will send the Messiah, Jesus, son of Mary, to destroy the remaining infidels and kill the al-Dajjal or the anti-Christ. Al-Dajjal is usually depicted as the worst of all villains, with one eye on his forehead, that will seduce humanity and lay waste to the entire world except Medina and Mecca. A second important person is the guided one or the Mahdi (Messiah). Within the Sunni tradition, identity of the Mahdi is ambiguous, although he is often associated with Jesus Christ.[51] In the Shi'ite tradition he is not identified with Jesus; some Shi'ite Muslims believe that the Mahdi is the 12th Imam. What is most important is that through his actions good triumphs over evil, ushering in a time of peace.[52] Nevertheless the end of time and the world as we know it comes to an end with a series of trumpet blasts. With the last trumpet blast, Allah destroys all creation culminating with the destruction of death itself: "Finally God commands that because of His word, all souls will taste death, even the angel of death himself must die, and so he does."[53] Once Allah's oneness and omnipotence are absolutely supreme, God then recreates the cosmos and resurrects humanity for the final judgment.

RESURRECTION

What the body of resurrection is remains a subject of debate for Muslims; however what is essential is that every human being will be resurrected for the final judgment. At this point barzakh ceases to exist and the resurrected persons are ushered to Jerusalem where they will be judged on the basis of their deeds committed in life. In one popular tradition, the righteous carry their deeds in a book, while the unrighteous carry their deeds on a scroll that hangs around their neck. After they have been judged by Allah, the righteous and unrighteous must cross a bridge (sirat).[54] For the righteous

---

50. Within the Islamic tradition, there are some exceptions to the rule that all persons have to wait until the resurrection to enter paradise. There are various prophets as well as martyrs in heaven.

51. Smith, 70, 128.

52. Sajjad Riziv, "A Muslims's perspective on a good death, resurrection, and human destiny" in *Death, resurrection and human destiny: Christian and Muslim perspectives*, 106.

53. Smith, 71.

54. Afsaruddin, 46.

crossing the bridge will be easy and they will do so and then enter into heaven. For the unrighteous it is a laborious process if not impossible: nevertheless there is hope even for the condemned that they can cross the bridge without falling into the pit of fire that is hell. Islamic mystic and theologian al-Ghazali describes the bridge as thin as hair and as sharp as a sword that stretches across hell, and the light necessary to cross the bridge will be relative to your good deeds. Thus the better you have lived your life the more light you have to cross. Even though your deeds in life determine your fate in the afterworld for all eternity, Muhammad pleads to God for the salvation of his people. In fact, many will be saved by his pleading. Allah's mercy overcomes Allah's wrath. For this reason Muslim theologians postulate that Allah will show mercy to the Muslims in hell as well as the possibility that all will be saved from hell one day.

HEAVEN AND HELL

For traditionalist Muslims, the resurrection of the body and final judgment indicate that heaven and hell will involve bodily pleasures and pains. Otherwise the bodily resurrection is unnecessary. Heaven is paradise where the blessed are free to enjoy the pleasures of food, drink, and sex, but most importantly a visitation by Allah. Note that relative to the distinction I cited above between traditionalist, modernist, and spiritualist, the pleasures of heaven are interpreted in a variety of manners: they are seen as physical pleasures (traditionalist), analogous but radically different from physical pleasure (modernists), or spiritual realities that lack any material analogy (spiritualist).[55] With respect to torments of hell mentioned in the Islamic tradition and Qur'an, we find the same plurality in interpretation. Whereas traditionalists interpret the torments of hell literally, modernists and spiritualist stress that it is ineffable and that the greatest punishment is distance from Allah.

Jane Smith made an important insight that these traditions are instructive rather than descriptive.[56] Her point is that albeit heaven and hell are realities in the hereafter, what we know about them occurs in the context of largely homiletic and polemical writings that are meant to encourage Muslims to lead good lives in submission to Allah. She argues that Islam allows for multiple interpretations of these traditions. Thus Muslims are quite comfortable advocating both allegorical and literal interpretations of the pleasures of heaven and pains of hell.

The plurality of interpretation is evident with respect to one of the most difficult traditions of the afterlife that I have found when teaching Islam to non-Muslim students, namely the heavenly virgins promised to faithful Islamic men in heaven, *the houris* (44:54; 52:20). The houris are chaste virgins of paradise that are rewarded to faithful Muslim men for sexual enjoyment.[57] In the most authori-

---

55. Cf. Smith, 134.
56. Ibid., 89.
57. Cf. Ibid., 164.

tative hadiths of Bukhari and Muslim every man in heaven is given one maiden in addition to his earthly wife. Nevertheless, while traditional Muslims accept that these are women given to men to satisfy their sexual appetites, modernist and spiritualist Muslims stress the incommensurability of the maidens and sex in heaven with sexual relationships on earth, or drop the tradition about the maidens from discourse by stressing that Islamic women become the houris. Other Muslims de-emphasize the hadiths that stress sexual acts with these maidens, and argue that these women are personifications of the good deeds of male and female persons. Some Muslims stress that they are simply attendants given to both men and women.

Nevertheless, the houris are only one aspect of Islamic heaven. Heaven is the penultimate expression of paradise and bliss. Heaven is a beautiful garden in which Muslims will enjoy life with their family and loved ones without pain, suffering, or any defilement. Life in heaven shares similarities to the life of the affluent on earth in as much as every person has a spouse, home, food, and servants.

For Muslims those in heaven continue to grow in knowledge and virtue. Following the tradition that Muhammad traveled through the seven heavens, heaven is divided into seven realms. There are a variety of traditions on the different pleasures and persons that populate each realm. Each realm is occupied by one major figure from the biblical tradition: the first realm is occupied by Adam; in the second are Jesus and John the Baptist, in the third is Joseph; in the fourth is Enoch; in the fifth is Aaron; in the sixth is Moses; and in seventh is Abraham who sits at the throne to the entrance to paradise. Paradise or the Garden is the closest analogy to Gan Eden or Christian heaven.

While heaven is a reward for the righteous Muslim, hell is the ultimate punishment, condemnation of the righteous. Hell is the inversion of heaven, and thus hell contains seven realms that also include certain types of persons and punishments. The main inhabitants of hell are infidels or unbelievers, who are further subdivided by their theological/ideological beliefs:

> 1-purgatorial fire [jahannan]-unfaithful Muslims; 2-flaminf fire [laza]-Christians; 3-raging fire [hutama]-Jews; 4-blazing fires [sa'ir]-Sabaeans; 5-sorching fire [saqar]-Magi; 6-fierce fire [jahim]-idolaters; 7-the abyss [hawiya]-hypocrites[58]

Traditions abound as to specific punishments relative to specific wrongdoings committed by persons in the different realms, and, in fact, there are various subdivisions of these realms in proportion to the sins committed. Although traditionalists, modernists, and spiritualists disagree as to whether literal or allegorical interpretations are appropriate for Islamic heaven and hell, they all agree that a continuum exists between life and the afterlife and that you are personally responsible for all of your deeds in life.

---

58. Cf. Smith and Haddad, 85.

Coping with Death, Dying, and Bereavement

The fact that even Muhammad, Allah's greatest prophet, died is very important, as it demonstrates that death is as natural as life. Moreover, the dying find comfort in their belief that Allah is with them and that suffering may be a part of Allah's plan for that person.[59] The Qur'an speaks to this: "To God we belong and to Him is our return" (2:15). Death should not cause fear, and the end of life offers opportunities to return to Allah. The upshot of this is that the preparation for death offers a final occasion to win the war against one's heart (jihad of heart). Thus end-of-life preparation involves prayer and reciting or listening to Allah's word, the Qur'an. At the same time, Muslims recognize that they have a mission on earth and Allah has determined our time for death in advance. For this reason the physical tasks are circumscribed by the spiritual task; in particular the idea that we cannot frustrate Allah's plan for us and that Allah wills life is very important. For this reason euthanasia or treatments that will hasten death are not acceptable.

With respect to the dying, when death is imminent, family members or friends will help prepare their loved one to enter into paradise at the final judgment. Their primary goal is to iterate the dying person's faith in Allah and Allah's unity. This will entail reciting the Qur'an, particularly the Surah Yaseen, or playing the Qur'an on a CD. Like a rabbi or priest, the imam plays an important role at the end of life. He will not only address the spiritual dimension of the patient, but also help the family make arrangements regarding special accommodations for caring for a patient, as well as planning the funeral service. In addition, supplications are made to help forgive the sins of the loved one.

For a Muslim the ideal death is to die knowing that you have lived a good life (i.e., knowing you have fulfilled your mission and duty on earth to submit to Allah in all things), but also surrounded by loved ones. In terms of the sociological dimension, dying at home in the presence of family is ideal.

Prayer is a central part of the preparation for death. Thus the dying will fulfill *salat* or daily prayer rituals to the best of their ability. Moreover Muslims believe that an ideal death includes dying after saying *La ilahaila-Allah* or "I bear witness that there is no god but Allah.[60]

Immediately after death several rituals are performed to prepare the deceased for burial. Reminiscent of Jewish custom, Muslims stress that the body must be respected and to avoid any action that may frustrate the resurrection or disturb the soul. Respect for the body is highlighted by the Islamic rituals that occur immediately after a Muslim dies to prepare the body for burial. Once a person

59. Ruqaiyyah Waris Maqsood, *After death, life! Thoughts to alleviate the grief all Muslims facing death and bereavement* (New Delhi, India: Goodword Books, 2001), 138-139.

60. Saleh A. Fetouh and Tarek D. Bahgat, "Al-Janazah" in *Guide to Muslim funerals in Greater Western New York*, 25. Note that this text is self-published and provides an invaluable guide to how Muslims in New York die, as well as information for Muslims with regard to burial expenses and Muslim cemeteries.

dies it is customary to recite *Inna Liillahiwainnailayhiraji'un*, "Verily we belong to Allah, and truly to him we shall return." The eyes and jaw are then closed and the body is covered with a white sheet. Supplications or *dua* is made to Allah on the behalf of the dead, so that Allah forgives the loved one for any sins. Excessive mourning is not permitted, as it demonstrates a lack of faith and inability to accept Allah's will, which is beyond question.

Because the respect for the body is an essential element in this tradition, cremation, autopsies, and embalming are inappropriate. Autopsies are only permitted when it is necessary to determine cause of death. There is debate on the ethics of organ donation regarding mutilating the body but also donating an organ to a non-Muslim. Muslims are generally open to organ donation after death provided that there is good reason to believe that the organ will save a life. Even though organ donation would complicate or at least impede the speed of burial, Islam stresses that Allah wills life and that to save life is a great good, and thus organ donation can be a final act of charity.

Before the funeral there are three main rituals performed: ritual washing (*Ghusl*), ritual shrouding (*Kafan*), and funeral prayer (*Salat-ul-janazah*). The ritual washing involves two to five individuals. While invoking the name of Allah, the washers begin at the head and respectfully clean the body following at least fifteen steps. With exception to spouses and children, washers are the same gender as the deceased. Washers will perform *wudu* or ritual cleansing that is performed before *salat* and then shroud the body. The shroud (*kafan*) consists of three white unstitched sheets and three seven-foot ropes for males or five white garments that included two sheets, a long loose sleeveless shirt, waist wrapper, and a head veil for women. The dead are then carefully wrapped and bound by these garments and then covered and tied with the remaining cloth and ties.[61] Afterwards the shrouded body is then transported to the funeral site, usually outside the mosque, where the funeral prayer is performed. This is an obligatory salat for the community. The service is serene and simple. The funeral attendees line up in three lines horizontally facing Mecca (Line 1: men, Line 2: children, and Line 3: women), and they recite the first seven verses of the Qur'an or *Fatihah* silently:

> In the name of Allah, the Entirely Merciful, the Especially Merciful. [All] praise is [due] to Allah, Lord of the worlds. The Entirely Merciful, the Especially Merciful, Sovereign of the Day of Recompense. It is You we worship and You we ask for help. Guide us to the straight path -The path of those upon whom You have bestowed favor, not of those who have evoked [Your] anger or of those who are astray. (1:1-7)

The mourners then recite prayers that invoke the peace and blessing of Muhammad (*Tashahood*), and make supplications on behalf of the dead. Service concludes with the prayer "Assalamualay-kumwarehmatullah" or "Peace be upon you O people of the graves."[62]

---

61. Fetouh, 28.
62. al-Janazah, 29.

The community then processes with the corpse to the grave. The deceased is laid on the right side facing Mecca. Note that one of the problems that Muslims living in the West face is the lack of a facility to perform the abovementioned rituals, especially when death occurs in a hospital setting, but also access to a Muslim cemetery that will allow the dead to face Mecca.[63]

Nevertheless, after the body is lowered into the grave, "Bismillahwa ala millatirasulillah" or "In the name of Allah and in the faith of the Messenger of Allah" is recited. The ties on the head and feet are undone. Those present then throw three handfuls of soil on the grave, reciting one verse in sequential order from this prayer with each handful of soil: "1-From earth did We create you; 2-And into it shall We return you; 3-And from it shall We bring you."[64] The mourners ask Allah to forgive the deceased: "O Allah! Forgive him, and have mercy upon him. Surely you alone are the Forgiver, the Merciful."[65]

After the burial, a three-day period of bereavement begins. During this period it is customary for members of the community to supply meals and for the family of the deceased as well as the bereaved to spend these three days focusing on their departed loved one. They may engage in acts that benefit the dead including prayer, charity, fasting, pilgrimage, and reciting the Qur'an. Nevertheless, Muslims can continue to benefit the dead by visiting the grave, reciting the Qur'an on behalf of the dead, and asking Allah to forgive the dead and lessen their punishment. This is particularly an important responsibility of children, as the Prophet teaches that a righteous child benefits his dead parent.

End-of-Life Care and Decisions

Like all of the other religions that I have presented in this book, the spiritual task, which for a Muslim is to be judged by Allah as righteous, dictates how religious persons approach the other dimensions of care. This is clearly evident when we consider the importance of prayer, cleanliness, presence of the community, and diet of the dying patient. Effective healthcare needs to respect these aspects of the Islamic tradition.

For religious Muslims, end-of-life preparations involve fulfilling salat. This will require caregivers to schedule times for uninterrupted prayer five times a day. Note that each prayer session takes ten minutes on average and requires the full attention of the Muslim; thus it is not appropriate to disturb a Muslim during prayer—the Muslim will most likely not respond unless there is an emergency. Prayers may be performed in the bed but the Muslim must face the Ka'ba in Mecca.

---

63. Maqsood, 169.
64. Ibid., 30.
65. Ibid.

Because the Islamic tradition stresses purity and cleanliness, before prayer, Muslims ritually wash their face, forearms, and feet. On Fridays or the Islamic Sabbath, Muslims will want to take a ritual bath (*Ghishul*). Illness complicates these important rituals, as illness that results in bleeding, defecation, and vomiting render the person impure. (Note that the obligation for purification before prayer is lifted when patients are physically unable to fulfill it and *tayammum* is performed, which involves touching clean sand that renders the person ritually pure.) Having conversations about patients' need to be cleaned in order to fulfill their religious obligations is important and helps instill respect for their autonomy (psychological dimension). If it is possible, make accommodations so as to make it easier for patients to undergo the ritual washing (e.g., making the sink more accessible to the person or placing the bed near the sink). Note that these prayer requirements must be taken into consideration when discussions about palliative drugs occur. Although there is no prohibition against them, Muslims will want to maintain equilibrium between pain control and cognition, so as to fulfill these very important rituals.

In addition to the importance of cleanliness for prayer, Islam stresses modesty in dress and social interactions. Regarding dress, although there is no prohibition to wearing clothing appropriate to a hospital setting, care must be taken to avoid exposing the genital region. If this region must be checked it is very important to ask for permission to do so. With respect to social interaction, caregivers of the same sex as the patient are ideal. It is not uncommon for Muslims, especially Muslim emigrants from the Middle East, to avoid unnecessary interactions, including shaking hands, with persons of the opposite sex. When this is not possible and the patient is a Muslim woman with a male health professional, it is not uncommon for a female relative or friend to accompany the patient. Moreover, male healthcare professionals should not take offense if female patients do not make eye contact with them as this is a sign of modesty in certain cultural expressions of Islam. Since modesty is stressed and it is therefore an important aspect of how a Muslim defines his/her autonomy, it is important for health professionals to knock before entering a Muslim's room.[66]

Caregivers should note that Muslims are forbidden to consume porcine products and drink alcohol. Traditionally, Muslims will only eat meat products that are prepared by a Christian, Jew, or Muslim. Also, if patients are healthy enough, during the month of Ramadan, they will fast from food and beverages from sunrise to sunset. If not, patients will make the fast when their health improves or do acts of charity in place of the fast.

Islam, like many of the religions we have discussed, stresses the social dimension for coping with dying; it is important for family to be present at the end of life. Islam encourages Muslims to visit the sick, and thus caregivers should expect many visitors in their Muslim patient's room. Therefore addressing the social task may require that the caregiver accommodate these visitors to the best of the

66. Cf. al-Shari, 433.

caregiver's ability. The more you can accommodate these visitors, the happier your patient will be. Note also, especially in Middle Eastern Muslim communities, it is not appropriate for family members to display affection in front of nonfamily. Thus what non-Muslims in the West may perceive as dysfunction and discomfort on the part of the patient may not be so. If this is witnessed and the healthcare professionals are concerned for the patient, ask the patient about the relationship before jumping to conclusions. Nevertheless, as death approaches Muslims seek forgiveness from one another, and tend to become much more emotional. Ideally family members will be present with their loved one as they die, reciting the Shahadah and the Qur'an with them. Once the patient has died, a family member will close the eyes and begin the rituals mentioned above.

Because Muslims stress the importance of respecting the body, it is very important for health professionals to help facilitate the documentation necessary to transport the body of the dead as soon as possible to the facility (funeral home or mosque) where the dead will be prepared for burial. Communicating the intention to help support Islamic rituals demonstrates respect but also may address the spiritual and psychological dimensions of the patient.

With respect to the physical care, Islam teaches that life is a gift and the importance of ending suffering. Thus while euthanasia is prohibited, palliative care is acceptable. The spiritual task also guides Muslims in their decisions to withhold or withdraw treatments. Doing Allah's will requires Muslims to take lifesaving medications. [67] This somewhat complicates decisions as to whether extraordinary treatments can be withheld—we should note that this terminology is not indigenous to Islam and thus the position on end-of-life treatments is obscure. Nevertheless, in both Shi'ite and Sunni Islam nutritional support (food, water), at least when the patient's gut can absorb the nutrients, it is considered basic and obligatory care.[68] Consensus exists that it is never licit to withdraw these ordinary means. With respect to extraordinary means in the context of withholding or withdrawing life support, the Islamic teaching that life should always be saved is circumscribed by these principles: nonmaleficence, justice, autonomy, and beneficence.[69] Withholding life support, even if it is futile, is immoral if any of these principles are violated. Because there is not a clear teaching on this topic and traditional Muslims tend to view withdrawing life support as maleficent, it is crucial to discuss this matter with a patient or proxy. Also be aware, especially in Sunni Islam, that many Muslims rely on their imam to inform them about the Islamic perspective; thus it is not uncommon for Muslim patients to desire that their imam be a part of this discussion. Nevertheless, the stress on life as a gift from Allah needs to be respected. For this reason, according to Dr. Mohammad Zafir al-Shahri and Dr. Abdullah al-Khenaizan, it is always prudent to provide at least the minimal amount of hydration and nutrition to Muslims in the last moments of their life. When directives are not clear this will

67. Maqsood, 141.
68. Cf. Shabbir M. H. Alibhai and Michael Gordon, "Islamic and Jewish end-of-life ethics" in *Muslim modern ethics from theory to practice*, 186; Jaffer, 180.
69. al-Shahri, 433.

help spare the family and patient the stress of feeling that they violated Allah's commandment to save life, as continuing ordinary treatments does not frustrate Allah's will.

Interestingly, while open to modern medicine, Muslims may also employ spiritual and traditional treatments to address their physical dimension. The most prominent spiritual treatment is to recite the Qur'an, which is believed to have healing powers. Muslims may also wear protective amulets that include verses from the Qur'an. It is not uncommon for Muslims to drink or wash themselves in water from the well in the holy mosque in Mecca.[70] In certain Islamic cultures honey and black cumin are also considered to have healing properties. Thus end-of-life preparations will require time for prayer as well as awareness of any healing treatment that the patient undergoes in addition to his/her Western medical treatments. Note that health professionals should understand that Muslims stress that all events are predestined by Allah, and thus are very skeptical in terms of being given a definitive life expectancy. Although Muslims value truth-telling, phrasing this information in such a way that avoids usurping Allah's will may be more effective to convey life expectancy. To do this effectively, if comfortable, one may simply qualify life expectancies with "but this is in God's (Allah's) hands."

Note that although Sunni Muslims generally accept the neurological criteria for death, Shi'ites tend to favor the traditional cardiopulmonary criteria (e.g., lack of heart beat and breathing). Thus healthcare professionals should be mindful of this and seek to be understanding of difference in opinion.

Conclusion

Islam is a religion that stresses submission of intellect and will to Allah the author of life. For this reason end-of life care is approached in the context of doing the will of Allah, so as to receive the reward that Allah will give to those who are faithful to Allah after the final judgment. It is the duty of every Muslim to prepare for his/her final judgment. In this manner the end-of-life preparations and funeral preparations should be the culminating actions in a life lived in submission to Allah. Living out this relationship requires specific dietary, prayer, ethical, social guidelines that healthcare professionals should respect, so as to help the patient have a good death.

---

70. Mohammad Zafir al-Shahari and Abdullah al-Khenaizan, "Palliative care for Muslim patients," *The Journal of Supportive Oncology* 3.6 (November/ December 2005): 432-436.

Interview

Imam Chawla is a scholar of religious sciences and holds master degrees in philosophy, political science, and Arabic and Islamic studies. In January 2011 he moved to the United States and since then has been working as the imam and community religious leader at Jaffarya Center. Before moving to America he served as imam in different communities for more than a decade. Imam Chawla also serves as Muslim chaplain and religious counselor with various organizations including Buffalo Psychiatric Center. Imam Chawla has delivered numerous lectures around the world and throughout the United States at different occasions and venues including universities, colleges, media channels, mosques, and Islamic centers. Imam Chawla is an author, translator, and researcher. He is fluent in five languages. Imam Chawla emphasizes inter- and intrafaith activities and is an active member of the clergy association and Imam Council.

Q: What is your role at your mosque?

A: I am an imam, which is a religious guide or leader. I lead worship and religious rituals as well as guide the members in my community in their affairs related to their religious life. In regard to end-of-life rituals, I provide spiritual and psychological support for the dying and bereaved family members.

Q: How do you define death?

A: Death is a transition from one life to another life. It is not the end of life. In Islam we examine death from the perspectives of the dying person, the bereaved family, and the Islamic community. We have certain teachings that address each perspective. For instance, in regard to the deceased, there are rituals that are performed while death is occurring as well as after death has occurred. We also provide grief counseling for the bereaved family members, and advise the members of the mosque about what they should do to support the family during this difficult time.

Q: In other religions that I have discussed in this book, end-of-life rituals gain merit for the dead. In Islam do these rituals gain merit for the dead?

A: Yes, in fact, we do believe that these rituals benefit the dead. They can be a source of blessings for the deceased person's soul, and good deeds performed on behalf of a dead person can bring joy to that person's soul. They also establish a spiritual connection between the living and the dead, which is of benefit to both of them.

Q: What do you teach your congregants about what happens in the afterlife? Do you teach that souls enter the barzakh when they die?

A: Yes, this is correct. The details of this state are not known, but it is mentioned in the Qur'an and in the hadiths of the Prophet. The Prophetic and Quranic texts tell us generally that when the body is dead, the soul departs from it and enters the heavens and then this intermediate state. The barzakh is a transitional world or in-between state. We must remember that in Islamic theology, the soul is not a material entity. After death the soul and this state are not bound to the body or to restrictions of space and time. Thus the Qur'an tells us that when the Resurrection occurs and the souls are called out of this state, there will be some persons who will say "we have just died" even though they died many years ago.

Q: Is it correct to state that the Prophet Muhammad is in this state now?

A: This is a difficult question that requires more space than this interview will allow to answer. However, it is important to note that death does not mean we disappear. Good souls visit from the afterlife and have the ability to amend their affairs on earth. Prophets and saints are no exceptions to this. They are spiritually among us, and they are able to communicate with us, though since we are not generally in tune to the spiritual world we may not perceive the connection.

Q: You mentioned a very interesting point that the dead communicate with the living. Are there any specific teachings about this? Does the reality of this communication influence bereavement customs?

A: Yes, we teach that the dead benefit from the assistance of the living. We help the dead by honoring them, mourning in the correct way, and performing charity on behalf of them. The Prophet teaches that any good work you perform benefits the deceased. This may include reading scripture on the anniversary of our loved one's death.

Moreover, honoring the dead is important for the living as well. By doing this you teach the next generation how to honor and remember you when you die. It also reminds the living that they will die, and that this life is only the beginning of our existence.

Q: What was your best experience coping with death as a pastor in this congregation?

A: I have not had a best or worst experience. However, the best death is generally a death when you are at peace, which is not necessarily without difficulty or physical pain. We teach that suffering can be a blessing that removes sin. Nevertheless, emotionally speaking, losing a small child or teenager is very difficult.

Q: You mention difficult situations, how do you respond to tragedies (e.g., suicide) in light of the fact that Islam teaches that Allah is just and merciful?

A: Indeed suicide is a difficult situation. As you have said, we believe in God's mercy. Although it is a sin to kill yourself, this is between the deceased and God. In Islam we teach that killing one person is like killing every human being. This includes killing yourself. But at the same time, we treat suicides with the same honor and respect that we would give to a person that died in any other way.

Q: Is suicide the worst form of death?

A: We cannot judge a person who committed suicide. Many times these persons are not mentally and emotionally healthy. God is the only judge.

The issue is not how the person dies, but rather whether or not the person has died in a state in which God is pleased. Traditionally, the best death is the death of a martyr, or someone who dies fully submitting to God. Any situation where a person dies rejecting God's mercy is a bad death.

Q: Suppose that someone from your congregation calls to tell you that he or she is dying. How would you respond to your congregant?

A: We call this the end-of-life movement. The body and soul have lived together for a long time, so there is a strong bond. This separation of the soul from the body can be difficult. I try to help the dying person transition in peace. We have rituals that we are advised to perform during this time. For instance, we teach that it is important to position the person so that they face the Ka'ba, the house of God, in Mecca. We face them so that they are sitting with their feet facing Mecca. When they pray, they are praying toward Mecca. We also remove worldly things from the room where the person is dying. The point here is to help them transition to the next life, by removing distractions. It is also important to read verses from the Qur'an, particularly the chapter known as Surah Yaseen. Preference is always given to persons that can recite the Qur'an accurately in Arabic. But if this is not possible, then any language is acceptable. If the person is having difficulty, we bring the dying person to the room or place where they used to pray. Obligatory prayers are recited in the mosque. But there are also optional prayers, such as reading the Qur'an; these prayers are recited at home. There should be a designated place for these optional prayers. It may be important to bring the person here to die, as it helps to create a peaceful environment. We also have something called the "Reminder." This involves asking the person a series of questions, such as "Who are you?" and "Who is your Lord?" among other basic belief questions. Reminding the individual of these fundamental beliefs and values is seen as both psychologically reassuring and spiritually beneficial.

Q: Does the "Reminder" have anything to do with the tradition that after death we are questioned by Munkar and Nakir?

A: Yes, we are preparing them for this questioning by divinely appointed angels. When we are reminding the dying of their basic beliefs, it is like going through a checklist. Tradition tells us that these are the questions that will be asked in the grave before the grave closes. This tradition is not a substitute for healthcare. It is very important to call a doctor if the person is dying. You do your best to attend to the person's spiritual needs without neglecting health needs.

Q: What should a member of your community do once their loved one has died?

A: It is customary to straighten the body, close the eyes, and close the mouth. If this does not happen immediately, it becomes very difficult or impossible to do this once the body is cold. This makes performing the ceremonial bath difficult, as we are commanded to be gentle with the body. For instance, it is very difficult to straighten an arm of the deceased that is bent without causing damage to it. Thus I remind my congregants to do this immediately after the death of their loved one. After this we wash the body and wrap it in a shroud. Then we perform a congregational prayer and bury the body.

Q: Can you walk us through the ceremonial washing and shrouding process?

A: The washing is gender specific: men do not wash a woman or vice versa. Private parts are always covered. Usually the imam and persons from the congregation perform the washing. We start by undressing the person, and then remove worldly things (jewelry, etc.). We then remove any impurities. We may suture bleeding wounds. In Shi'ite Islam, there are three ceremonial baths: a bath with water containing lotus leaf, a bath with water containing camphor, and a bath with pure water. After the body is washed, it is shrouded. There are certain clothes for men and women. A minimum amount of clothing should include one piece of clothing for the top and one for the bottom, in addition to a shroud that covers the whole body. The clothing should be unstitched. During this process we want to make the body at peace and prepare the soul for the questions. For this reason we may recite Qur'anic verses as we do this, as well as perform the "Reminder."

We teach classes to show our congregants how to do this, because in order to wash a body with proper respect you need help. You cannot physically do this alone. You need three to four people to carefully move, wash, and shroud the body. We have a facility here to wash and shroud the body. But you can do this at the funeral home.

After shrouding the body we then place the body in the coffin, if there is one. The body is now moved to a place for prayer. This may occur at the mosque, Islamic center, cemetery, or funeral home. Prayers are different from normal prayers, as they do not include prostrations; we praise God, testify to our faith, praise God for the Prophet Muhammad, pray for the Muslim community, and conclude with a particular prayer for the person who has died. After this a grave is dug. When the people carrying the coffin see the grave, they will set down and pick up the coffin three times. On the third occasion, the mourners place the coffin into the grave. Usually the person laying the body in the grave is a relative.

The face of the body is moved so that it faces Mecca. The body may be buried in any direction, but in Muslim cemeteries all graves are in one direction facing Mecca.

After they close the grave, there are many traditions. Prayers are said for the dead. A close relative may address the people at the cemetery and say that he wants his relative to be at peace, so he will offer to pay any of his relative's debts, if there are any.

Q: Is there a specified bereavement period?

A: There is no limit. The length of the period depends upon the community. Islam does not paralyze the life of the bereaved. Usually in Islamic communities, meals are cooked by the community for the bereaved for the first three days after death. But the three-day period is not obligatory.

Q: What do you do if there is no body?

A: If there is no body, then you cannot perform the rituals that I mentioned. It is important to pray for the deceased.

Q: Should the burial occur within twenty-four hours after death?

A: Yes, you bury the person as quickly as possible. Sometimes it is difficult because of holidays and time of day. For instance, funeral homes and cemeteries close at night. There is no sin if you delay the process.

Q: What is the Islamic position on autopsy?

A: It is not permissible to disturb a body unless there is good reason to do so (e.g., it is required by law).

Q: In a traditional hospital setting, is it a problem if the body of the deceased is moved to the morgue before the family arrives?

A: Yes, this is an issue. If the healthcare professionals can prevent the body from being moved until the family arrives, this is ideal. Nevertheless, we are reasonable and recognize that a hospital has limited resources and rooms.

Q: Besides the aforementioned issue, are there any other difficulties regarding practicing Islamic end-of-life rituals in a traditional hospital setting?

A: No, I am not aware of any other issues. Health professionals in my experience are very accommodating. And there have been various legal rulings that protect religious rights. Many of the morals and values of our society are not in contradiction to Islam.

Q: Do Muslims accept the neurological criteria of death?

A: Traditionally, Islam considers a person dead when the pulse and bodily functions have stopped. There are occasions when it is permissible to allow a person to die even if there is a pulse. Muslim scholars and authorities do have different views in this area. Nevertheless, when a person is declared to be dead by his/her doctors, we accept their diagnosis.

Q: In terms of Islamic end-of-life rituals, what should the healthcare provider do if their Muslim patient is dying and there is no one around?

A: First, Islam teaches that we must do our best to save life. Do everything you can to save your patient's life. Second, all prayers are beneficial. If the provider is comfortable, he or she is welcome to pray for or with the patient.

Q: In closing, do you have any advice for health professionals who will care for dying Muslim patients?

A: I have two parting pieces of advice: Number one, health professionals must learn more about religious rituals and duties; this is important because it will help them to be sensitive to the needs of their patients. Number two, they should immediately call the family and/or the imam. If there is a Muslim at the end of life, a pastor or person related to that Muslim should be present. It will make not only the person at peace, but it will also make the work of healthcare easier. I have seen that simply reading the scriptures helps the dying person to die in peace.

In closing, I think the work you are doing and the work that has been accomplished prior to you is excellent in regard to teaching healthcare providers and givers how to care for religious people.

CONCLUSION

This text has provided an overview of the challenges of dying, and examined important theories on coping with dying and grief, ethical dilemmas related to death, NDEs, and how persons who identify with a world religion define a good death.

Interestingly, although every religion has a distinct history, culture, and doctrines, there is perhaps more in common between the great world religions than what is generally supposed. This is evident particularly in the world religion perspectives on the afterlife. Every world religion shares the general sketch as to what happens after death (e.g., first, there is a transition period, and second, the spirit enters a new state of existence), respect for the deceased, and their spiritual task (i.e., enlightenment or salvation) influences end-of-life decisions and care.

Regarding similarities in afterlife beliefs, Hindus and Buddhists believe the spirit remains close to the body immediately after death and then ascends to a transition state. While for Hindus this state is the world of pitrs, for Chinese and Tibetan Buddhists it is a bardo where the spirit remains for no more than forty-nine days. In both Hinduism and Buddhism, the spirit eventually moves from this transition state to more fully experience the effects of accrued good and bad karmas, which may occur in the realms of heaven and hell if liberation is not attained. Although not sharing the tradition on karma, Jews and Muslims also teach that the spirit of the deceased remains with the family for a period of time, and there is a period of transition before the spirit attains its final rest-ing place. In the western traditions there is a postmortem judgment before the spirit enters this transition state. Postmortem judgment is also a feature of Hinduism and Buddhism; however the judgment is interpreted within the context of accrued karma and ability to perceive reality. For Jews this transition period may last nine months and is usually associated with suffering in Gahenna. While many Christians speak of this transition state as the middle/intermediate state or purgatory; Muslims call this state the barzkah. In all of these religious traditions, after this transition period albeit forty-nine days (Buddhism) or until the resurrection of the dead (Islam), the spirit enters a new realm of existence. Interestingly all religions accept the existence of heaven and hell and respective pleasures and punishments relative to good or bad deeds performed in life. However, for Christians and Muslims, heaven and hell are eternal realities of existence; whereas for Hindus, Buddhists, and to an extent Jews they are temporary. Whether these similarities are evidence that these traditions are expressing within their context, theological language, and syntax the experience what millions of Americans have purported to have, an NDE, is debatable; however, it is of interest to note that the similarity in experiences in the afterlife across cultures and religions are one of Dr. Long's proofs that there is life after death. Note that Long examines the experiences of persons that identify with these traditions as opposed to what the authorities (e.g., revealed texts and religious teachers) in these traditions teach about life after life.

Respect for the body of the deceased is another feature of the world religions. With exception to Christianity, world religions perform various postmortem rituals, including a ritual washing of the corpse that evidence reverence for the body. For Hindus and Buddhists, the body housed a great spirit, and for this reason it must be respected. Cremation, which is the ideal manner to dispose of the corpse, does not contradict this respect for the body since the cremation of the body is a sacred event and the body is burned to benefit the spirit. If the body remains, the fear is that the spirit will be unable or unwilling to liberate itself from attachments to material existence that will result in a negative rebirth. Within the Jewish and Islamic traditions however, the ritual washing and burial of the body not only convey respect for the dead person's body, but also helps prepare the dead for the general resurrection before the Day of Judgment. For this reason, cremation is inappropriate. Although Christianity, in particular Catholicism, dropped the ancient Jewish burial traditions, the body remains important, and thus even in the case of cremation, the cremains must be respected.

Turing to end-of-life care, we again find remarkable similarities. Religious practitioners define what a good death is in the context of their religious tradition. Within each religious tradition, the spiritual task (e.g., attaining liberation from rebirth, good rebirth, or salvation) guides decisions about medication and treatments (physical task), expression of autonomy (psychological task), and evaluation of interpersonal relationship (social task).

Nevertheless, in all of my interviews with religious leaders from the western New York region, the religious leaders were impressed with the dedication of North American health providers that they encountered. Moreover all traditions, including traditions that have complicated end-of-life and funerary rituals, stress that if a nurse, doctor, or caretaker wants to provide effective healthcare, then they must first be the best nurse, doctor, or caretaker that they can be! Consistent with this statement, this text is not meant to change healthcare but rather functions as a guide or supplement to provide culturally and religiously sensitive care that will help those caring for terminally ill persons who identify with the discussed religions cope with their dying. I have employed Corr's model for coping with dying and creating tasks relative to this coping because his research offers a simple but effective means to approach end-of-life care that is consistent with how religion influences end-of-life decisions of people that identify with a religious tradition. All of what I have said in this book is circumscribed within the ability, time, and administration of health providers and their facilities. As evidenced in my interview with Monica Sleap there are health facilities that make pastoral care a priority for religious patients. Hospice in particular offers a valuable alternative to traditional hospital care that has the resources to help patients address their spiritual task. For this reason hospice care is attractive to religious people.

All of my interviewees were realistic and sensitive to the fact that allowing their congregants to have their end-of-life rituals performed may not be possible in all settings. For this reason the religious leaders greatly appreciated attempts to be informed about their congregant's needs and religious tradition.

Sensitivity to the needs of religious people provides segue to the generalization that religious people share the same concerns about their healthcare: that health professionals communicate with them clearly and that they respect their decisions. The terminally ill, in particular, never want to be treated as a corpse-in-waiting, but a person of value. The more respect that can be shown, even if this entails simply habituating a nonjudgmental demeanor to alien customs, demonstrates respect for an individual's choice to live a life in fidelity to their God, Supreme Reality, and religious philosophy. In the end, religious people do not want anything that is different from most Americans: to have the freedom and ability to define what they deem to be a good death. Thus this text serves to provide a resource to help health professionals provide culturally sensitive care for their patients, in hope that through understanding people with different perspectives on life and death we will further engender a more tolerant society that values all people, especially the most vulnerable in our society, the dying.